Dat e

WRITERS AND WRITING

WRITERS AND WRITING

by Robert van Gelder

Charles Scribner's Sons New York 1946

PRINTED IN THE UNITED STATES OF AMERICA

DESIGNED BY PAUL MCPHARLIN

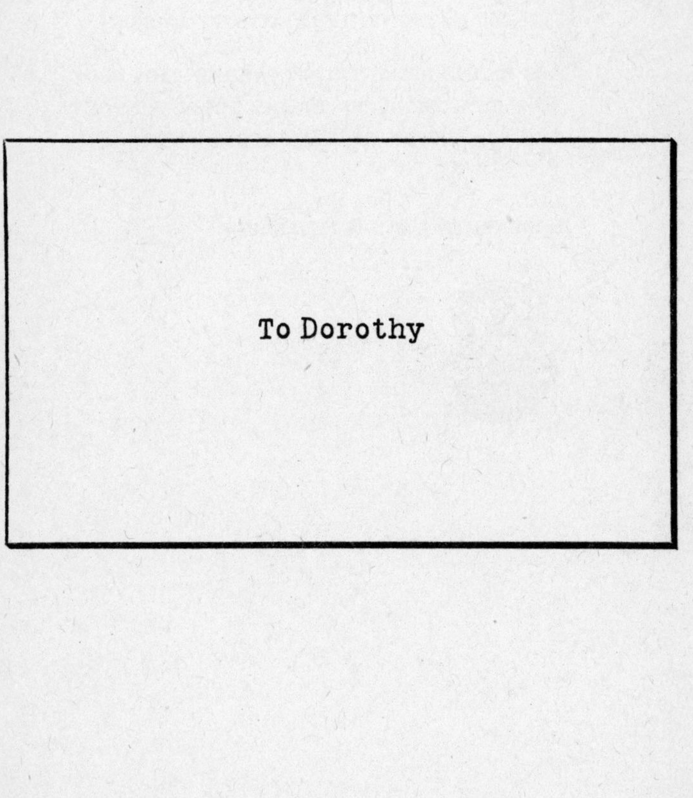

To Dorothy

CONTENTS

WRITERS AND WRITING

These interviews first appeared in the *New York Times Book Review* and are re-published through the courtesy of the New York Times Company.

NOTES ON THE LITERARY LIFE

By Robert van Gelder

My introduction to the literary life came about a dozen years ago through the late Theodore Dreiser, who seems to me to have been a strong embodiment, not necessarily pleasing, of the traits that a man needs to hold himself together through a long career as a creative writer. It was Dreiser's birthday and I—a reporter on *The New York Times*—was assigned to go to his suite at the Hotel Ansonia to do a birthday interview with him that everyone involved—the City Editor, Dreiser and myself—knew probably wouldn't be printed at all or at most would get into the paper only as a couple of paragraphs.

Dreiser usually attacks the rich and the religious when he is interviewed, but on this day he spent most of the time that I was with him bragging about his dog. He said that dogs are naturally very intelligent but that they are commonly retarded by the people who own them. People who don't talk to their dogs beyond something like "Here, Towser," or "There's your supper, Mike," get about what they give, according to Mr. Dreiser. They are dull with their dogs and their dogs are dull with them.

But when the owner is smart, he continued, the dog is made into a real companion and very quickly becomes smart also. His own dog, said Dreiser, with a somewhat heavy and entirely sincere enthusiasm, was brilliant. This dog was an Irish setter and often it would come to him, in the study of his house outside Mt. Kisco, hunting for something to do.

"When I'm in my study I'm there to work," said Dreiser. "I'll want to get rid of him, do you see, but instead of saying, 'Scat, go on, get out of here,' as you might to a cat, I make a suggestion. I may say: 'Why don't you go to the lake and have a swim for yourself, old fellow?' There is a lake on my place. I have quite a place up there.

"He'll look at me and think it over, then trot out. The next time I see him his coat is wet. He has understood me, don't you see? He has gone to the lake and taken himself for a swim."

"He likes to swim, doesn't he?" I asked.

"Yes," said Dreiser.

"Then why wouldn't he swim anyway, whether you suggested it or not? How do you know it is your suggestion that makes him take a swim?"

Dreiser scowled. His heavy-featured face was made for scowling and it is likely that he had found years before that his scowl was quite impressive.

"What are you trying to do?" he asked, menacingly. He had been tossing and catching a paperweight. Now he held the paperweight as though in a position of readiness. Dramatic. "Are you trying to knock the pins out from under me?"

How the little quarrel ended I don't remember. I do know that before the interview was over I had told a few stories about our own dog, a massive shepherd with an I. Q. of at least 150, and that Dreiser and I had agreed that our dogs should meet. And when I was leaving, Dreiser pleased me enormously by telling me that I seemed to be a good guy and that he would like to have dinner with me some night to talk over books and newspaper work.

Months passed. Then one afternoon I was out on assignment with Jack Beall of *The New York Herald Tribune.* We had some time to kill in the middle of the assignment and went and loitered in a restaurant. In our talk it came out that Beall also had interviewed Dreiser on Dreiser's birthday, that he also had been told by Dreiser that he seemed a good guy, and that he also had been asked: "How about dinner?"

We both had accepted the invitation as meant when we had heard it individually. The first thought of both of us when we learned that it had been extended to the other was that it was quite possibly a trick designed to persuade reporters to work harder to get the interview into the paper.

"But on the other hand," I said, "he could have meant it. After all, there's nothing wrong with either of us."

"I'm a lion hunter myself," said Beall.

"Call him up," I said, "and ask him to have dinner with us."

"A great idea," said Beall. "You call him. I'm a lion hunter but I'm sort of afraid of lions."

We tossed a coin. I lost.

"Yes," said Dreiser. "Sure, I remember Beall and I'll be glad to see him again. But what's your name? . . . Spell it. . . . Well, never mind, you come along too."

I left the booth, sweating. The date was made but Dreiser never had been able to recall seeing me. I felt that I was crashing the dinner, an interloper, but Beall insisted that I keep the date, as I had helped get him into it.

We met in the lobby of the Ansonia and went up to Dreiser's suite. There Dreiser showed us an invitation to a party that Harrison Smith, the publisher, was giving that night.

"Now I suggest," he said, "that we don't drink much at dinner. Save your money. After dinner we'll all go to the party where there will be plenty of liquor and we can drink all we like."

He wanted to have dinner at Barbetta's—an old Italian restaurant on the West Side.

"We'll talk about newspapers," he said. "Barbetta's is the kind of place that I knew when I was a newspaper man."

As it turned out, however, he didn't want to hear stories of newspaper days. There was an Italian travel poster on the wall at Barbetta's and that became the topic—the Dreiser dog—of the meal. The colors of travel posters, and the colors of water and sky as seen from various points along the Italian shore, made practically the entire conversation through the long dinner.

Dreiser and Beall seemed to have followed much the same routes in their wanderings through Italy and they went on and on about the colors they had seen—from this little inn, from that little hill, at this or that turn of the shore.

Hemingway talked somewhere on how a good book stays with you, on how you know afterward how the people were, and what they ate, and what the weather was. Perhaps that was good conversation because to this day I know quite clearly how Beall and Dreiser were as travelers, where they were, what the weather was and what the colors were.

Beall made several honest efforts to include me in this conversation but I never had been in Italy.

I felt a complete dullard, a bore. And at the party it was not much better. There were a number of pretty girls around and as Dreiser came into the apartment he caught one and settled himself in a large chair and called to me to bring him a drink.

Neither Beall nor myself was introduced to anyone. Beall went off lion hunting but I had had enough of lions.

I brought Dreiser his drink and he explained jovially that he couldn't get one for himself as if he got up the girl would escape. It was true that she was struggling a bit, though not very vigorously, as she probably was confused, for she had been caught so suddenly.

Looking back I realize that it was a rather lively party, with some running through the rooms, a couple of minor spats going on, and so forth. I remember Heywood Broun pacing slowly about, like Kant beneath the lindens, and absent-mindedly brushing away with one big paw a man who promised that he was going to tell him a funny story.

In one corner of one room, alone most of the time, John Dewey sat in a comfortable chair, just looking about.

Squatted on the floor across the room from Dewey was Max Schuster, of Simon and Schuster. Cass Canfield of Harper and Brothers stood near the kitchen door. A member of the left-wing intelligentsia, whose name I don't recall, was deeply tanned, having just returned, he said, from Miami.

This last man seemed to feel about as out of place as I did and we drifted together a couple of times and spoke. But by this time I was pressing, as the saying is, and in a heavy attempt to be humorous made some crack about Communists lolling on

Miami's beach while bankers starved. He looked grieved at my tactlessness and our brief contact ended.

I walked through the rooms, reflecting that here were the people who were influencing a whole generation's response to life—the creators of ideas and the distributors of ideas, but that reflection did not, of course, last long.

A friend of mine came over to say that he felt a little drunk, but good. He had been poking about in one of the bedrooms, he said, and had noticed a woman's hat that looked as though it was decorated with horns.

"I put it on to surprise the girl I'd been talking to," said he, "and at that minute John Dewey came in.

"I said: 'Mr. Dewey, I'm a cuckold,' and pointed to the horns on the hat.

"He said: 'That's my wife's hat.' Oh, he was perfectly all right about it, but he took the hat."

Dreiser kept calling to me to bring him another drink. The girl was quiet now, just sitting there, staring off into space. I made him the drink and then, to avoid further butling, went into the kitchen and leaned against the wall, and thought about Dreiser. The central fact about him, I decided, was that he was peculiarly able to be himself without shutting himself off from others.

I put together the evidence indicating his belief in himself, a belief that extended into every corner and trifle of his life.

For example: the interview. Instead of sweating around for some topic that might have made newspaper copy, he had chosen to talk about what interested him at the moment—his absent dog. At dinner, color had pleased him; he had been momentarily as fascinated by color as Goethe was, Goethe, who had believed that because of his work with color he would survive for posterity less as a creative artist than as a natural scientist.

And now here Dreiser was with the girl on his lap.

The people, Dreiser and the girl, were in sharp contrast. The girl was busily snubbing Dreiser—a lot of good that did her but she was doing her best to keep from any involvement with him;

her attitude was that of a memsahib who has strayed into a native village, there been received, astonishingly, as an equal, and is making the best of it until help arrives.

But Dreiser was snubbing no one. For all of his self-centeredness he had no private-world remoteness. Physically he was treating the girl as though she were a stage property, a night-club rattle, but at the same time, through talk and grunts and cries and whispers and songs, he was trying to arouse her to the party spirit.

He was not afraid of being the object of either boredom or distaste. He hoped to entertain and interest but he had no slightest idea of losing himself for one minute in making that effort.

Probably he felt that same way when he wrote. His books read so. They are the work of a man who is, first of all, himself.

Years later I sat with George Jean Nathan in Twenty-one and he told me of a time when he and Mencken had kidded Dreiser into trying a story of Life in Society.

Dreiser had come through with a description of a member of the carriage trade sweeping down a marble staircase dressed for the opera, her slippers and fan red and her gown made of rustling green silk, or some such combination.

Dreiser had been furious when they'd laughed at him. But after that one excursion into the Diamond Horseshoe he had returned to what he knew, into material that he could honestly deal with, that meant something to him.

The joke is on other writers. How many thousands are there who wear out frustrated lives trying to give editors what they, the editors, think they want, and doing none too well at it, and getting by on sufferance after a short time, or not getting by?

And then beyond that those who seek, nervously, simply to please—to please "the public"? When all that the public wants is the best that some whole man, who is no more than normally concerned with pleasing, can do well enough to satisfy himself.

My second evening in the literary life was spent with a writer who had written to please, to make money by pleasing. He was very bitter about it. Three of us sat in a hidden little beer stube on the West Side while he told of all the money he had made and how much dissatisfaction he had had with it.

"Now let's say this," he said. "Let's say that life is as wide as this bar is long. Life stretches from the mind of the lowest aborigine squatting in the shade of a rock to the mind of a Shakespeare, a Spinoza, a Dante, a Lincoln. Life stretches economically from the poverty of a Chinese peasant, an Indian untouchable, a feeder on carrion, to a man smoking dollar cigars in his limousine as he drives with his sweetie to his yacht. Life covers the world—grass, trees, amoebas, prizefighters, flowers; it covers the world. Life takes in hells of misery, torments of the damned, degradation down here at this end of the bar, and up there at that end of the bar," said the speaker, with the merest glance toward a girl who had just come in, "lies ecstasy."

"Watch that stuff," said my other companion. "That's a detective she's with."

"All right, then, not my ecstasy," said the bitter man, philosophically. "But I hope that I have given you some conception," he said to me, "of the vast space of life, the range of it."

"Yes."

"Now look at this match," said the writer. "How long is it? An inch, an inch and a half? Compared to the length of this bar it is nothing. And yet it is into the length of that match as it is in ratio to the length of that bar that you must confine yourself if you want to write stories that sell to editors.

"To editors—to the magazines! They want stories of life, they say, and certainly they do. But only of so much life, the span this match represents. You can learn the tricks if you want to—it isn't tough—and then you can play them, and be just as clever as you know how to say that love is sweet and horses are funny. Not people. People aren't funny. They are all wonderful and good and they will raise a fine howl if you don't say so. Dogs are all wonderful and good, too," said the writer, shaking his head mournfully over his beer. "But horses you can like or dislike when you deal in this little range of life no wider than the length of a match."

This writer, of course, felt sorry enough for himself. Soon after, his name stopped appearing in the big weeklies, and since then I have seen it nowhere else, so it may be that he gave up the whole struggle and went into some other kind of work. Since then I have heard the same sort of talk from other men and women. Their position is most unenviable, certainly, but they are paid very well and it would seem that it should be possible for them to cut their standard of living and thus allow themselves considerably more time in which to write the books that they believe they want to write. The limits that the magazines and the movies and radio place on themes do not, happily, apply in books.

The people who have the really rough time, as it seems to me, are not those who feel that they have sacrificed their art for pottage, their freedom of expression for a measly swimming pool, but those who spend their lives as would-bes, caught by the desire to write, like fish upon a hook, and moving through frantic and vain rituals.

I think of one man who ran his life as by a timetable; it was all a preparation for the day when he would begin to write. He started each day by reading an act from Shakespeare or a chapter from the Bible. This, as I gathered from stray hints, for he was never specific in revealing his purposes, was to put himself into the mood of greatness. He would then move on to a certain restaurant where he always arrived for breakfast at precisely the same time. The same waitress had kept for him the same table, and there was always orange juice and grapenuts set out for him. She would bring him his coffee after he had sat down, but this was merely her acceptance of his whim, for had she set out the coffee by the clock it would have been hot when he came. He arrived at that restaurant on the split second, finished his meal on the split second, and always had the correct change so that the cashier would not hold him up. His days then consisted of so much time for museum visits, of a two-hour session of reading French, an hour of reading German. He had a number of word games that he played, privately, to increase his vocabulary. All in all, he did not waste a minute, but neither did he, so far as I could ever make out, ever get a lick of work done. Whatever standard he had set for himself, it was too high, a perfection that he could not attain.

I think of another man who might almost have been the brother of that first one. This one had an eight-hour job, but it was very easy in the first place, and in the second place he had a quite disagreeable temper and had bullied his immediate superiors on the job into the feeling that they were cads and destroyers of genius if they asked him to do any work. His boss was a timorous man and as whenever he suggested that my acquaintance interrupt his reading there was always an explosion, he usually tried to avoid trouble by giving the work to the other members of the staff. This man was always going to write a novel when he could find a place in which he could be happy at his work. During the winter I knew him he moved twice and for each move he had to swap and buy furniture, measure the windows for curtains, buy curtains, arrange for the place to be cleaned, threaten suit against some noisy neighbor, and so on. After a time he left New York and became a traveler, ranging the world, I suppose, for the perfect place in which to write.

At the other extreme from him, but, I suppose, always coming toward the same place, was a man I knew who once leased a large unfurnished apartment at an excellent address. He was perfectly sober when he did this. However, the rent for the apartment came to within $8 a week of his salary. To buy furniture was impossible. It was all he could do to keep himself in enough soup and sandwiches to sustain life. I went to see him in his new apartment and had a bad time getting in, for he could not but agree that there was something rather odd about his sleeping on a pile of newspapers in a corner of a room looking out on Fifth Avenue with the rent paid up, and I suppose he did not want anyone to see the conditions that he had chosen. Anyway, whether it was the apartment or something else, this man did produce some stories and poems that were published in little magazines, which is more than the other two accomplished.

I tell the stories of these three men not to laugh at them. Writing is desperately hard work for most of us, and we avoid it when we can. These people had simply built up more elaborate barricades against work than most of us do, although perhaps they were really only more elaborate in performance, for the barricades of alcoholism and just plain loafing are just as strong. I remember Eudora Welty, one of the most talented and natural of writers, closing a discussion of the difficulties of getting down to work with the only sigh I've ever heard from her and the comment, "There's always something else you'd rather do."

One thing that makes writing so difficult is that it is such a lonely job. It may be that it is in an effort to get away from this loneliness that more and more of the successful writers have taken to dictating what they have to say. Running a typewriter is practically automatic after you have worked at one for years, and I suspect that it is not only to avoid this purely automatic chore that people turn to dictation. The effort, rather, is to change the conditions of work. The writer in middle age has behind him hundreds of hours of work alone and the guilty feeling that most of these hours did not produce anything much, and there comes a time when he cannot face, or thinks he cannot face, more hours under the same conditions, so he changes the setting by getting someone else to do the typing for him. In this way some of the weight of apprenticeship is lifted.

J. P. Marquand told me that he could dictate best to someone who showed no particular interest in what he was talking about, who spent most of the four hours reading while he prowled the room and thought of a paragraph now and then. Christopher Morley said that his secretary was invaluable to him because she kept him on the main line of his effort. He said that, naturally, he preferred to write letters because that was easier than working on a novel, but when he started to branch off into a letter she would ask him what he was supposed to be doing that day, letters or his novel. Morley has a set-up that indicates a great deal of thought given to the subject of getting to work. He maintains a hide-away office in the West Forties. To this he goes three mornings each week, bringing notes that he has made during his days off in the country. When he is ready to work he turns over an hourglass that is somewhat inaccurate and does what he can in the way of creation as the sand runs through. Thus the demands that he makes upon himself are not those unlimited demands of apprenticeship. They are for just one little word after another, so many words for each gram of sand, and when the sand has run out Morley can go with good conscience and good appetite to a neighboring Italian restaurant that serves an excellent lunch.

Another writer told me—he's an old master of the pulps—that he was greatly aided in producing by dictation because of a strong streak of penuriousness. "I pay my secretary $30 a week," he said, "and I hate to pay for anything without getting full value. The more I work, the harder she works. Why, I've sometimes turned out as much as 30,000 words a week."

For those not gifted with quite this degree of penuriousness H. G. Wells' system for producing may be more to the point. Mr. Wells told me that when he is writing a novel he simply pours out the words on the situations that most interest him. When his interest diminishes and he comes to a gap, he simply jumps it and goes on to any further point in the story on which he feels like working. When he has about 30,000 words down on paper he then goes back and begins filling in the gaps, again following his own impulse as to which gap he is most interested in filling. Finally, he either fills the last gap or leaves it.

The advantages of deadlines hardly can be overestimated, and one reason that the fiction field is no more crowded than it is probably is because there are so few deadlines in it. The writer of an article is told when he must have his copy in, and he does everything possible to produce it on time. But fiction is, in general, not ordered; the ways of telling a story are many, the work that can be done is endless. When you consider that most article writers make almost a fetish of gathering vast quantities of material that they know they will never use simply to put off for a time the actual writing, it becomes plain how much greater are the temptations to procrastination of the writer of fiction. Few men have ever written with less to say than Harold Bell Wright, but I once read somewhere that Mr. Wright always drew up full genealogies for his main characters, noted the sturdy goodness that had activated the hero's great-grandfather, explored the courtships of his grandparents and dealt in considerable detail with his parents, even though these people were not to be part of the story. This, it is very likely, was simply Mr. Wright's way of doodling before getting down to turning it out.

I could go on almost endlessly about work habits, because I discovered early when doing these interviews that the best way to warm a writer up for talk was to ask him about his work habits. This is a wonderful question. It is just personal enough, it is a topic to which the writer has given a lot of thought, and is one that he explores eagerly.

For these interviews I have followed nature rather than a technique. I have not read up on anyone before hand, have asked few questions, made no notes. I'd simply meet an author somewhere, listen for about an hour and a half, then sometime that day or the next go to a typewriter and put down at top speed all that had been said that I felt was of any use to me. These rough notes usually ran about 2,100 words—three pages of single-space typing. Later in the week, about three hours before my copy was due in the composing room, I would look over these notes and write the interview in final form.

This sounds slapdash—but it isn't. I didn't read up on people before I went to see them because I didn't want a lot of stale, secondhand notions of what they were like. I tried that with a few of my earlier interviews and found that if I went to see a man with a little collection of anecdotes about him in my mind I tended to spend much of my time trying to verify whether he was the kind of man that his friends and others who had written about him said that he was. I would bring away the same sides of him that had been brought out before.

There is that same blurring effect when you ask a lot of questions in an interview. You may be finding what the man thinks on a large number of topics but you have less of him. The way to know a man is to listen to him ramble and just give him a nudge now and then to keep him going.

The practice of not taking notes also fitted in. The interviewee just jogs along, figuring that soon you will get out the pencil and the copy paper but that until then he needn't start straining to be this or that for the public; he need only be himself. He talks at his natural rate, says what he means, doesn't raise his voice, is not stuffy unless stuffiness is really a part of him, does not act unless he is a born actor. The interviewer also gains by not taking notes because he misses less. When you are just sitting there smoking a cigarette and drinking coffee or Scotch you notice the words that are stumbled over, the characteristic repetitions and back-home phrases, the subordinate clause that doesn't seem to mean much when it is heard but that makes a double point when it fits into the whole pattern. Also, you are much more apt to ask the "why" or the "why-not" questions that would never be asked through forethought, that are born of the instant, and bring out the best stuff.

As for the fast writing—that also fits. If you work slowly and hard over a profile you are all too apt to go creative and try to build up this or that idea of a person. That is, the interviewer becomes concerned with points that he wants to make and is apt to ever so slightly falsify some aspect of his subject—for example, by leaving out a couple of untidy facts that seem to have no place in his scheme for the effect that the interview is to produce. But if you draw the sketch at high speed, just putting down everything that seems interesting, the untidy facts get in and modify the portrait as they should, and the picture is freehand, it is individual.

To use this method successfully, of course, you should have a kind of movie memory that plays back the scene for you when you are at your typewriter. I found out by accident when I was quite young that I usually could recall fairly precisely the phrases and inflections of talk that I had heard if the talk had been of special interest to me, and I believe that a great many people can do that trick but don't realize it. For me the trick does not work if the talk follows an at all artificial rhythm or if it contains any considerable proportion of words that are not part of my own working vocabulary. When the words are strange I'm like a dog watching the finger and disregarding the direction in which it is pointed.

Necessary, too, for this method is an uncritical and unselfconscious attitude with people. When you are with a person you must be ready to accept all that he is—there must be no second man sitting back picking what he says to pieces or wondering what impression he has of you. All that can come later, when the interview has been written and sent to the printer. But if it is to be a true picture it must be made without prejudice, with every aspect that you have managed to see drawn in, but with no conscious process of like or dislike interfering.

Several people have asked me, "How'm I doing?" as they talked or even, "You won't pillory me, will you?" and always I have assured them with entire truthfulness that they were fine, that I liked them—I always did. A few of these have come out in the interviews as braggarts and bores and I suppose they think now that I was lying to them when I reassured them, but I wasn't. I never have even been tempted to try to "take" anyone in print and think badly of the practice. It is unfortunate that if you simply report truthfully what people say it so often looks as though you hit them in the eye with a tomato.

On the whole the fast method has worked fairly well. I have had only one blast for inaccuracy—a Frenchman became furious because I had said that he lived at the Ritz. I had been told by a man in his publishers' office that he lived at the Ritz and had used this as a fact without further verification. But he didn't, it seemed, live at the Ritz, and I received a two page letter calling me down for my mistake. One poet thought at first sight that he had a complaint but decided on second thought that he hadn't; M. Lincoln Schuster believed, rightly, that I had misquoted him in my interview, and Harry Scherman felt that I had overplayed one point in my interview with him, but otherwise it has been pretty much roses all the way, so far as kicks are concerned.

The subject of this introduction is supposed to be the Literary Life. I want to write about it honestly, avoiding both windy generalizations and gossips. Before starting to write I did some work and found I know 1,500 people who have to do with books well enough to write a paragraph about each one. In fact, I even wrote the paragraphs—but of this mass I can use little, for it is very subjective stuff. There are some people so big that they cannot be harmed by factual, intimate reminiscence—and there are some hens that are supposed to have teeth. Too many true accounts, to be interesting, must nudge at gossip—and I'd rather not be that interesting.

One writer talked to me about another at lunch not long ago. "B," he said, "has such strange and awful and so many personal troubles that he must be a great artist. The ordinary man can't think up ways to get himself into such messes as B arranges for himself. When you read the life of Dostoevski you see what a genius can do to himself when he really sets to and tries. B isn't far behind. Up to now he hasn't been under sentence of death and he hasn't had to skin out of the country. But I guess he's saving the electric chair for the climax—or maybe a lynch mob will get him first."

This speech was a mere skirting of the gossip—which I hadn't heard but which my acquaintance had taken for granted that I knew. He took it for granted because gossip about authors and publishers and book reviewers and book editors is very easy to pick up and, in fact, difficult to avoid. It reminds me of a conversation that I heard on a bus one day recently; a young man who had the stigmata of a chorus boy was telling a couple of girls what a third girl thought of them. "You'd hardly gone," said the boy, "before she said: 'I hate those tramps; they make me gag.' And then she told a lot of dirt about you and some firemen."

"I don't like her, either," said one of the girls, thoughtfully. "Especially now."

The whole tone of the talk was such—there was no heat in it—that I felt sure that the boy was merely trying to get a reputation of being a pretty interesting conversationalist.

That same hope sparks most of the gossip of the literary life. It is not mean by intention, for there is no outrage in it unless politics or some suggestion of censorship is at the center.

Fury up to the point of frothing at the mouth may accompany a description of political frightfulness of which some writer has been guilty—a doctoring of facts on iron-ore production, a faked interview with a Commissar, a kind word for T. V. Soong. But intimate recitals of what led to the divorce or the psychopathic ward or suicide are just talk and not much emotion accompanies them, because the heat has gone out of discussions of personal morals and into political morals.

In some of the more political-minded sets to say that a man has run away with his secretary because his wife tried to interfere with his drinking is considered less of moment, than would be a statement that his reaction to a speech made at Ajacio was one that differed somewhat from the reaction of the people in the room.

A generation ago the career of one of the most popular and able and intelligent essayists that America has produced was ruined when a girl clerk sued him for breach of promise. His books were withdrawn from circulation, magazine editors returned his contributions unopened, and he was discharged from his job as a professor of English. He died bankrupt and a suicide.

It would be demeaning to try to show with hints how much times have changed, but they have not changed enough, for now a man can conceivably find himself in just about as much trouble if he offends politically.

In the Spring of 1945 W. L. White's yarn of his six weeks in Russia, "Report on the Russians," was published by an entirely sound and responsible publisher. To me this book sounded like the talk of a prosperous Emporia, Kansas, matron busy running down the clothing, manners, house furnishings and so on of a family that lived on what the matron considered the wrong side of the tracks and that was—again as the matron believed—too big for its boots and too eager to rise in the world and become acceptable to nice people. I felt that this attitude was snobbish and little and mildly ridiculous. But, on the other hand, the prejudice was frank and the report was readable, and was put forth as one man's view and not eternal truth—which is more than can be said for most books on Russia.

The storm that met "Report on the Russians" was as out of proportion as was the punishment meted out to the essayist thirty-odd years before.

One man I knew actually had foam on his mouth as he denounced as Communists every reviewer who had been critical of the book. And from the Left came an expensive throwaway to cry "Fascist" at everyone who liked the book.

That was the line-up. One must hate the book and its author or one must admire the book and its author. "Coward" was the word from both sides for those who tried to stand on middle ground. Men whom I know, through years of association, to be entirely American in their political viewpoints, who never were in the slightest degree tempted to swing further to the Right than the bulk of the Republican Party were shouted about as Communists or Fascists simply because in doing their jobs they have said what they thought instead of trying to trim and twist to appease one side or another.

"The attack on this book is a Communist plot!"

"The book is part of a Fascist plot!"

And so they saw plotters everywhere, not honest reviewers and commentators speaking their minds, but foreign agents malevolently conspiring. The row kicked up about "Report on the Russians" is important because it is symptomatic; the real football was not the White book—it was free speech.

In the midst of the turmoil a man of my acquaintance wrote an impassioned article on the right of a publisher to print any book that he pleases. It was partisan-inspired but had a high tone, and its Miltonic position was hardly to be assailed. Every idea in it was about three hundred years old and thoroughly tested.

A couple of days later this man dropped into my office and I passed on the rumor that a certain very wealthy man of markedly liberal views was entering more deeply into publishing.

At this news the face of the defender of liberty turned turkey-red and he pounded the floor with his umbrella. It was not a showman's gesture but a perfectly straight reaction.

"That man," cried the defender of liberty, in a thickened voice, "must be stopped!"

A newer trend in publishing that might be commented upon is a curious limiting tendency that seems to me to be sneaking out to replace the old genteel tradition. There are a few men in publishing, and they are quite smart men, who have come to mistrust their own reactions to the printed word because they have become convinced that they do not represent the public, that there must be a division between the caviar on which they can feed with satisfaction and the mackerel that is the proper food for the mass.

These are very alert men who like to keep themselves on the "inside" of many fields. Cultivating a wide acquaintance, they know that such and such a promotion was no promotion but a kick upstairs on the way to the exit, that the story of a controversy that makes the newspapers was only half the story and that the added facts, known to them, probably will not come out until months later.

Such knowledge after a time is apt to seem to its possessor confusingly like an evidence of exceptional mental powers, and it leads to the conviction that those who are not so well informed on what is behind the tickings of the times are not quite bright.

It is out of this conviction, I often have thought, that the great emphasis on writing for dunderheads has emerged. A vast audience through centuries has enjoyed Shakespeare, but it is a quite general belief that readers and auditors today are best catered to if all thought is presented to them in the style of a primer for the backward.

Certainly I am all for clarity and simplicity in writing but I feel that the state of mind that rejects any expression that might be beyond the scope of a lazy child is as unhealthy as would be the activities of a farmer who controlled vast valleys of the richest earth and in that earth planted year after year only a crop of peanuts, bad for the land, and bringing into being too many peanuts. There also can be too many primers for the dull.

During these last few years more books have been distributed than ever before, and the next few years may see a further rise. That means more money in books, and it is interesting to speculate on what the money will do. In other fields of writing it has had a stifling effect: magazines filled with tame hacks, Hollywood filled with roaring boys who also are tame hacks.

The often-asked question, "Will it make money?" has been like a question in a game. The money involved in nine books out of ten is not much. And so books have supplied the range for a free company, adventurous and intelligently exploratory, reasonably sure, reasonably kind, warmly optimistic. With all the sincerity of which I am capable I hope to see it ever so.

MENCKEN ON LITERATURE AND POLITICS

"Print it!" cried Mr. Mencken. Opinions on writing in the Thirties

February 11, 1940

RUSSIA AND ROOSEVELT are responsible for a ten-year decline in the quality of American writing, said H. L. Mencken.

"The writers fell for the current blah, and no good art can come from men who believe in the blah of their times. The writers of the Thirties have been enslaved by the bushwah of the Pinks."

It was a typical Mencken interview. "Print it!" Mr. Mencken would say after delivering himself of what appeared on the surface to be the grossest libel. "I've known so-and-so for years and in my considered opinion he is a jackass and a simple-minded stooge."

The setting was the comfortably furnished board room and library of the Knopf offices on Madison Avenue, where Mr. Mencken had spent a part of the morning writing autograph cards for insertion into copies of his new book, "Happy Days: 1880–1892."

"Imbecile, boob, idiot," said Mr. Mencken, talking of politics and Pinks. He has a way of pressing his cigar against an ashtray and pushing it around when he is emphasizing his opinion of the editors of *The New Republic* or *The Nation*, or when he is talking of members of President Roosevelt's Cabinet. Naturally, the cigar frequently goes out. The wonder is that it remains lighted as well as it does.

He credits the World War and the peace that followed it with the rise of literature during the second and third decades of this century. Artists could stand aside and see through the abject falsehoods, the rosy glow of optimism, that warmed the common man in the years immediately after the war, and as a result they performed their true functions as artists.

"Red Lewis. His 'Babbitt' was incomparable, wonderful, great. As George Nathan said of 'The Merry Widow': 'Nobody wrote it—God wrote it.' You can say that same thing, truthfully, about 'Babbitt.' Babbitt at that time was the greatest man in the country, he was America. And Lewis saw him truly and fully, had a little fun with him, too.

"Then he wrote 'Elmer Gantry.' We had prohibition and Elmer was the great man behind prohibition. Some people said he exaggerated Elmer. Nonsense, I know those fellows. Elmer was one of the best of them; he was a scholar and a gentleman compared to some I've known, a prince among his kind. Lewis had a little fun with him, too, but basically it was a true portrait.

"But Red is a humble fellow. What other good novelist do you know who speaks well of other novelists? None of 'em do—none of 'em. That's proof of Red's humility. He always speaks well of other novelists. And probably because of that basic humility of his he was caught up in politics. He lambasted the Fascists and then turned around and tried to lambast the Communists in the worst novel ever written in America. That was—let's see, yes, 'The Prodigal Parents.' Frightful stuff. Imbecilic."

The main trouble with American literature, says Mr. Mencken, is that other writers also went into politics, and lost their gift of disbelief.

The shock of depression caused the mouth of all America to hang open—adenoidally receptive to some belief. The majority of men always need a rock of ages, a cave of brotherhood, a staff and diaper of belief.

"The kids came out of college with degrees that weren't worth anything. They couldn't cash in, they couldn't get jobs, they hadn't anything to sell. So they turned to Messiahs—to Russia and to Roosevelt.

"They believed that Roosevelt was going to make America more wonderful than it ever had been before. They believed that the Russians had found a system of government that would permit every one to be comfortable and happy.

"Believing and trusting, they were out of the hurricane, free of the loneliness—but they weren't artists. They couldn't perform the artist's function. They were enslaved by the Pinks."

Best of the up-from-slavery writers, Mr. Mencken believes, is James T. Farrell. "Wonderful stuff in those Chicago tales. Whoever doesn't like Farrell is an idiot or a liar." Farrell had considerable critical backing three or four years ago, has been less prominently mentioned since. Mr. Mencken puts that down to politics. "Farrell refused to go along with Stalin's boys, and as a critic he took a fall out of new authors they were bringing up. So they ganged him." Farrell's latest effort, a tale of the Christian Front, does not appeal to Mr. Mencken, who found it "idiotic, imbecilic, rot." "But, after all, every writer may crack up occasionally."

He also likes William Saroyan: "the only one of the 'advanced' writers with pungency, with something fresh to say and a new way of saying it."

John Steinbeck "has a great talent, but he must have been flattered by the pigs. The political essays in 'Grapes of Wrath' are terrible. They might have been written by one of the kept idealists of the liberal magazines that run on a deficit. But the story is wonderful. I assume that he'll outgrow the stupid politics."

WRITING CONTEMPORARY HISTORY

The author of "Only Yesterday" and "Since Yesterday" talks about the methods he employed

February 18, 1940

FREDERICK LEWIS ALLEN talked on writing contemporary history. He said that since 1931, when he completed "Only Yesterday," his best-selling history of the Twenties, he has pretty much known that he also would review the Thirties. But for years his magpieing of materials was casual. He drew rings around a lot of news stories and editorials, but about as many ringed pieces ended up in the trash basket as in folders.

"It was no loss. The stuff that seems significant at the moment has a way of wearing off with the months and years. The best material for books such as mine are the things that you take for granted as you live with them. And it is this material that is the hardest to find when you need it.

"I wanted a photograph of people at the door of a basement speakeasy. I searched the town and couldn't find one. Pinball. When and where did pinball start and when was the craze at its height? I vaguely remember that I first discovered it in a bar in June, 1935, probably at the Jones Beach Hotel. How long had it been going on? I pester every one I run across with such points as this."

It seemed unlikely that Mr. Allen would do much pestering on any subject. He is a courteous, hard-working man. You have the feeling that—for one thing—he is too busy ever to be a pest.

His notes were not elaborate. One of them, made in the Spring of 1936, is fairly typical. It read: "Knock, Knock. Handies. People have been playing Monopoly—must check on Monopoly."

He did quite a bit of research on Monopoly but only barely mentioned it in his book. He printed a sample Knock, Knock.

"Who's there?"

"Eskimo, Christian, and Italian."

"Eskimo, Christian, and Italian who?"

"Eskimo Christian and Italian no lies."

He did not mention Handies at all.

Useful in writing of the Bank Holiday were such trivia as the Radio City Music Hall advertisement that checks would be acceptable at the box office, and the tooth-paste manufacturer's announcement that a three-month supply could be bought with checks dated ninety days ahead.

He was under the impression for a long time that he would make extensive use of solemn anti-New Deal arguments. He collected a fat folder of these, but there was nothing in the folder, as it turned out, that he could use. The casual gossip at dinner tables, the anti-Roosevelt jokes told on suburban trains, were far more useful in rendering the spirit of the criticism.

"I tried to write objectively of course, but with events so close at hand that was difficult. An objective statement on the Supreme Court plan, though written by one who is against it, might seem to another who is against it to be an out-and-out plunking for it."

When he really got down to work on the book he found the *World Almanac* useful because, though its type is cruel on the eyes, it contains an extended chronology of the main news stories of each year. He studied these lists, checking off the stories that he wanted to look up in the files of *The New York Times.*

"I didn't read only those stories. I'd go through into the back pages. It is fascinating to look through the real estate advertisements in the issues for September, 1929. There was a great boom in Park Avenue co-operative apartments—they were selling at fantastic prices. And the automobiles and women's fashions, the theatre and book reviews, help give one the feel of the time."

He kept a notebook, devoting one page to each month, "only

to remind myself of the various things happening at the same time." He searched out the dates he needed: "going through year after year—it was a lot like cramming for an exam." The Variety yearbook is very useful in providing material on the amusement zone, for it contains lists of hit songs, popularity ratings of radio programs, moving pictures, and so on. He went to magazines for information on special subjects, and read enormously in books. The Thirties were far better reported than the Twenties, he says, citing "Middletown in Transition," by the Lynds, the Moley and Farley memoirs, and the Beards' "America in Midpassage," "which I was afraid to read for fear I'd be too much influenced by their findings, but which I couldn't resist poking about in." The original, unpublished material that comes to him in his job as associate editor of *Harper's Magazine* was "enormously helpful."

He wrote the book during four months of leave and on nights and Sundays, through a year.

"My writing process is something like shoveling snow. I go into the bank until I get stuck, then get up momentum in a new start. That is, I dive into a chapter, keep on going as long as I can. After stalling I go back to a point where I found smooth going and gather speed for a new thrust. It seems to work."

He writes two or three drafts on an average and can go back through the book and pick out his good days and the days when the work was hard to get through.

The "big people" of the Thirties, he believes, were the "social salvationists"—the reformers whose ideas were interpreted and dramatized by President Roosevelt.

"They are prominent all through the period, but the real key to the period, it seems to me, is not in them but in that greater thing—the force of economic maladjustment—the depression."

PEARL BUCK TALKS OF HER WORK

Her Discovery of America

March 10, 1940

Pearl Buck says that in American life she has found a limitless reservoir of material for writing. She never "became Chinese," she always knew that she was American, yet her discovery of this country has had a certain Columbian freshness.

"The Good Earth" was, in a way, "a pot-boiler," written on "borrowed money and it had to be written at the time it was because I needed—oh, a lot of money. Not just needed it. Had to have it." And out of this desperation came almost overnight a—seemingly from her point of view—unqualified success. That success brought her here, completely changed her life; it gave her the chance to spend all her years "writing only what I want to write."

She came here a stranger to the present, but well grounded in the past. Her family memory stretched deep back to frontier living; her parents had lived as children through the Civil War and they had not left America until the Eighties. Since coming here she has studied the years between, not systematically, but as a pervading interest.

"I find so much that interests me, that seems exciting and strange and revealing, that I'll keep right on turning out books, one after another. I've enough to work on for years. And no two of the books will be alike. I may write what reviewers call trash at times, but I never will write to pattern."

Work for her is about as painless as work can be. She writes rapidly—with great concentration and a consequent ease. Four hours a day—the hours from 9 to 1—five days a week. "She covers eight to twelve pages of foolscap each morning—an average of about 2,500 words a day," Richard Walsh, her husband and publisher, broke in.

The place of the interview was the Walsh apartment, which looks down on Park Avenue a few blocks north of the Grand Central. Mrs. Walsh spends very little time there; as a general thing she comes to town only one day each week. Her real home is in a "close-knit Pennsylvania-Dutch community," in Bucks County—well away from the settlements along the Delaware into which many New Yorkers have moved.

Since coming here she has been a "fascinated student" of the present and of recent history. Two aspects of life here on which she has done a good deal of mulling are hero worship and the status of women. Her new novel, "Other Gods," is on hero worship—the story of a young mechanic who captures the American imagination by a feat of daring and of the behind-the-publicity troubles that result.

"Of course, nothing like it could happen in China. Hero worship was something new to me. I missed the Lindbergh flight and the parade and great turnouts, but I was here for Corrigan, and the New Dealers who have been worshipped. Our all reading the same books at the same time, and knowing about the same people, are part of this."

As for women, she says that even though it may be true that the individual man in this country is rather awed, perhaps bossed, by his woman, the male attitude toward "women" is something else. In England a woman who really accomplishes something becomes a personality in her own right, escapes inequality. And in China, Mrs. Walsh declares, there is no inequality between the sexes.

"All through childhood and youth in America girls are allowed—they are educated—to believe that they are, if not the equals, the superiors of boys. And then, suddenly, the shock as they start to earn a living. Of course, if they stay in the home they do not necessarily make this discovery of inequality. But why should they stay in the home? They're not taught to, particularly. Why should only the home be the stronghold for women?"

There are many curiosities of the American scene that she may write books about. Her novels are not planned well ahead of the writing; they grow out of her preoccupations. She does no research for discovery, merely for immediate production.

"That is, I don't go digging facts from their contexts for possible use in future plans. But when I finally settle on a subject I do a lot of talking about it and questioning, and all my reading, every activity, centers on that one subject. Not even war breaks in."

She disclaims certainties, does not know sure answers. "One thing that I do know is that I am extremely happy to be here in America, so happy that I must check myself against being too fulsome, too sentimental about it."

THAT DARING YOUNG MAN, WILLIAM SAROYAN

He talks on writing as he pleases, on horses, the theatre and graciousness

March 24, 1940

William Saroyan—author of "My Heart's in the Highlands," "The Time of Your Life," "The Daring Young Man of the Flying Trapeze" and other stories and plays with equally excellent titles—straddled a narrow and thoroughly uncomfortable round iron railing in the skylighted fourth-floor corridor of the Theatre Guild Building in West Fifty-second Street and talked eagerly and hastily and well.

He is extremely friendly, one of those rare people who have managed to get along without, seemingly, erecting any barriers against others. Even his courtesy is no barrier, for it apparently has grown directly out of an extraordinary sensitivity, an inescapable consciousness of the reactions of those about him. His talk is colorful, bright with images, and delivered in a hurry because there is so much more talk where it came from.

Saroyan is thirty-one years old. He started writing when he was sixteen years old and determined to give himself until he was thirty to the task of proving that he could write. "Recognition," as he calls it, came some time ago. For several years even those commentators on the state of letters in America who heartily dislike Saroyan's work have found that he opened up for them great mother-lodes of expression. The author of a recent article on the current literary scene, for example, spent more space berating Saroyan than he gave to praising all the writers he liked.

Saroyan is black-haired, about medium height, with a jutting nose that is not so large as the nose of Cyrano de Bergerac. His voice is almost as deep-toned as John Steinbeck's, and there is a suggestion of considerable vitality beneath a nervous manner that is just surface.

Saroyan was hanging around the Theatre Guild as co-director with Eddie Dowling of his new play. He said that he was there to keep the stuff natural and to explain what it meant. "They are apt to go wrong on scenes from lives with which they are not familiar. And sometimes they are confused. They think they know what it means when they don't.

"Like one fellow wanted to produce a play of mine as a fantasy. You know, not play it straight but with a lot of dreamy angles. 'Fantasy!' I said. 'Hell, it is damn near all fantasy now!' "

Theatrical people, he explained, naturally want to use theatrical tricks. They have vast backgrounds on which they draw for theatrical effectiveness, and they want to play up scenes to get a sure kick out of them. Saroyan guards against many of these aims.

"We have this hoofer who hoofs a little, does a few dance steps. They wanted to go to town with those dance steps—make them symbolic of something. I said no—just let him hoof. Any simple little hoofing. The audience will take care of the symbolism."

In response to a comment that he was the current golden boy of the theatre he spoke of his "recognition." He is writing a lot of plays now, not because he is a flash in the pan, he said, who is trying to clean up while he's hot. "It is just that a door was open to me. My first show was put on and the people liked it. Naturally I'm turning out more. I'm not the kind of guy to knock at a door and then when the door is opened not to go in. You knock at a door and the people open it and if you don't go in they say, 'What's he doing? Picking daisies?' But all this work in the theatre is part of my general plan. I'm still writing short stories and I'll go on from this to novels—anyway, long prose pieces. But right now the theatre is wide open. No one's been making full use of its possibilities."

He said that George Jean Nathan woke him up to some of the

theatre's possibilities and suggested a course of reading for him. He has "discovered" Strindberg and Molière—bought a beautiful old set of the latter writer's work at 10 cents a copy in the moldy basement of a Fresno bookstore—and has immersed himself in these old plays. "They got inside people—they were naturals."

Did he consider himself a "natural"? Yes. Certainly. His writing flows without impediment. And he always has stories to tell. "What else is a 'natural'? I knew when I was a kid that I was going to be a writer. And when I was 18 I learned that I had to write in my own way. I'd been trying for a couple of years at that time. Then no editor would pay any attention to my stuff. Well, I was doing a great deal of very hard and quite disagreeable work. I wanted to live like a writer, since I was one, so I studied the pulp magazines and aimed at getting $50 for a story—that seemed like riches then. I studied them carefully and wrote ten stories that followed the pulp story pattern. But the trouble is that when I try to be phony I am a lot phonier than other people. The pulp company kept my stories a couple of months and then sent them all back. So I knew that I had to write my own way."

He said that it is a mistake to say that his work is formless, that everything he writes has very definite form. The lines of the problems make clear starts, move on through climaxes and are resolved. But the material, the way of handling it, is new and unfamiliar, and the accusation of formlessness is a result. "Once a magazine asked my agent if I'd write a Christmas story. He warned them that I'd probably write something they wouldn't see as a Christmas story because I write my own way and can't write on ideas from outside. They said for me to go ahead. I was willing to do it because it was the Christmas season and I felt like Christmas. So I wrote it as a story of the children's day and not only small children but the day for the childishness—I mean the childlikeness—that is in all of us. That is Christmas to me, more important than wreaths and trees and the rest of it. But they'd wanted more the wreaths and trees and didn't find much Christmas in my story at all."

The gossip that he has been losing his play royalties at the race tracks is "purely a fable." He always has bet "a buck or two" on the horses when he had the money, partly because he likes to go to the tracks and watch the horses run, and partly because "on a day when you want to take it easy, don't want to shave, don't want to work, it is nice to stop around at a bookie's place and listen to the talk and watch the people—it is a fine place to loaf. And these idlers, too, are part of the American scene. It is good to know workers—to be able to write well about them—but the idlers are people too and they also are interesting. Don't get me wrong. I don't hang around a bookie joint in the name of art. But art comes into it; it comes into every department of life. You've to see all people in all actions in all moods to do the thing I want to do. And gambling is American."

If he had not been "recognized," that would not have ended his program. In fact, he might have done better work, he believes, but on another plane, another level. Now he must be gracious. People praise what he does, and though it often is evident that they praise him with the wrong reasons in their own thoughts, he is appreciative, he respects their praise because praise must always be respected when it is sincere. All sincerity must be.

Had a strong person such as himself been allowed to go on butting his head against stony indifference, he could hardly expect to avoid an attitude, not of bitterness, but one that would reflect the world as it looked to him in his anger and frustration. He would have called attention to the frauds, the foolishness, the meanness of the world, because that would have been the way the world looked to him. Now there is a glow over it—"I won't need to change, can go on with the work, with the program that I laid out for myself many years ago."

We were in the corridor on the fourth floor of the building, because all the doors to the rehearsal rooms were locked. Saroyan, whose talk so often seems overself-confident when quoted or read in print, was shy about returning through the waiting room—which was crowded like a subway car at 5:15 with actors and actresses futilely waiting for parts—to obtain a key. There are forty dark theatres in New York most of the time, he said, and the unemployment problem is an evil. He has been trying to talk up an idea that might ease this situation. If theatre owners and unions and actors and directors and writers could get together and agree to keep costs down to a minimum, why wouldn't it be possible to run shows at a dollar-ten or even a fifty-five-cent top? "Maybe the people in the cast would only get $25 a week, but that would be better than wasting their time and their talents."

He jockeyed for a more comfortable position on the iron railing, unwilling to meet again the hopeful, expectant looks of the people he was powerless to help.

A TALK WITH ERSKINE CALDWELL

It used to bother him that people found his work humorous. Now he doesn't care

March 31, 1940

THE STORY IS that in the early days of the record-breaking run of "Tobacco Road," Erskine Caldwell, from whose novel the play had been taken, came down from Maine to have a look at the performance. But every time he went into the theatre the laughter of the audience drove him out. The laughter—golden to the commercial-minded—sent him wandering the streets in rage.

Questioned about this, Mr. Caldwell said—not complacently, but not sadly, either—that all this, if it happened, happened a long time ago. "Seven or eight years, wasn't it?" A play that runs that long can wipe out a considerable amount of woe. It probably is true, said Mr. Caldwell, that he found the laughter provoking. "I don't write things that are supposed to be funny. But if people want to laugh at what I have to say, that is up to them. There's nothing I can do about it, and nowadays I've found that out."

As for wandering the streets in a rage, there would have been nothing new in that. "I was cooped up in this town when I wrote my first novel. My room was in one of the houses torn down to make a place for Radio City. When I lived there they were making sample drillings and doing some preliminary work, and I'd come out about three o'clock in the morning, pick up a loose board that workmen had left lying around, and go to Fifth Avenue, where I'd bang a lamppost with the board. Other times I'd pick up loose bricks and crack them together until they broke. That's one reason I live in the country. I need exercise."

When he is working on a novel he spends much of his time chopping wood and cutting down brush and digging ditches. He is tall, unusually well built, with sizable, very capable-looking hands, and he keeps his hands busy while he broods about his work. He spends about a year thinking a novel before he does any writing at all. No notes; no outlines. He has made only one note in his life. That was for a name that he considered using, but eventually he threw the note away.

He writes "as it comes to me; I can't change it." When he wrote "God's Little Acre," he ripped the pages from the typewriter and threw them on the floor; never looked at them again. Some one else gathered them up and sent them off to the publisher. His new book, "Trouble in July," just published by Duell, Sloan & Pearce, was, in a sense, rewritten. That is, he typed a manuscript copy and made changes in phrasing. There were no structural shifts, however.

When he finishes something he likes to have one person agree that it is all right. When he gets an agreement the story or novel goes out for sale. His wife, Margaret Bourke-White, the photographer, does most of the first reading. (Mr. Caldwell has since been divorced and has remarried.)

He has written 125 short stories, 100 of which have been published. Most of the stories and all the novels concern life in the South. He is not trying to do a "Southern panel" but he is trying to cover the various aspects of the Southern scene that seem most important to him. "But not a planned cycle—nothing like that."

His novels and stories crackle with violence. In one an old man falls into a pigpen and is eaten by the hogs; there are lynching scenes and scenes of torture; people are burned with turpentine and the tails of dogs are sliced off for sport; heads are crushed and bodies mutilated.

"Well," says Caldwell, "it is a violent country. I've seen a man beat a mule to death because the sun was hot and he was tired and tense, sick of the endless sameness of his life. I've been in a barnyard at the end of a day in the cotton fields when the boss came over to ask why a mule was lame. A Negro explained that the mule had stepped in a rabbit hole. The boss beat the Negro unconscious—knowing the Negro couldn't fight back. I've been an unwilling witness at a number of lynchings."

Caldwell first tried his hand at writing when he was eight years old; went to work in the fields when he was nine. The son of a country preacher, "and maybe you know how country preachers are paid," his view of the world always was "economic." He did not go to school until he was sixteen; then he had a year of high school and moved on into a prep school, where he paid his way by playing football. He played semi-pro football also, and football earned his way for a year at the University of Virginia.

The fact that his position was center and that he weighed only 98 pounds when he started playing football for a living is perhaps a pretty good scale to indicate the strength of his determination. Ninety-eight-pound centers have a rugged time on the football field. Caldwell still wears the marks of his career in sports.

Cutting loose from the university and from a newspaper job that he held for a time in Atlanta, he set out to live by writing.

He decided to settle in Maine, for a number of reasons. One was that there he could view the South from afar, an aid to perspective. Another, he thought the life there would be simple and cheap. Another, he anticipated that his neighbors would let him alone while he worked.

"I suppose it is all right to save up a thousand dollars and then go off somewhere to write a novel. That wasn't possible for me, and I'm not sure that I wasn't better off. I never let other people or extraneous things interfere with me at all. They could turn off the lights and cut off the water—it couldn't be helped. I wanted to work at writing and I did. I never have let any one influence me or turn me aside."

The best writing, he believes, is the work of people who are moved, driven by life—not the manipulators of life. Theodore

Dreiser and William Faulkner "dig their stories out of life with both hands."

He feels sorry for the people who go to writing classes—sorry for them because he believes they are wasting their time. "The important thing is to live first, have something to write about. If you have enough to say, you'll say it all right."

Though in his own work he concentrates on the South, he roams the rest of the country and believes that there are great areas alive with material that have been too long neglected. Our literature is not yet all plaster and niches; all life today has a place in it, and if writers would realize that, our books and magazines would be far more exciting than they are.

As for his own reception in the South—"they still write editorials against me every now and then; but I think that what I'm doing is having its effect." He is not, he says, an evangelist or crusader; he doubts that much good can be accomplished by preaching.

"I try to hold up a mirror to nature in the South—and to my own nature, to human nature. I don't say that lynching is evil or that cruelty is bad. But by showing people as they are cruel, and by showing their victims, by showing people oppressed to hopelessness and impoverished to hopelessness—perhaps in that way I'll have some effect on many lives."

MARQUAND UNBURDENS HIMSELF

Writers need egotism, discontent, and usually are happier for their ignorance, he believes

April 7, 1940

IN HIS NOVEL "Wickford Point" John Marquand said: "A writer of fiction is usually happier for his ignorance, and better for his having played ducks and drakes with his cultural opportunities. All that he really requires is a dramatic sense and a peculiar eye for detail that he can distort convincingly. . . . It is safer for him to be a self-centered egotist than to have a broad interest in life. He must take in more than he gives out. He must never be complacent, he must never be at peace . . ."

In person Mr. Marquand gave me, at least, no hint of ignorance or egotism—maybe in these respects he falls short of his ideal. Also, it may be suspected that he is rather more at peace than he seems to be—that his gusts of impatience are in part the workings of his dramatic sense. As one friend puts it, he is an "unchanging sort of man." He has stuck to the same magazine and book publishers, the same literary agent, the same friends with whom he started, and though the bulk of his work has consisted of stories for the popular magazines, the essentials of practically all of these tales have been laboriously mined out of his own experiences, not drawn from stock.

Twenty-odd years ago Mr. Marquand got together a $400 stake, quit his job in an advertising agency and went to work on his own as a novelist and short-story writer. Since then everything that he has written has sold. *The Saturday Evening Post* bought one story and never printed it, but that doesn't spoil the record.

Earlier, while working on *The Boston Transcript* when not long out of Harvard, he collaborated with W. A. Macdonald—a fellow newspaperman now on the staff of *The New York Times*—on a novel called "Yellow Ivory." The scene was India, a land with which the collaborators had become familiar through reading Kipling.

They assigned themselves alternate chapters and worked ambitiously, spurring themselves on with many cases of Sterling ale—which in those pre-prohibition times sold at two quarts for a quarter—and hundreds of Richmond Straight Cut cigarettes.

The novel ran to great length and the express charges for shipping it to publishers and paying the freight when it was returned collect finally forced them to withdraw the manuscript from circulation. Many years later, poring over one of Mr. Marquand's serial stories, Mr. Macdonald saw long stretches of familiar material. His own half of the novel never has seen print, but not all of Mr. Marquand's effort was wasted.

First as a romantic writer and later as a satirist, Mr. Marquand has made a long search for surroundings that would give him that sense of absolute aloneness that is almost a necessity for the taking of that step between reality and art. "Yellow Ivory" was written in a windowless room that provided an almost overwhelming sense of privacy because it was lighted only by a skylight.

His present New York apartment is as private—as islandlike—as one is apt to achieve. You go into an apartment house that seems merely normally guarded by doormen and elevator operators, but instead of rising, the elevator drops down. Several floors below street level the operator escorts you through a long corridor to a heavy, locked door and presses a bellbutton in an unheard, Morse-code signal. The door clicks open and after negotiating a fairly easy labyrinth the visitor arrives—like a hungry rat in a psychologist's laboratory—at the Marquand apartment door. The East River rolls past the windows of Mr. Marquand's study.

For summer use Mr. Marquand recently acquired a true island. This island is said to be about two-thirds salt-water marsh and its mosquitoes are creatures of legend. Mr. Marquand intends to transport an old house that he owns over some twelve miles of land and water and set it up on his island. To a writer there are few feelings more fundamentally satisfactory than that of inviolable privacy. "But not that I get it," Mr. Marquand commented. "No matter what workroom I use the whole damn family gets into it at one time or another every day."

He works with great concentration, but actually writes for only four hours a day, except in emergencies. When a piece of work has been hanging on too long he works for six hours. Last week he was on an emergency basis, trying to finish the first draft of a novel.

"For weeks I've been leading up to a crucial situation and haven't known exactly how I'm to handle it. That situation has been buzzing around everything else I've done. When I straighten it out the first draft will be finished and I'll break off to work on short stories."

He heartily dislikes writing, always has and always expects to, "but the pleasure of finishing a job takes a lot of the curse off it." He tries to plan his work so that when a set task is completed he can get away on a trip. These journeys of reward have taken him over most of the world.

After one trip through the West, Carl Brandt—who has been his literary agent for more than twenty years—remarked: "I hear you had some trouble with your shoes in Barstow, Calif." Mr. Marquand's face took on a purplish tinge as he saw privacy again destroyed—and in how remarkable a manner! "Good God!" he cried. "How did you—?"

It developed that another writer on Mr. Brandt's list had passed through Barstow not long after the Marquands and had found the night clerk of the principal hotel still muttering about a curious adventure he had had.

"This man Marquand," said the night clerk. "He's English, ain't he?"

"No, no. He's American."

"Whatever he is, he's been readin' too many novels. Bellboy come up to me and says, 'Funny thing. There's two pairs o' shoes standin' in the hall outside one o' the rooms.' I went and looked at 'em. Man's shoes and woman's shoes—both pairs dirty. 'What they put their shoes there for?' says the bellboy. 'Because he's been readin' too many novels,' I said. We come away."

According to Mr. Brandt, Mr. Marquand commonly responds rather vaguely to the details of ordinary living. When he has a cold he is likely to telephone friends, describe his symptoms, and helplessly request advice. He then follows the course of treatment specifically outlined by those he trusts. "When you write fiction," says Mr. Brandt, "you have something more to think of than whether the water is turned off or how much spinach to eat."

Mr. Marquand said that last summer he read the novel that he had quit his advertising job to write. It was "The Unspeakable Gentleman," a highly romantic tidbit that was published serially in *The Ladies' Home Journal.* Reading it over was an upsetting experience. "I almost lost my lunch."

"But though I don't like it now, could never write it now, I meant every word of it when I did the work. It was in every way the best I could do at the time—and that goes for everything I've done since. I can write on order—get a real kick out of doing adventure serials—and when I'm doing a job, whether on order or on my own, I'm sure that it is good. I believe that the serial and the short story are more difficult to write than the novel. In the novel you have room to make mistakes. In the short story there can be no mistakes—every sentence must count. And serials are short stories strung together.

"I have very little patience with the standards of the professors, the essayists, the writers of *belles-lettres.* They copy and quote. The writer for the pulp magazines—however close to pattern and formula he may stick—must be more creative than the professors or he can't survive."

KATHERINE ANNE PORTER AT WORK

The crystal clearness of her style, the perfect imagery, are achieved at white heat

April 14, 1940

KATHERINE ANNE PORTER stated with evident surprise that her papers are now in order and in her own house. Formerly she traveled a great deal with a suitcase for personal effects and a steamer trunk filled with manuscripts and notes. "Always I was up to my chin in paper." Now she has burned numerous short stories and four novels that she decided not to publish. But the material that she kept to work over is enough to occupy her well into her eighties. There are notes for novels, for a biography of Cotton Mather, and for some forty short stories.

Miss Porter's books are long anticipated. Each season Harcourt, Brace & Co. hopefully announce the coming publication of her study of Cotton Mather. Each season publication is postponed. Now she has completed eleven of the twenty chapters. And more, she expects to have a novel finished in June.

One difficulty is, she explained last week—when she came here from her home in Baton Rouge, La., to receive a gold medal in recognition of her work—that she requires absolute privacy when she does her writing, and as she likes people very much and thoroughly enjoys everyday living, she finds the gift of privacy not much to her taste.

Her neighbor in Baton Rouge, Robert Penn Warren—poet and author of the novel "Night Riders"—amazes Miss Porter with his ability to make full use of even thirty minutes of free time.

"He simply goes to his typewriter, picks up where he left off, and pounds ahead. 'Night Riders' was a tremendously complicated book to write. He went through it as though he was simply making notes in a journal."

Miss Porter is generally thought of as a stylist—her writing as a "connoisseur's product." Actually she is not much interested in writing for connoisseurs, and certainly she does not strive as a maker of phrases or wielder of rhythms. To write a story she goes through a long "brooding period," then stocks a room—preferably a rented room in a place where she is a stranger—with oranges and coffee, and goes to work, writing as rapidly as possible. Each of her three novelettes, "Old Mortality," "Noon Wine," and "Pale Horse, Pale Rider," was written in a week.

"I was just back from Europe and had no ties, no immediate responsibilities. Carl Van Doren told me of an inn at Doylestown, Pa., and I went there and took a room and started writing on a Saturday. I worked all week and on the next Saturday that first story was finished. I immediately commenced the second story and finished it on the Saturday after. Then it was necessary for me to return to Baton Rouge. I took a room in New Orleans on a Monday and finished the third story on the next Monday."

In the interest of speed she works on a typewriter, has evolved a kind of typewritten shorthand. When the first version is down she revises by interlining the script, makes more changes in a clear copy, and that is all. The crystal clearness of her style, the perfect imagery, are achieved at white heat.

Miss Porter never shows her manuscripts to any one until they are ready for publication. "If you go about showing what you do and asking advice and perhaps taking it, then the work isn't yours any more, isn't entirely your own." Through her long apprenticeship she said nothing about her work. She earned her living by writing—but that was writing done on order. Once on order she wrote an entire Mexican issue for a magazine. That issue continued to sell for eleven years, according to Paul Crume, who wrote on Miss Porter recently in *The Southwest Review.* Miss Porter hadn't heard of this record sale.

During her apprenticeship Miss Porter made a living for a time here in New York as a book reviewer. She also "ghosted" books and articles. While she was ghosting books, she said, she was bewildered and even a little frightened. "It seems perfectly incomprehensible to me that any one should want to sign a book that some one else had written. I think it a kind of insanity. I hated to be alone with people like that."

Miss Porter is a Texan, the descendant of soldiers and scholars. One of her ancestors was a colonel on Washington's staff and she is "quite proud of him; it seems that he went where he was needed and did the best he could. There is nothing in the record to suggest that he was a careerist or politician." Other ancestors established Porter Academies in various parts of the country.

Miss Porter started work as a newspaper reporter in Dallas—"but they let me go after a brief time." She had more success on a newspaper in Denver, but the influenza epidemic of the armistice year brought her so close to death that she believes she learned that it is true that the moment of death holds something like revelation. "Pale Horse, Pale Rider" is an attempt to record that experience; Miranda looks over the precipice that she recognizes as death:

"There it is, there it is at last, it is very simple; and soft, carefully shaped words like oblivion and eternity are curtains hung before nothing at all. I shall not feel or remember. Why can't I consent now; I am lost; there is no hope for me. Look, she told herself, there it is, that is death and there is nothing to fear. But she would not consent, still shrinking stiffly against the granite wall that was her childhood dream of safety, breathing slowly for fear of squandering breath, saying desperately, Look, don't be afraid, it is nothing, it is only eternity."

Miss Porter believes that this is the best story she has yet written. But she never has written anything that was not "the best I could do at the time."

BENÉT'S WORK IN PROGRESS

The author of "John Brown's Body" is writing a new long narrative poem with the American frontier as the theme

April 21, 1940

WHEN INTERVIEWERS HUNT—as interviewers should—for color and anecdote, Stephen Vincent Benét has a stock answer to the effect that he never has shot any elephants. Miles of paper covered with handwriting: "I've spent most of my life at a desk." A long illness last Summer "gave me some fine material. I learned a lot about a hospital from the inside." Slight of build, the illness has had an effect on his posture. He cultivated a mustache in his twenties in an effort to add a little to his age. He wears extra-large glasses for eyes so weak that they frustrated his desperate effort to get into the army in 1917. He learned an eye chart by heart and was accepted, but when they put him to peeling potatoes the sergeant noticed that the way he was carving the things he was likely to nick his nose. Brought up for another examination with a different chart he failed and was discharged from the army after three days' service.

A great-grandfather, a grandfather and his father all were graduates of West Point. Each year Mr. Benét goes to the Military Academy and lectures the cadets in an English course where his "John Brown's Body" is required reading. Through special rulings his son and daughters were baptized in the West Point chapel.

When Stephen Vincent Benét came back from France a dozen years ago his grand, 100,000-word narrative poem of the Civil

War, "John Brown's Body," was rolling up a million-dollar sale and making him the most discussed poet of his day. Poetry always has been his primary interest—while still a penny-pitching Yale undergraduate he contributed poems to well-edited magazines and published two volumes of verse. It seemed that "John Brown's Body" would subsidize considerable poetry—"but that was in 1929," said Mr. Benét last week. "I invested in good, sound, New Era stocks." And so his second major poem has been delayed while he has worked at short stories, a novel, movie scripts, verse, lectures, some librettos; while he has employed himself as odist for the tercentenary celebration of New Haven, as an editor of Farrar & Rhinehart's "Rivers of America" series, as an editor for the Yale series of books of younger poets.

Now the poem is about one-quarter written: "I'll have it finished in a year—I hope." It has been, he said, a difficult job, with 150 years of American history to cover. Its theme is the American frontier—the folk migration into the West.

"I've been reading a lot lately about Indian captivities. One woman who had been captured by Indians and made a squaw was resentful when she was rescued because she'd found that there was a lot more work to do as the wife of a white man. With her Indian husband she'd been able to sit around most of the time—doing a little hoeing and some cooking but not much of either. It was hard to go back to the job of being a pioneer."

He told of a man who had been captured during the French and Indian War and didn't know whether he was to be tortured or not. Most of the Indians in the camp went to fight the English under Braddock, and when the battle was over a giant Indian in war paint came into the captive's hut and the captive thought his time surely had come. But it seemed that the Indian had picked up a book on the battlefield and had brought it back with the idea that it might be of some use to the captive. There was another yarn about a small boy who was in a river boat with two oarsmen and an old lady who wore very full skirts. Suddenly Indians leaped from the shelter of bushes on the river bank, killed both boatmen, captured the boy, scalped the boatmen, overturned the boat. The last the boy saw of the old lady she was floating downstream held perfectly erect by her billowing skirts and stiff corsets, majestically rounding a bend of the river.

The excitement of walking in new land—and particularly the smell of new land—described usually as a "clean" odor—enlivens most of the records that pathfinders in America put down. Gratitude for cleanliness, for virginity, was noted at Jamestown and Plymouth, up the Hudson, in western Pennsylvania and so on West. It seems that the prairie when first seen was more beautiful than it ever has been since. There were many kinds of little flowers growing; these flowers did not return after the land had once been plowed. The wonders of the virgin land, the emotions of the pioneers are best recovered from wholly personal writings—letters and diaries—and it is in these sources that Mr. Benét has done much of his digging.

The Benéts maintain a large house in the East Sixties. Mr. Benét does most of his writing from two to five in the afternoon and from eight to eleven at night. He makes a first draft in long hand, revises as he copies that draft onto a typewriter. John Farrar says that he always has written with considerable ease; that the poems he wrote when at Yale were excellent; that he was certainly a "born writer." Mr. Benét, however, says that the best example of a born writer he has known is Thornton Wilder, who "really could write like a streak when he was in college."

Mr. Benét keeps a work-sheet on which he lists titles that seem to have the promise of a good story in them. One such title was "The Devil in New England." "At first I thought of having the Devil come to a small town in New England—a modern small town. Then I tried shifting it back into the past. It seemed a good idea but I didn't know what I'd have him do when he got there. Then I thought of Daniel Webster—how about if he met the Devil? From then on it was easy, of course. Webster's strong point was oratory, so naturally he'd have to meet the Devil in an oratorical contest and win."

He said that for many years he supported himself writing "he and she stories," but that he'd had to quit because "when you get along in your thirties you simply don't know about young love on Long Island."

"I never did know anything about love on the great estates—at least, nothing firsthand. But when you're young, you have friends who are going through it. After a while, though, your friends settle down and the key is lost."

The tales, like legends with which he has been almost wholly successful, had their predecessors some years ago. "I wrote some historical yarns that *The Country Gentleman* published. No one made any fuss—that is, readers didn't write in to say that they'd liked them or disliked them—so the idea went to sleep for a while."

His main concern at present is with the poem, at which he proceeds at no known rate. "I keep at it as much as I can and on some days I get through a lot of work. But pretty often I get stuck—it is an awfully difficult job. I can't jump around on it—that is, write part of the one section, get stuck, and start on another section. When I stick I must experiment until I find the way to get unstuck—and sometimes that takes days. But I'm hopeful now—hopeful that I'll be through it in another year."

ASCH RETURNS FROM THE PAST

After long labor on "The Nazarene" he plans a novel of modern New York

April 28, 1940

"THE DIFFICULTY OF the young writer in America," said Sholem Asch, happily, "is that in this country every one must earn a living. It is demanded; starvation is not allowed. He who serves his apprenticeship in Paris, for example, may starve if he pleases. He may starve and work. Who cares? His hunger is his own affair. But over here it is necessary to learn quickly—or earn a living by some other means. Starvation is against the American principle."

His gesture took in Fifth Avenue, a likely spot to bring this particular American principle to mind. He had just left the West Forty-fifth Street offices of Putnam's, his publishers, and was heading toward the Public Library like a duck to water. "I truly love the place; the magnificent books; I require books as I require air." He is not, at present, engaged in special research. "I am not thinking of a novel. No, I am thinking of the East River. I do not sit down and decide that now I must do a novel, but only think of a subject. And then, if a novel is there for me, it evolves."

His next book, according to his present plan, will deal with Jewish life in America, more specifically in New York. "In Europe wealthy Jews mingle with wealthy gentiles, but the masses of the Jewish people keep and are kept strictly to themselves. Here, it seems to me, that situation is reversed, for the masses mingle and intermarriages are frequent. I think this is a healthy condition."

He told of some difficulties he encountered in writing "The Nazarene," his novel about Christ. He could not, he said, as a Jew, accept the New Testament whole—"yet, what other authority had I to work with? What greater book? But there are details impossible, in scholarship, to accept. As an example, the statement that after Pontius Pilate had passed sentence he washed his hands, as a way of showing that he was purifying himself of the deed. Tell me, would Hitler rend his garments to show grief? No. And neither would Pilate wash his hands to purify his soul. The act is utterly Jewish."

To guard against error he took those chapters that he thought might contain errors, or points open to dispute, to the greatest authorities on Biblical times that he could find. His own scholarship is not inconsiderable. For research into the life and times of Christ he assembled a working library of 1,200 volumes; and, more important, the subject had fascinated him for more than thirty years.

He said that he started to write "The Nazarene" in 1907, during his first visit to Palestine. Several scenes of the first chapters were published, but the result was unsuccessful. "I was far, far from ready." In 1914 he again went to Palestine and spent many months traveling through the country, visiting places of note mentioned in the Old and New Testaments, studying and taking notes. Again in 1929 he returned there and spent several months. In 1936 he made a fourth visit, collected more hundreds of notes, and then the next year returned to this country to settle—he had become an American citizen in 1919—and started to write. The book was published last Fall.

When actually at the job of writing he works with great application: "I do not understand these writers who find inspiration only between eleven and one; when I write I do nothing else." For many years he did most of his work in Paris and in the south of France because he found life in New York too distracting. "There was always an appointment to be kept, a speech to be made, an invitation to accept." The profits of "The Nazarene," which has sold more than 250,000 copies, have enabled him to buy a house in Connecticut where he expects to do much of his future work. His rule for writing, he said, is his own amusement. "If I like what I am doing, others will like it. But I must be amused or it is not good."

Mr. Asch is a well-fed-appearing man, with tired, red-glazed eyes, an unusual capacity for quick enthusiasms, a manner that seems to reflect a deep and extraordinary kindness. He was born sixty years ago in the small town of Kutno—a Russian town at that time, then Polish and now, in all probability, Russian again. Brought up in a Jewish, strictly religious atmosphere, he was prepared to be ordained as a rabbi, but readings in Shakespeare, Goethe and Schiller instilled in him a desire to write. When he was twenty, he started his literary career by writing short stories in Hebrew, but at the age of twenty-three he switched back to his mother tongue of Yiddish and published an epic of patriarchal Jewish life under the name "Village." His first play was produced the next year and at the age of twenty-five he was a full-fledged playwright with productions in St. Petersburg, Warsaw and New York.

Asked how many languages he uses, he said: "I am not one of those Jews with many languages at my command. Yiddish, of course. All my thoughts are in Yiddish and I write in Yiddish." (The Sterling Library at Yale asked for and exhibited the manuscript of "The Nazarene.") "My second tongue is Hebrew; I have done some work in Aramaic—" "And the European languages?" "Yes, certainly, Russian, German, French, Polish and so forth—and a little English."

He said that for many weeks he has been trying to draw himself back into the present. "For years I have lived in the past, in the temples and roads of Jerusalem, studying and writing and rewriting, until the life of today seems less real to me than the life of that day. Now I am beginning to feel at home again in these times and to take an interest—a very great interest—in life in New York as it is lived today, particularly along the East River."

THURBER'S LIFE AND HARD TIMES

An account of the humorist's rather confused start as a writer and as an artist

May 12, 1940

JAMES THURBER said that when, in the mid-Nineteen Twenties, he returned from France—where he had been working as a newspaper reporter—he went round to Brandt and Brandt, the literary agency, to ask whether the stuff he'd been writing in his spare time had any chance of publication.

"Some one there told me that I was most likely to sell to *The New Yorker. The New Yorker* was about a year old but I'd never heard of it. I went over to the magazine office with some thirty pieces. They sent them all back. I wrote more and they sent those back. Then my wife—my first wife—said that she thought I was spending too much time on each piece; that I was worrying the life out of the ideas. I set an alarm clock so that it would ring when I had worked on a piece for forty-five minutes. I decided that was all the time I'd give myself on each job.

"The first thing I wrote under that system not only sold—it caused Ross (the editor) to send for me. I went to see him and in some way or another Ross convinced himself that I was an old friend of Andy White (E. B. W.). In fact, I'd met White only a few minutes before meeting Ross.

"But because he liked my piece and because he thought I was a friend of Andy's, Ross hired me. I started as managing editor, of course—every one starts as managing editor on *The New Yorker*. I didn't know that I was managing editor—I thought I was a writer. But each week a girl would bring me slips of paper to sign and the third week I asked her why I had to sign slips of paper. She explained that these slips were the payroll and that signing them was part of my job.

"I went to Ross and told him that I didn't want to be managing editor, that I wanted to write. He said, 'Nonsense!' He said that he could get a thousand writers but good managing editors were hard to find. I could write if I wanted to but wouldn't be paid for it because my job was to be an editor and he wanted to discourage my writing. But I kept on turning out pieces and after quite a while Ross decided that since I was willing to write for nothing perhaps I was a writer after all."

He had been a member of *The New Yorker* staff for several years when one day E. B. White—they shared an office—picked up a drawing that Thurber had tossed toward the wastebasket and sent it in to *The New Yorker's* weekly art conference. The conferees thought this was whimsey and returned it. It was a picture of a seal—a penciled drawing on a piece of yellow copy paper.

White reinforced the lines with ink and again submitted the seal. Rejected a second time, the drawing was returned with an added sketch made by an artist at the conference and a note: "This is the way a seal's whiskers look."

"Along about then Andy and myself wrote a book, 'Is Sex Necessary?' And Andy insisted that my drawings be used as illustrations. Harper's weren't exactly fond of them, but when the book came out the drawings made a kind of hit. So the next time I met Ross he said: 'Say, why can't you give us some of your drawings?'"

Mr. Thurber hasn't stuck to his system of writing by the clock. When he goes to work on a piece he writes a first draft "just for size." "That draft isn't any good; it isn't supposed to be; the whole purpose is to sketch out proportions." He polishes this first draft, building up the material, perfecting the prose. The first page may be rewritten as many as fifteen times—not counting brief, warm starts. A passion for flawless typewriting causes him to recopy each page with a mistake on it, "and, of course, every time you copy a page you make changes."

Despite these labors, he enjoys the actual work of writing, he said.

"I rarely have a very clear idea of where I'm going when I start. Just people and a situation. Then I fool around—writing and rewriting until the stuff jells."

He is not doing any writing now. "I've had one bad eye for a long time and now I've a cataract on what was the good one. I can see that chair over there but I couldn't recognize any one in it." (The chair was about a yard away.)

He has learned that there are at least 300 varieties of cataract, named, like stars, for their discoverers. His, he said, is one of the simpler kinds, comparatively easy to be rid of, but two operations will be necessary. One this Spring and one in early Fall.

Tall and thin, with a pleasant voice, an exceptionally narrow mouth, a streak of white hair mounting from just above the ears. It is complimentary but true that neither in manner nor talk does he give indication of consciousness that he is a humorist with a reputation. No epigrams.

He commented that he is forty-five years old and that the forties are very hard going. He quoted John Jay Chapman, who said in his autobiography that he would have killed himself when in his forties except that he was sure he wasn't worth the powder and shot and the trouble of burial. Mr. Chapman reported that the fifties were better and Mr. Thurber hopes he was right.

"When you get to be forty-five the only thing you really want is another shot at the ten years since you were thirty-five, or better, at the fifteen years since you were thirty."

He was to fly to Bermuda the next morning, and some one who worked for the airplane company telephoned to make sure that Mr. Thurber knew what time the plane was to leave and where it was to leave from. Mr. Thurber returned to the interview not quite patient. "That's the third time they've called," he said. He feels that his reputation for being uncommonly vague and a little mad is not justified. His writing is based in truth distorted for emphasis and amusement—but truth. "It is reality twisted to the right into humor rather than to the left into tragedy."

"The Male Animal," the play that he wrote with Elliot Nugent, "is fundamentally the story of the break-up of a marriage—but with a twist. If you told a friend that so-and-so and so-and-so had broken up, the friend would say, and mean it, 'That's too bad. I'm sorry.' But in the play we say, 'No, it isn't too bad. It is funny.' And we give it the twist that makes it funny.

"Some of the reviewers said that there were 'mad Thurber touches' in the play. You'd think if there were 'mad touches' I'd know about it. It all seems sane enough to me."

THOMAS MANN IN PRINCETON

He talks of the work he recently has completed and of his immediate plans

May 19, 1940

PROMPTLY AT five o'clock Dr. and Mrs. Thomas Mann entered the drawing room of their Princeton house accompanied by a French poodle who, in spite of the heat, was wearing unconventional full dress. The drawing room is, as Mrs. Mann said, "of concert hall size." A grand piano at the far end looked not much bigger than an office desk. The house is a massive structure located on Stockton Street, surrounded by gardens and a high brick wall and further screened from the street by large trees. A weather-worn sign that reads "For Sale or Rent Furnished" shows above the wall. The Manns are leaving soon to spend the summer in southern California. Whether they will return to Princeton in the Fall "is not yet decided," Dr. Mann said.

"My friend Max Reinhardt has a house in California, and there are many German-speaking people in the movies now. The skies are a heavenly blue. It is a part of your great country that is very much alive. Yes, we will go there for a time."

It was one of the first really warm days of the year and Mrs. Mann commented that one who had not lived well into middle age could not possibly appreciate the change in the season.

"Oh, no," she insisted. "You have given it no attention at all. Probably you are not even aware that it is Spring. You were quite as well satisfied in the Winter."

Erika Mann came in, exclaimed, "Oh, an interview!" and left

swiftly by way of a French window. It seems that interviewers not uncommonly concentrate on Dr. Mann's opinion of how long the war will last, who will win, and what country will next be attacked—questions that neither he nor the members of his family feel he adequately can answer. Dr. Mann asked whether this interview was to be "political or literary," and on hearing that it would not be political he, Mrs. Mann and James H. Meisel—formerly an influential German editor who now is Dr. Mann's secretary—appeared to be relieved.

Dr. Mann mentioned his coming birthday—he will be sixty-five years old on June 6th—and recalled a special theatrical performance that was part of a quite elaborate celebration of his birthday five years ago in Zurich, Switzerland. There had been one almost comparable event here, he went on, when his lecture room had been as gayly crowded as the theatre at Zurich.

"My lecture was given at a time when many young ladies were here for one of the annual Princeton parties. But not only the boys came to my lecture—the girls came too. A heartening victory for a man of my age."

His manner was animated as he spoke of this. On the subject of his work he was cool, matter-of-fact. He hopes to get on with his "Joseph cycle" in southern California this summer. His most recently completed work is a novel "based on an anecdote in the life of Goethe," he said. Frau Charlotte Kestner, the Lotte of Goethe's "Sorrows of Werther," for whom Werther committed suicide, comes, at the age of sixty-three, on a visit to Weimar, and is entertained at dinner by the aging Goethe.

"The anecdote interested me, but relatively it is unimportant. The novel is a study of Goethe, the artist—a portrayal of the inner life of a genius."

The time of this novel is 1816, he continued, and he found it difficult to go back from that period directly into the time of the Joseph cycle.

"So I am working on a novel based upon an old Indian story—not American Indians—no, no—a legend of India."

He said that his work habits have changed little with the

years. He wakes at about seven-thirty or eight and after breakfast goes immediately to his study, where he writes "slowly, in longhand." His average rate of production has stepped up somewhat in these last years, but it still is no more than about a page and a quarter of manuscript each day. He stops work at noon.

"Yes, that is my unvarying schedule—seven days each week. I believe I would find it impossible to do anything else than work in the morning. I have no temptation to read, to lie down, to talk. Without opening my mail or reading a newspaper I go—with fresh energy and a clear mind—to my desk."

At noon he walks for an hour—"thoughts come clearly while one walks." When he was a younger he covered considerable distances on foot or on a bicycle, he said, but now a walk of an hour is enough. The afternoon is given to correspondence, reading and "receiving friends."

He touched upon the war in a comment on the difficulty that the artist today encounters in his attempt to give all of himself to his work, and again his manner changed. His tones became harsh with strong emotion as he spoke of "the detestable forces of evil that are loosed upon the world." He sat rigid, staring straight ahead, the teacup that he held chest-high, an incongruous object.

Later he led the way to his study, a workroom very near perfection. The room is lined with books. "The Nazis took my library—but I have acquired these volumes in the last few years." A big desk that he smuggled out of Germany dominates the room—it is placed between a wide fireplace and the south windows. Books were scattered on the couch and there were large, comfortable-looking chairs with books on the arms.

"A good place to work," Dr. Mann said. "Here we have the security of a strong, great country behind us. But even here in this room the explosions that make the world unfit for living I can hear. There is no escape until the enemies of mankind are driven out."

JOHN O'HARA, WHO TALKS LIKE HIS STORIES

The author of "Appointment in Samarra" and "Butterfield 8" is working on a musical show and contemplating the writing of a play as well as another novel

May 26, 1940

John O'Hara said that when quite young he had made up his mind that he would write three novels—one about his home town of Pottsville, Pa., one about New York and one about Hollywood. In 1933, when he was twenty-eight years old, he decided that it was time to get started, so he went on the wagon and commenced to write. But the Pottsville material at first took the form of a series of long, integrated short stories and he hadn't gone very far before he decided that he was trying to cheat himself.

"That was in August. I was in Pittsburgh working on what was laughingly called a news magazine. I got out of there and came back to New York—tried to make a living free-lancing mainly to *The New Yorker* and *Harper's Bazaar*. I threw over the short-story idea in December and began on a novel, living in a nine-dollar-a-week room in a place called the Pickwick Arms. There was no desk—only a chair, a bureau and the bed. I used the bed as a desk—put my typewriter on it—and each night I'd work until my back began to hurt.

"My working time is late at night. Evenings I'd go to Tony's and sit around drinking coffee and talking to people until about midnight, then go back to my room and write. Sometimes I'd quit after a paragraph or two, but usually I kept going until about seven o'clock.

"The novel interested me and after a while I discovered that I had only three dollars and that because I'd spent all my time on the novel I had no short pieces out—that is, there was no chance of a sale that would bring in some cash. This worried me. I was not so good on the touch, either, because I owed a lot of people.

"I had 25,000 words of the novel completed. At various times in the last few years three publishers had seen my short stories and asked me—well, said that if I wrote a novel they'd like to see it. I wrote three identical letters saying that I had 25,000 words written and that I'd submit the manuscript under two conditions. The first condition was that if they liked it they would subsidize me while I finished it. The second condition was that they'd read the manuscript overnight.

"I finished these letters early in the morning, put them in the mail and came up to Times Square and went to the movies. I spent the whole day in ten- and fifteen-cent movie houses along Forty-second Street. When I went back to my room at about five-thirty that afternoon I found messages to call all three publishers. There was nothing wrong with the mails that day—Cap Pearce of Harcourt, Brace had read my letter and called me at eleven-thirty that morning. His had been the first call, so I telephoned him and he said that he'd read the 25,000 words that night. The next day he telephoned to say that Harcourt, Brace wanted the book and to ask how big a subsidy I needed. I told him I wanted fifty dollars a week for three months and he said to come on over and sign the papers."

O'Hara completed "Appointment in Samarra" within four days of his self-imposed deadline. The book was unquestionably first-rate and well before publication a movie contract was offered and accepted and O'Hara went to Hollywood as a writer for Paramount. Much of his time since then he has been under Hollywood contract. His Hollywood rating is that of a "polish guy." That is, in general he works on scripts that already are partly completed but require dialogue or comedy angles.

His Hollywood novel "Hope for Heaven" was an effort to show

the young people of its year just as they were, to compass in a brief book the current moral attitude, the manner of speech, the political view, the type of humor that appealed—in short, youth in an America temporarily stunted. The book brought him a number of letters from people of college age asking him how old he was—a sound indication that the novel had accomplished its purpose, he feels.

O'Hara's next novel will have as its central figure an older woman. He is in New York now working on the book of a musical show based upon his "Pal Joey" stories—they have been appearing in *The New Yorker.* When he finishes this he intends to write a play—a tragedy. And next year he will start work on his fourth novel, a story of encroaching age. Meanwhile he has completed a number of sketches and short stories that will appear in magazines this Summer.

Tall, with good shoulders and capable hands, O'Hara is not a man to avoid arguments. His energy is sufficient to form a basis for legend—old friends recall the night some years ago when, feeling that a soldier had insulted him, he made a determined attempt to reach Governor's Island with the intention of taking on the army.

His talk is spiced with an entirely agreeable note of challenge that, as it has no itch of nervousness about it, merely adds to the interest. Blessed with a really magnificent memory and an unerring instinct for vivid and significant detail, his talk has much of the quality of his writing. The fact that his writing is all first-draft, that it goes to the printer just as it comes from his typewriter, becomes readily believable after an hour or so of talk.

THE ROAD UP FOR JESSE STUART

With four well-liked books published, the young Kentuckian has three more volumes planned

June 2, 1940

"I STARTED WRITING soon as I could write my name," Jesse Stuart said. "That wasn't any too early. Couldn't write my name before I was eight or nine. But I knew then I wanted to be a writer and I know it yet. Sir, they can't stop me. If people won't read what I write, that'll be too bad. If people won't publish what I write, I'll suffer. But they can't make me quit writing. They'll have to kill me first."

He said this with great seriousness—not so much as a man who really expects a murderous attack as a means of keeping him away from a typewriter, but as a man who would be thoroughly prepared.

He put another match to his cigar and pulled up a chair on which he rested his feet. Though about six feet tall, he is rounding out considerably. He explained that he hadn't put on weight, but looked bigger because he was going soft: "My muscles are running to fat. I don't do so much heavy work. Why, sir, I had to work in a quarry. I had the toughest job of anybody on the quarry crew where I went to college. And before that I worked in a steel mill. Used to swing a twenty-pound hammer that was too heavy for my weight. I'm no butter ball right now, but I'm nearer to one."

Mr. Stuart was here to attend the final dinner of the booksellers' convention at the Hotel Pennsylvania. His manner is expansive but considerate; a mixture of energy and eagerness enlivens his conversational style. When introduced he sticks to character: "Where you from?" he asks briskly, and when this is answered he tells of Kentucky—"That's where I come from; out where the hoot owls holler in the daytime."

"I could keep right on writing for a hundred years and I couldn't tell you all there is to know about Kentucky. Everywhere I go I see things I want to tell about. Went to see an uncle of mine one time and he and his sons—they were great people. I didn't just say they were wonderful people—I wrote about them and put down the truth just as I saw it—called 'em by name, told what they did and said, and what their pasts had been. Well, you know when you're writing the whole truth the people it's about may not like it, and when the manuscript had been bought I tried to get the names changed. But the type already had been set up and nothing could be done. It was published, and I didn't know what would happen. Turned out all right, though; no one in the family ever read it."

Mr. Stuart said that he was the first of his father's people ever to go to college. He ran into debt putting himself through high school, worked in a steel mill until the debt was paid off, then quit his job and hitchhiked to Berea College. Before registering he was asked why he wanted to enter Berea and whether he thought Berea was the finest college in the country. He said, no, that Harvard was better, and Vanderbilt and the University of Virginia, but of the small schools he liked Berea. He was told that there was no room for him in Berea and advised to go to Lincoln Memorial. So he hitchhiked on there, was admitted and worked his way through.

At Lincoln Memorial he dug ditches, worked in hay fields, quarried rock, waited on table, wrote poetry, ran the school paper, and met two other able writers. They were Harry Kroll, best known for his writings about Southern shantyboat people, and the author of an excellent autobiography, and James Still, one of the best of the younger poets and short-story writers, a stylist with a decidedly uncommon talent. Mr. Kroll was a teacher at Lincoln Memorial during Jesse Stuart's freshman year. James Still worked in the college library.

Finishing his course in three years, Mr. Stuart returned to Greenup County, poured out a flood of lyric verse. Most first volumes of poetry are slim little books; Mr. Stuart's was a lusty tome of 730 pages. It was very well received. Since the publication of this book, "Man With a Bull-Tongue Plough," Mr. Stuart has written "Beyond Dark Hills," an autobiography, "Head o' W Hollow," a book of stories and sketches, and "Trees of Heaven," a novel. He has completed enough short stories to make up at least one more book, and he has two other works in mind.

He said that he works at night, starts in the evening after supper and often keeps at his typewriter until dawn. He turns out enormous amounts of copy during some stints—in one night's work writing sixty-five typewritten pages, double-spaced, which is in the neighborhood of 20,000 words. He writes for his own satisfaction and thoroughly enjoys the work.

"I believe we should have more regional literature in America, and a lot of my stories I give away to little magazines in the sections that are trying to build up a regional literature. That's something I think is very important. I wish we had a dozen, two dozen writers telling about Kentucky.

"I suppose I could go out in Nebraska and write if I had to. But not for long. Before many months I'd have to go back to Kentucky. Because all that I am is right there. In a town like this I'm lost. I don't know a lot of the things they talk about; I don't know the little signs and what they mean. Back with my own folks in my own fields I'm my own man and I know it. I certainly do enjoy it there. I enjoy it all."

VAN WYCK MASON'S WAY OF WORK

A practiced craftsman, the author of "Stars on the Sea" outlines his technique when writing a novel

June 9, 1940

Van Wyck Mason had come to New York to attend a party at the Rainbow Room—a "literary tea" in something of the old style—that was given to mark the imminent publication of his new historical novel, "Stars on the Sea." He said that the long novel had occupied him for two years, despite the fact that his usual daily working speed is thirty typewritten pages a day.

"I spent eight months reading books, digging out maps and visiting the regions where the scenes are set. Then for sixteen months I wrote—or, rather, dictated. I'm an old pulp-paper magazine man and accustomed to getting through a great deal of work in every working hour. Also, I've a Dutch thrift that makes me hustle so that my secretary will have something to do.

"On this novel I kept up my usual pace of about 9,000 words a day, but I was a long time finishing it because I rewrote the book five times.

"And that wasn't because I was fussy about phrases. Novelists are up against such tough competition for a reader's attention, what with newspapers full of news, hell popping on the radio, movies to see and automobile drives to go on, that I doubt whether pretty phrases sell many books. There is still a respect for the very polished kind of writing, of course, and that's fine. But I wonder how many people have a go at a book in order to savor the prose. I believe the majority prefers a well-plotted, fast-moving yarn, with plenty of incident."

Mr. Mason said that before starting a book he makes a chart showing the physical characteristics and speech traits of the characters—"so that when I've once given a girl blue eyes and black hair I'll have a check against talking about her red tresses." He has the time of the more important happenings roughly worked out, names settled, and settings planned and properly furnished.

"Then for the first draft I'm interested primarily in getting the whole thing down. I let descriptions run on for pages, introduce incidents whether they really belong or not, let the characters spout at any length—anything to get the story swinging and keep it swinging.

"That first draft is a version without self-consciousness. In the second I try to get my proportions right. That is, I decide when making the second draft how much space will be given to a fire or a fight, and how much emphasis should be placed on this or that encounter.

"When I start the third draft the proportions are pretty well settled and I get down to polishing—cutting up the action with change of pace, chopping down the speeches, that kind of thing.

"The fourth draft is further polishing and for much of my work four drafts are enough. But 'Stars' took another going over."

Mr. Mason hunts and fishes, goes in for a good many outdoor sports, which probably accounts for the obvious authenticity of the outdoor scenes in his novels. He saw enough fighting on the Western Front in the last war to explain his skill in battle descriptions—incidentally, these descriptions are the easiest for him to write.

He lived through two years of war, then entered Harvard. The contrast still amazes him. After college he became an importer, traveled around Europe and northern Africa as a part of his trade.

"One evening, here at the Harvard Club I met John Gallishaw, one of my old teachers. He asked me how my writing was getting along. I said: 'What writing?' He said: 'You ought to try it. You wrote some pretty good themes.' I said that it was very nice of him to say so and Gallishaw said that he wasn't being nice, exactly, that he was starting a short-story course and would like me as a student, since every little helped.

"But I was just about to be married and the course cost $200, so I said I couldn't take it. Gallishaw said that he'd gamble, that he'd take fifty dollars in cash and the rest out of my sales. That suited me. I took the course and Gallishaw gave me a fine start.

"I have a Continental respect for the arts. I think that an art must be learned and I set about learning by writing in the most popular vein, presumably the easiest vein. Instead of trying to write opera I wrote jazz. My first markets were the pulp magazines. That was in 1928 when there was money for all of us, and in that first year of writing I earned $18,000. I wrote eighteen stories before turning out one that didn't sell.

"Of course, I went into the pulps with certain advantages. I'd seen a good bit of action and a great deal of the world. I could use uncommon backgrounds."

His work in the pulp-paper magazines he looked upon primarily as an apprenticeship, and that apprenticeship was cut short when, as the depression deepened, rates for stories dropped and the range of the market lessened.

His aim always had been to write historical novels. He said that he has a strong interest in the ideas and the people of America's early days and he said that he is interested in teaching some essentials of American history "with a sugar coating over the information so that it will go down easily."

"This country didn't just happen, our way of life isn't an accident, but too few people realize the ideas and ideals and sweat and blood that made democracy work. If, in books read simply for pleasure, I can help spread the realization of what our form of government means, I'll feel that I've done all right."

BEN APPEL OF HELL'S KITCHEN

He has ranged the country for material but his native scene remains his primary interest

June 16, 1940

BENJAMIN APPEL recently returned from a buttonholing swing around the country. He went out to find how people were talking and discovered that most of the talk was about trouble. In the South they complained about "the li'l' feller" not making enough to live, and he says that he heard pretty much that same complaint in New England, in the Midwest and on the Coast except that in those regions they said "little" rather than "li'l'."

He made a special point of getting down the accents and personal and regional turns of speech for his new book, "The People Talk." "I went out in Wisconsin, for example, and pitched hay with a crew. Whenever any one made a comment that I thought I could use I'd stop and make a note—right there in the field. Just as well I did. I wasn't used to heaving hay around and the notes gave me a breathing spell."

Before ending a visit he typed out all the information he had collected. In this way he kept his notes from jamming up and discovered shortages of fact and inconsistencies before it was too late to fill in what he lacked and inquire for corrections at the source. He and Mrs. Appel were on the road for about eight months, stopping with farmers, haunting the dog wagons where factory workers and taxi drivers ate, probing beneath the casual talk of groups gathered at country stores.

He had gone out armed with letters of introduction from his

publishers, E. P. Dutton and Co., and from union leaders in the C. I. O. But much of his material came from keepers of small stores, from housewives approached as by a canvasser, from men stopped in the streets.

"The People Talk" was Mr. Appel's first effort in nonfiction. A native of Hell's Kitchen—New York's midtown West Side—the bulk of his writing has been fiction; the characters gangsters and politicians.

"Of course, I never found any glamour in crime. It is just part of the life that I knew, and you can't call the life of Hell's Kitchen glamorous. There are quite a number of people up the river in Sing Sing who were just neighbors. For instance, for a while my father did very well as a real estate operator. He had an office at Fortieth Street and Eighth Avenue, and a lot of other people who were doing well in politics or one thing and another would come to his office and sit in a very big poker game that ran there.

"I was about sixteen years old, but very naïve for that age, when we had a chauffeur, Red. I hung out a lot with Red and on many afternoons he'd take me downtown with him on visits to the Tombs. He'd bring presents to men in the Tombs, and once I said something about it being kind of funny that he should have so many friends who were in jail. Red said that lots of people were in jail and that their friends on the outside should help them. I asked what his friends were in jail for and he told me they were all in for speeding.

"Red was good to me but I guess the money he saw kicking around my father's office made him restless. One day when the poker game was big, some stick-up men came in and knocked it off. A couple of months later there was another stick-up in the office. And this time there was proof that Red was the finger man—that he had tipped off the stick-up crowd that there was a lot of cash available. But as I say, Red was just some one I knocked around with."

He spoke of the rigorous social rule of the Hell's Kitchen boy town. "The Irish Catholics were the top dogs and they considered that they outrated Americans, Germans and Jews in that order. After that came the Italians, the Greeks and the Negroes. Every block had a gang, and when you went off your own block and a gang caught you there was considerable chance that you'd be beaten up. But, of course, there was also some chance that you'd be beaten up on your own block. When I went to the University of Pennsylvania I talked from the side of my mouth the way they do in prison pictures and I pronounced words in what is the Hell's Kitchen accepted style."

As a sophomore he shifted to New York University, transferred again in his junior year, going to Lafayette College, where he remained until he was graduated. He published a book of verse while still an undergraduate, but he had been out of school for some time before he discovered that his best material was that which stemmed from his native place, the West Side. In the last ten years he has published three novels with Hell's Kitchen settings and has written sixty or more short stories. Some of these have been reprinted in anthologies.

"I haven't made much headway in the more popular magazines because they want you to write to pattern and I've tried that and can't do it. The attempt to milks the originality from my own stuff—and what orginality is left ruins the pattern.

"At present I think about the war a lot and can't get set to do anything. I'm fooling with a play but don't expect to make much progress until something is decided over there. There is only one thing I'm certain of, and that is that I'll keep on writing."

JAMES WARNER BELLAH ON WRITING FOR MONEY

He credits his success as a dealer in light fiction in part to his expensive tastes

July 7, 1940

JAMES WARNER BELLAH took over a story-writing course at Columbia University one year and the students earned double the cost of their tuition by the sale of their writings. Mr. Bellah thinks of himself as a craftsman and he taught craftsmanship. He says: "My stories are better than pulp-magazine stuff, but I know better than to think they are art." Behind this statement and contradicting it is a stubborn conviction that any man who writes as much as he does and works as hard must, at one time or another, write something that will be remembered. But this is a hope that he does not permit to interfere with the practical business of earning a very good living by writing.

He credits his success as a dealer in light fiction in part to his expensive tastes.

"I was in the advertising business here in New York, but I wanted to write and the writing got in the way of business. So I took a year off, went to Vermont, and determined to hit *The Saturday Evening Post* before that year was over—or go back to advertising and forget stories. Through most of the year I wrote plotted stories, trying to turn out what I thought was wanted. None of them sold to the *Post*. In the eleventh month I wrote a yarn based on the fear I had as an aviator with the Royal Air Force during the last war. It wasn't plotted, it wasn't trick—it was fear translated into words.

"It sold—to the *Post.* It has been in all kinds of anthologies. So far as I know every aviator who ever read it knew that it was true, had known the same emotion in the same way. So that was a good story. I followed it up with more stories of the same kind—all true, the real thing.

"But you can't go on writing aviation stories forever. The vein petered out for me. I had life insurance policies to pay and people to look after so, naturally, I went back to plots. I'm a glib writer—too damn glib. I can write myself around improbabilities, slough over facts that I don't know, hide reality in humor, change what is ugly into romance."

He said that these talents hadn't helped him much in Hollywood—that no matter how fat a contract he'd gone out there with he'd never managed to put any of the take away. Neither have his book sales been considerable. His best medium has been the magazines. He is one of the writers editors of mass-circulation magazines can trust to turn out a serial story that will follow advance specifications, that will not shock, arouse or offend, but will amuse and please the readers. This market at present, however, is much confused, he said. "I'd hate to be an editor right now." Material that seems timely when ordered is apt to be very stale fish when ready for publication; while material that is not timely seems dull, unnecessary, not worth reading.

"A couple of months ago I started a series with an army background. Luckily, I wrote only two or three of the stories that I'd planned. Who wants to read about an army in peace time with the world turning upside down?"

He likes to keep three jobs going at once because it is a relief to turn from one to another. Currently he is writing a serial story, putting together—with the aid of a collaborator—a long series of brief histories of famous regiments, and making a compilation of family letters. The Bellahs settled in Delaware when this country was new. Mr. Bellah's workroom is decorated with the swords of his ancestors—they fought in all the wars in which the United States has engaged—and his own swagger-stick, carried in the last war, is in a far corner. The Bellahs were good correspondents and saved their letters. Mr. Bellah is putting them together to make an informal history of sidelights on great events of the last 150 years.

Mr. Bellah maintains three homes with correct addresses; lives and spends most of his working time in a walk-up flat six stories above the East River. In this hide-out he starts work at six in the morning, keeps at it until twelve-thirty or so, looks after family, business and social interests through the afternoon, and goes back to work at six or seven o'clock in the evening. He writes in longhand bent over a coffee table at an angle that would be decidedly uncomfortable had he not kept in trim for years as a fencer, small-boat racer and big-game fisherman. A callus as big as a dime decorates the middle finger of his right hand as evidence of diligence at his craft. He averages about 2,000 words per working day.

Most of his time off during the last year has been spent with the United States army. Through four and one-half of the last twelve months he has been on duty as a reserve officer. He works at army tasks instead of going on vacations. Formerly his vacation schedules were simple. When he finished a piece of work he bought a ticket for some faraway place, traveled until he found a port that pleased him and stopped there, entering into the life of the place. Now the range for such traveling has narrowed and, anyway, he considers the army of first importance in American life.

"We ought to train a million men and get started at it right away. We're bound to lay a lot of eggs at a job of that size, and we haven't any time to lose before learning just what it takes to get a million men in shape for fighting, because when we get one million trained we'll have to start at once to train another million."

WILLIAM ALLEN WHITE TALKS OF WRITING AND READING

He thinks the main change in recent years has been "the swing away from 'dirt'"

July 14, 1940

William Allen White said that the writing of fiction is largely a matter of glands. He said that when he was biologically fit he wrote novels; with age he turned to biography. Behind all writing worth its ink is feeling—"and I believe that holds even for the columns on the market page of a newspaper. But when you can no longer, because of age, share the more elemental emotions, you had better quit trying to create a world and stick to reporting the world as it is.

"I spent five years working on 'A Certain Rich Man,' and I thought it was a fine novel. So did plenty of other people—it sold 250,000 copies.

"A friend of mine who knew George Meredith once told me that Meredith had remarked to him about the way in which all his experience, all his knowledge and ability and feeling concentrated at his fingertips when he wrote, when he was going full steam ahead on a story.

"That is inspiration. You get it by applying your sitter to the seat of a chair and getting at the job with all the energy you have. You don't get it by going across the street for a drink or by drowsily reading something some one else has written.

"I've known that same thing that Meredith described whenever I have written anything that I could be particularly proud of. When I was writing 'A Certain Rich Man' Mrs. White and I went to Colorado, where there'd be no distractions. I'd read the sections of my novel to her as I finished them and we'd marvel. Neither of us could think where that flow of prose had come from. Why, we wondered as much about how that book was created as we did about our son Bill. We'd look at Bill and say, 'How do you suppose such a fine fellow as this ever came about?' With the novel we were that same way."

Mr. White has written some hundreds of words daily for sixty-five years. As owner and editor of the *Emporia Gazette,* one of America's best-known newspapers, he gives himself time off from his job only when traveling in Europe. On his American journeys he reports.

When interviewed—over the breakfast table of the tradition-haunted National Arts Club facing Gramercy Park, which, as Mr. White commented, "is just about the only co-educational club in town"—Mr. and Mrs. White had just come here after fascinated attendance at the Republican convention in Philadelphia. Mr. White had been writing a daily "obbligato on the convention news."

Despite the energy with which he employs his style he has said that its directness and conciseness were in large part the result of youthful laziness. While in his teens he became a reporter on a Kansas newspaper where his duties included setting type. He jumped the middle step of composing his stories on paper and wrote them with type. The typesetter White was saved a good deal of work by the writer White learning to express himself in short pieces made up of short words.

Mr. White said that he didn't think much of the current crop of books. As one of the judges for the Book-of-the-Month Club he must read widely, and he said that the last book that he has been ready to go all the way out for was "Native Son," by Richard Wright. To objections that this book is the work of a Communist who seeks to obtain wider expression for his ideas through fiction, Mr. White's answer is that Communism, like typhus, is a disease spread among the undernourished by lice, but that if a Communist is an artist in fiction, his work should be considered only on the basis of art.

"The people who might be infected by Communism are not, by and large, readers of first-rate novels."

He believes that the Book-of-the-Month Club readers are divided into three groups.

"There are about 100,000 of them—probably more, but we'll settle on 100,000—and among them are about 20,000 readers who will accept subtlety in literature, who like stylists, who do not mind 'dirt,' who quickly fall in with new literary fashions.

"Then there are about 60,000 readers who are solid professional people—doctors, school principals, and so on—who don't appreciate subtlety, are made impatient by stylists, and are not much interested by fashions, by newness.

"The other 20,000 are people who have made good but have not had much education, who like the look of the books on their living-room tables, who intend to read but never get around to it."

The main change in taste in recent years, he believes, has been a swing away from "dirt." "Five or six years ago John Steinbeck's 'Grapes of Wrath' might have sold for the dirt that was in it. But that has changed. It has had its big sale in spite of the dirt and wholly because of its great qualities as a novel."

SINCLAIR LEWIS TALKS OF WRITING—AND ACTING

He likes the gregariousness of the stage—"Writing is such a lonely business"

June 30, 1940

SINCLAIR LEWIS is fond of the stage much as good tennis players are fond of tennis. "Arrowsmith," "Babbitt," "Main Street" are books that he liked fine a long time ago, that he still has a perfectly friendly feeling for, but that are no use right now. If he met Gottlieb or Dodsworth or Doremus K. Jessup, they'd be people to act, not to write about. Currently the most valued book he owns is a paper-covered copy of Eugene O'Neill's "Ah, Wilderness." As guest star for the Maplewood (N.J.) stock company he is as eager to impress Robert Ross, his director, as Martin Arrowsmith was to impress Dr. Gottlieb, and he goes about it in much the same way—by diligence and hard work, with a humble eagerness to be taught. His play script averages from twenty to thirty markings to the page—blue and red ink, green pencils, hard pencils, soft pencils, all have been employed for these markings at various times—and the print is blurred in spots as though the ink had been stroked out of the paper by a too affectionate hand. In the rehearsal hall in West Forty-sixth Street the other members of the cast read their lines. Mr. Lewis lounged at ease, his script in his pocket. He knew the play to the last syllable.

For two hours in his hotel apartment just east of Park Avenue he had been champing to get down to the rehearsal hall. As an actor he is handicapped by a habit of early rising. He needs little sleep and wakes at five, six, or seven o'clock. As most actors get up reluctantly at about eleven o'clock—"and that's necessary, you know; they must be fresh for their evening performances"—he daily faces practically an entire morning with no actors for company. Some of this time can be spent in the acquiring of personal props.

"I smoke a pipe in 'Ah, Wilderness' so, let's see, I need some fuzzy pipe cleaners and one of those pick and shovel things they dig into pipes with. And where's a good pawnshop where I can get a heavy gold watch chain, not quite as big around as my little finger—I want the audience to see it but it shouldn't be too gaudy—a simple, heavy pattern, but not too flash?"

He is impressed by the "professionalism" of the theatre. "Writing isn't any fun until you write as a professional. Same with the theatre. Dabblers and amateurs don't know the best of it." He says that he never did like formal society and that now he can't stand it. "The people of the theatre are intense—and so they're alive. An actor always will listen to another actor, and gladly, because he knows that if he listens the other actor will have to listen to him. And where can a playwright find an audience as good as a bunch of actors? When the playwright comes in and says, 'I—ah—am pahticularly int'rested in the paht you play, because I felt when I wrote the paht that there was rather moah to it than the lines bring out,' 'I felt the same thing, something sort of mystical,' says the actor, and in a flash he's going through the lines. Who else would listen to that playwright? Actors do, and like it."

Asked if he found that his own acting helped him to write better plays, he said that he couldn't say about that because he had yet to write a play that was a success; that he could hardly credit himself with improvement until he had clearly improved. "But my acting does keep me thinking in terms of what can be done on the stage."

He said that he liked the gregariousness of the stage. "Writing is such a lonely business. I almost always discourage kids who tell me that they want to be writers. The only reward is in what you do, the actual doing of it, and the writer has a lonely life. Of course, discouragement does no harm. It is impossible to discourage the real writers—they don't give a damn what you say, they're going to write. The others are better off if they are out of print."

He said that he didn't know why he became a writer, that back in Sauk Center every one in the gang could lick him and that psychoanalysts probably would make a lot of this fact. For himself he didn't think much of it.

"In every gang there is some one every one else can lick—and they don't all turn out to be writers."

His own work first received notice when he was eleven years old and in the fifth grade. "The teacher read a short story of mine to the class and said some nice things about it. But I'd written a lot of stuff before that."

He spoke of the time when "Ivanhoe" was his favorite book—though Dickens was his favorite author—and when the character he liked most in all the books he had read was Richard the Lionhearted.

"The people there at the tournament didn't know the name of the strange knight in black. But I knew—boy, did I know! And they didn't know who would win—but I did. A man who is an authority on that period told me that Richard was the best literary critic of his day—he criticized books in his letters. Another thing, Richard collected castles. He'd be riding along through the country and a castle would catch his eye. . . ."

A castle caught Lewis's eye and he peered sidewise, speculatively, and rubbed his chin. "But, Your Majesty," said Lewis, plaintively, "that castle won't do us any good. We don't need it. And you have so many castles. . . ." "Um-m-m," said Lewis, as Richard Coeur de Lion. "We don't need it, eh?" "No, Your Majesty. It would be just a waste of time and men. . . ." "Better take it. Protect our flanks." "Your Majesty, our flanks don't need . . ." "Besides, I think he defies me."

"So the King would ride to the castle and yell, 'Do you defy me, you dog?' 'Hell, yes,' the guy in the castle would say. And then they'd have to sit around there and fight over it until Richard had collected it and could go on with his main war.

"Maybe that was his literary temperament. It is a bad thing when the artistic temperament gets loose in the world. Look at Mr. Schicklegruber and Benito. Mr. Schicklegruber wanted to be a painter and Benito wanted to write. What hell breaks loose when the artistic temperament runs amuck! They do a lot worse than bankers or merchants or straight out-and-out politicians or aristocrats. And Churchill, Reynaud, Roosevelt—all good writers —opposing them. A dangerous business.

"The artists believe what they want to believe and you can't knock it out of them. Tom Wolfe made me a character in that book of his that will be published in the Fall. He says that my nickname is 'Knuck' because I have enormous knuckles. I doubt that my knuckles are any bigger than yours." We solemnly compared knuckles. Lewis's fingers, like the rest of him, are long and thin. "And he claimed that I was drunk twenty-three hours a day and did an astounding amount of good work in the other hour—that I never slept, just went on eternally drinking and working. How could that be so? Who could write a dozen books and be drunk twenty-three hours a day?

"Writers kid themselves—about themselves and other people. Take the talk about writing methods. Writing is just work—there's no secret. If you dictate or use a pen or type or write with your toes—it is still just work. I know that people want to hear about methods. They think, now if I knew exactly how that fellow or this fellow does it, I could do the same thing.

"And the writer gets thinking the same way. He works his little idiosyncrasies into a system like a scheme for beating roulette. If he has tried some method and it doesn't work out, he is as intolerant as an old lush who has quit drinking because his doctor has asked him to pay his bill so that he won't have the trouble of collecting from the estate, and who hates, despises every one who takes a drink. He says that method is no good.

"I have a—well, chaotic mind. So I do a lot of rewriting. But I can't fold my hands across my belly and cough and say that rewriting is the thing to do. Arnold Bennett once showed me the manuscript for the best book he ever wrote, 'The Old Wives' Tale.' And it was in a beautiful hand and all fixed up, the capitals practically illuminated, and there were only two or three changes of words to a page. He had each sentence clear in mind before he put it down—and it was his best book. He showed me later manuscripts and they had all kinds of changes—paragraphs scratched out, interlining. He never again had been as sure of himself and his material . . ."

Mr. Lewis popped his watch out of his pocket for the fifteenth time in thirty minutes. Time for the rehearsal. And in the rehearsal hall his manner changed. A supremely companionable man before eleven o'clock, he was, after that hour, the man who had written some of the best books ever written in America putting all of his amazing energy into a new and for him completely fascinating job.

WRITING BIOGRAPHY AND HISTORY

Allan Nevins talks about his working habits—he plans a long history of the United States

July 21, 1940

To THE REQUEST, "Please tell me a sparkling anecdote about Allan Nevins," friends of the historian usually answer: "He is the hardest-working man in the world." One man tells of telephoning Mr. Nevins early one Christmas morning and finding that Nevins already had left for the public library to get in a good day's work. "If he comes for dinner he'll play one game of ping pong afterward, then, as often as not, go home to write." For years he has been under family pressure to take a vacation, but his idea of a holiday is a chance to write without interruption. He finds this opportunity for brief periods at his Summer home at Windham, Vermont.

When questioned on this subject Mr. Nevins says that he feels that he hasn't done any real work since about 1908, when he was eighteen years old.

"I grew up on a western Illinois stock and grain farm. We'd start to labor at dawn and really labor until we were ready to drop. My father, a strict Scotsman, considered industry the highest virtue. And he was convinced that the devil found work for idle hands. He saw to it that the devil had no opportunities in my case.

"I was set at hard labor when very young. Not until I was in college did I realize that there was much of anything else in life. Of course, that farm-boy background has had its advantages. As a fledgling newspaperman I heard a good many people grumbling about how much copy they had to turn out for too little pay. It didn't seem too much work or too small pay to me. It seemed like a vacation."

He likes to get started at work before eight in the morning, has a brisk, no-nonsense way with food, keeps on whatever job he is doing until bedtime.

He rewrites so much that he complains that his typing bills eat up large amounts of the profits of his books. He writes a first draft on a chapter, has it typed, goes over it in pencil. This process is repeated four or five times with all the work he turns out. His early drafts are always too long, he said, and are very apt to be dull. Revisions are necessary to cut them down and to brighten the phrasing. He does most of his research himself, making extensive use of old newspapers. However, he spent more than a thousand dollars obtaining records in the Public Record Office in London for his biography of Hamilton Fish, and he always has an expert proofreader check the dates and name spellings in his books. "I've gone over these dates so often that I can't trust my own eye by the time a manuscript is in galleys."

Mr. Nevins has just completed a biography of John D. Rockefeller that Charles Scribner's Sons will publish this Fall. It is not an "official" biography—"there was not one cent of subsidy"—but the Rockefeller family gave him access to, "so far as I know, all the material they had." He said that he'd rather not talk about the subject of the biography.

"As an impecunious teacher I feel somewhat self-conscious making table talk on Rockefeller. I'd rather let the book speak for itself. It is documented and as complete as I could make it."

This will be, he said, his last biography. He is starting work on a history of America from 1850 on, that, he expects, will occupy him for the rest of his life. The first volume will cover about four years and he will devote three years to writing it.

"My schedule calls for a volume every three years; that is, five volumes in fifteen years, ten volumes in thirty years, and so on, and on, I hope. There is no danger that I ever shall run out of material. History is being made faster than historians can write it."

His office and his home are filled with their attempts. Four thousand books crowded into high bookcases line the walls of his barrack-like study in Fayerweather Hall on the Columbia University campus. There are dozens of sets of American histories pressed against the south wall. Biographies by the hundred crowd the east wall. The desk, of the kind that hundreds of railway clerks use, is a little island in a sea of books. Books are piled on tabletops and overflow from the room's one easy chair onto the floor. Another collection of equal size Mr. Nevins keeps at home.

Mr. Nevins formerly lived on Staten Island and his homeward journeys with enough books to burden a camel made him a memorable passenger aboard the ferryboats. He commented that it was perhaps unreasonable to buy so many books with a large university library that he might draw upon only a block away, but the buying of books was a habit that he formed early and has been unable to break.

He talked of his system of writing biography. The ideal sources, he said, consist of exhaustive diaries kept by the subject, used together with files of newspapers. Your subject lives in his diaries, his world in the newspapers.

Answering the question, "How do you make material for biography your own—that is, how do you acquire possession and the right to use the facts set down by other men?" he said that he reads exhaustively around every angle that he intends to treat, makes full notes but puts his notes aside before he starts to write. "It is a matter of digestion."

Another good method of learning what are the salient points drawn from wide research is to catch a friend who is interested in the subject and talk out what you have learned, at length. In this way you discover facets of interpretation that you might have missed, points of argument that had been unrealized, and the form most suitable for the story you have to tell.

Mr. Nevins believes that there are trends in both biography and history that to him are eminently satisfactory.

"I am Victorian by nature and I like biography in the Victorian manner: large, exhaustive books, filled with detail, showing a man in the round. I feel, too, that if a man is worth a biography he is worthy of the sympathy of his biographer. Essays that merely hold a historical personage up to ridicule—well, I don't appreciate them. Sandburg's 'Lincoln' and Freeman's 'Lee' are the kind of biographies I like.

"And in history, too, we are returning to an older style that was used before the German monographic school of history made such headway here in America. Accuracy, yes, but color and life, the flow of thought well expressed surely have their own importance."

THE FUTURE OF WRITING IN A WORLD AT WAR

Stefan Zweig talks on the plight of the European artist and the probable form of the literature of the coming years

July 28, 1940

"THE ARTIST HAS been wounded," said Stefan Zweig, "in his concentration." He rapped his breast with the knuckles of his left hand. "How can the old themes hold our attention now? A man and woman meet, they fall in love, they have an affair—that was once a story. Sometime again it will be a story. But how can we lovingly live in such a trifle now?

"The last months have been fatal for the European literary production. The basic law of all creative work remains invariably concentration, and never has this been so difficult for the artists in Europe. How should complete concentration be possible in the midst of a moral earthquake? Most of the writers in Europe are doing war work of one kind or another, others had to flee from their country and live in exile, wandering about, and even the happy few who are able to continue working at their desks cannot escape the turmoil of our time.

"Reclusion is no more possible while our world stands in flames; the 'Ivory Tower' of esthetics is no more bomb-proof, as Irwin Edman has said. From hour to hour one waits for news, one cannot avoid reading the papers, listening to the wireless, and at the same time one is oppressed by the worries about the fate of near relatives and friends. Here flees one without home in the occupied area, others are interned and ask for freedom, others wander about begging from one consulate to another to find a hospitable country which will accept them. From all sides every one of us who has found a haven is daily assailed by letters and telegrams for help and intervention; every one of us lives more the lives of a hundred others than his own."

He spoke of external hindrances occasioned by blackouts, by lack of freedom of movement, by inability to obtain access to research materials.

"For instance, I was just about to lay the last hand to my favorite book on which I had been working for twenty years, a large and really the first comprehensive biography of the great genius Balzac. Reluctantly I had to abandon this nearly finished volume because the library of Chantilly which contains all of Balzac's manuscripts had been closed for the duration of the war and brought away to an unknown and inaccessible place; on the other hand, I could not take with me the hundreds and thousands of notes because of the censorship. Just as in my case, for thousands of artists and scientists work of many years has been stopped, perhaps for a long time, by purely technical difficulties.

"And the internal difficulty—what means psychology, what artistic perfection at such an hour, where for centuries the fate of our real and spiritual world is at stake? I, myself, had soon after completing my last novel, 'Beware of Pity,' prepared the sketch for another novel. Then war started and suddenly it seemed frivolous to represen· the private fate of imaginary persons. I had no more the courage to deal with private psychological facts and every 'story' appeared to me today irrelevant in contrast to history."

He said that most of the other writers he knew had experienced this same distraction in their own work. Paul Valéry, Roger Martin du Gard, Duhamel and Romains all had confessed to him that they could no longer concentrate on their work. "I would be suspicious against any European author who would now be capable to concentrate on his own, his private work. What was allowed to Archimedes, the mathematician, to continue his experiments undisturbed by the siege of his town, seems to me quasi inhuman for the poet, the artist, who does not deal with abstractions but whose mission it is to feel with the greatest intensity the fate and sufferings of his fellow beings."

Yet out of this war will come vast realms of experience in which the artist may work, and Mr. Zweig paced the floor excitedly as he talked of this:

"On each ship, in each travel bureau, in each consulate, one may hear from quite unimportant, anonymous people the stories of adventures and pilgrimages which are no less dangerous and thrilling than those of Odysseus. If any one would print, without altering a single word, the documents of the refugees which are now kept in the offices of charity organizations, by the Society of Friends, in the Home Office in London, it would make a hundred volumes of stories more thrilling and improbable than those of Jack London or Maupassant.

"Not even the first World War drove so many lives to such crises as this one year, never has human existence known such tensions and apprehensions as today—too much tension to be dissolved immediately into artistic form. That is why, in my opinion, the literature of the next years will be more of a documentary character than purely fictional and imaginative.

"We assist at the most decisive battle for freedom that has ever been fought, we will be witnesses of one of the greatest social transformations the world has ever gone through, and we writers before all have the duty to give evidence of what happened in our time. If we reproduce faithfully but our own life, our own experiences—and I intend to do so in an autobiography—we have perhaps done more than by an invented novel.

"No genius can nowadays invent anything which surpasses the dramatic events of the present time, and also the best poet has again to become student and servant of the greatest master of us all; of history."

Mr. Zweig says that the one thing he can work on now is his autobiography, which will carry the title "Three Lives."

"My grandfather lived a life, my father lived a life. I have lived at least three. I have seen two great wars, revolution, the devaluation of money, exile, famine. The period of the French Revolution and the Napoleonic wars, the period of the Reformation—they were times not unlike this. No other times can equal the change we who are of middle age now have seen."

He commented that he was once "the most translated author in the world."

"My books were published in Italian, Japanese, in practically all the countries on earth. They had—how do you say—universal coverage. When Hitler came in, my books were banned in Germany, now they are banned in Italy, perhaps next week in France. There were large Finnish editions and Polish—no more. Every fortnight I lose a country.

"Oh, that is not important. So long as they can be published in one language, that is enough. And I believe that over here you will resist the death of freedom for a long time. It is inconceivable that liberty could be destroyed here. It will be regained in France; here it will not be lost."

Mr. Zweig is here only on a visitor's visa. He intended to leave shortly for South America, where he will lecture. Then he will return to England. "I cannot miss what is happening there."

He said that he is writing his autobiography as he writes everything else—"four times too long."

"I write the first time to please myself. I put in everything that I think of. I am a contented writer who can write all day and be happy. So the early drafts of my books are very, very long.

"On the other hand, I am a nervous reader. I become very impatient when any author—including myself—strays from his point. So when I read what I have written I cut it in great chunks. I chop and chop until there is not a spare word, a sentence that can be done without."

PROFESSOR LANCELOT HOGBEN, AN "AUTHOR IN FLIGHT"

The story of an escape from occupied territory and a hurried journey of 20,000 miles to safety

August 4, 1940

Perhaps the first British "author in flight" to reach here is Lancelot Hogben. Author of "Mathematics for the Millions"—an extraordinary best seller in that, although it is a book rife with symbols, it has sold 70,000 copies in this country alone—of "Science for the Citizen," "Dangerous Thoughts" and more than a score of scientific monographs, Professor Hogben is poised here, uncertain as to his next move, after a journey of escape that has taken him most of the way around the world. Regius Professor of Natural History at the University of Aberdeen, and honored for his research work on the pituitary gland and his work on the mathematical theory of genetics, his future, as he said last week, "seems to hold no probabilities."

Professor Hogben had been lecturing in Norway. Early on the morning of last April 9th, accompanied by his daughter, Sylvia, he drove to the airfield outside Oslo to board a plane that would take them to Sweden, where he was scheduled to lecture at Upsala. Their plane was due to leave at eight o'clock. Fifteen minutes before that time German bombs fell on the field.

"Traffic was disrupted and though we thought it was only a demonstration as a preliminary to an ultimatum we decided it was best to go back to our hotel. With the air filled with German fighters it seemed hardly the thing to go up in a plane even if one took off. We returned to our hotel with our luggage and then set out to walk to the British consulate. The British staff had already left when we got to that place—it is in a suburb—and an American had taken over. We thought it best to hurry to the Swedish consulate for visas that would admit us to Sweden. On the way there, however, we turned into the Karl Johans Gate, the main street in Oslo, and found silent crowds lined along the pavements watching German infantry march in. We waited in the crowd, as near to the marching troops as I am to you.

"It then seemed best to me to get to the border without visas. I inferred, rightly as it turned out, that the German forces were not yet sufficient to cover any but the main thoroughfares of Oslo, so we went to a stationery store and bought a map of the city with the aid of which we could follow little-frequented streets to the outskirts and then hope for the best in reaching the border. We were successful in that we scouted streets before turning corners and, when we saw German patrols, dodged down quieter streets. We came fairly near disaster when we attempted to board a bus. There was a rather large crowd getting on this bus and we were in the midst of this crowd before we noted that there was a Nazi guard at the door. This man asked me, in Norwegian, why I was traveling and I answered in my very best Norwegian that I was on my way to visit my mother, who was ill. My daughter then spoke up and said: "Don't talk to him, Daddy. He's a filthy Nazi." Fortunately, though the guard knew Norwegian—for the Germans sent men who had been adopted as orphans into Norway and brought up there—he did not know English. My daughter is very brave, but inexperienced in escaping from occupied territory. We went on—not aboard the bus.

"Out on a highway I succeeded in attracting the attention of a Norwegian lorry driver and told him that Oslo had been invaded. He didn't believe me, but I succeeded in persuading him to turn around and take us along the road to the nearest large town on the border. But so many German patrol cars passed us that it was evident that the large town was not the place to go. I talked with the lorry driver and he agreed to go back through

Oslo and take us to the remote and small frontier town of Han. It was a rather dangerous trip, as so much of the traffic was flowing out of Oslo and we were conspicuous in going in against this traffic. But we roughed up our clothing to look as much as possible like members of the lorry driver's family and made a successful trip through Oslo and over mountains to Han, stopping on the way at the lorry driver's house, where he fed us shrimp paste and brown bread. The trip was decidedly uncomfortable, for we were sweating hot during the day and very cold at night. There was snow on the ground, but the sun was hot; we had shed most of our heavy clothing for walking.

"We reached Han before the Nazis, but, as we lacked passports, were taken into protective custody by the Swedes. This was pleasant enough, for the Swedish customs men are often college students taking the law course, who hold customs jobs for a year to make up their tuition. Also, the captain of the guards was at that moment reading the Swedish translation of my 'Science for the Citizen,' so we were very well received and made as comfortable as might be. I wired friends in Upsala for money and asked them to make arrangements to get us into the country. We were set free inside Sweden after a three-day wait and went to Stockholm, then to Upsala. I had needed money because one was allowed to take only ten pounds out of England and the long trip by lorry had cost me all that I had—and little enough it was—one hundred Norwegian crowns. From Upsala I cabled W. W. Norton, my publisher and friend, for money and he sent it to me. There was at first the probability that we could escape by way of Narvik. That became impossible. It was then planned to take us and the rest of the British colony out by way of Petsamo. But then Holland was invaded and the plan was dropped. There were no ships and men available for the attempt.

"It was feared all through this time that Sweden would be invaded at any moment. My daughter came down with influenza as a result of exposure, and I earned my living by translating Swedish scientific papers into English. The suit I wear was bought in Upsala with the proceeds of one of these translations.

"Fearing that we could not get free through Norway, I started arrangements for Russian visas and finally they came through. We flew from Stockholm to Moscow, stayed there for a time in squalor in the best hotel in town—the table linen looked as though it had not been changed since the purge of 1935, and that was the Metropole, widely known as the best hotel, while the lavatories were like those I remembered in Portsmouth as a boy before the Boer War. We then boarded the Transsiberian Railway and for ten days traveled across Russia, where all of our money was taken from us, though we did manage to obtain passage to Japan.

"I cannot believe that every one who visited Russia and approved of it when it was fashionable to visit there and approve of it could have seen anything but a few show places. Surely all of them could not have lied. The country is one vast slum. Outside of Moscow I saw nothing that compared favorably with even the worst slums of Glasgow. Moscow offers little enough; the rest of the country offers nothing. It is perfectly evident that the attempt to industrialize has broken completely down. If the engine is running, it is not in gear.

"They talk of the new literacy of the Russian masses, the enormous sales of books and circulation of newspapers. All through that ten days on the train I saw only two Russians reading anything at all. I asked the Intourist guide when we reached Vladivostok for a newspaper. She said that she would get one right away. The next day I reminded her of my request—these little delays one learns to accept quickly in Russia—and within a few hours a copy of *Pravda* was given me, the latest paper obtainable. It had been printed two days before we left Moscow and had come to Vladivostok aboard our train. And the newspapers are only single sheets, folded, about the size of a tabloid page.

"Intourist no longer is at all efficient. We had paid, in advance, for private rooms at Vladivostok—when we reached there we were told that we must sleep four in a room. We finally figured out how that could be arranged in decency, and then were told that there would be an extra charge of 200 rubles for the room. As they had taken all of our money—just why I do not yet know, save, perhaps, that they simply wanted it—they suggested that we might sell our possessions. We had practically no possessions, but my daughter had managed to retain a three-year-old dress, worth when it was new about nine American dollars. We offered this for 200 rubles and it was accepted immediately, and the rubles paid over.

"The Russians are greatly in need of clothing. Outside Moscow —and with the exception of Red Army officers—I saw no one so well dressed as the men who wait outside Labor Board offices at home to receive the dole.

"I talked with a number of impartial newspaper men who knew Russia—Americans who have spent considerable time in the country. They told me that the present breakdown dates from the great purge of 1935, when, in a wave of nationalism, foreign experts were kicked out. There is simply no one to carry on the industrial work. It is believed that Stalin signed with Germany simply because he was too weak to fight Germany."

Professor Hogben formerly was the close friend of many British intellectuals who became Communists. He broke with them on this issue some years ago, explaining that his childhood had been largely devoted to reluctant religion—his father, a non-conformist minister, insisting that his spare time be given to learning the Bible by heart—and that he had no intention of giving his adulthood to communism, a dogma and faith in which he could not believe.

ERNEST HEMINGWAY TALKS OF WORK AND WAR

He has just completed a new novel set in Spain during the recent campaigns

August 11, 1940

Ernest Hemingway was here in New York copyreading and delivering to Scribners, his publishers, at the rate of 300 pages a day, the final draft of his longest novel. People who have read the manuscript agree that it is his best. Said one such reader encountered as he waited, rather bemused, for a chance to cross a cross-street on which there was no traffic, one afternoon some months ago: "I've just read the first three-quarters of the new Hemingway and you might as well believe me because you're going to find out that it's true—it is even better than 'Farewell to Arms.' "

Mr. Hemingway's stay here was supposed to be all for work, but cheerfulness kept breaking in. On the eleventh day of July's heat wave his rooms at the Hotel Barclay saw as lively company as any rooms in town. An electric fan droned on the coffee table, flanked by bottles of White Rock and fronted by a superb bowl of ice. A fifth of Scotch rested hospitably on the floor where it could be handily reached from three of the four chairs. Lawyers, old friends and visiting soldiers came and went. The telephone rang not quite continuously. Mr. Hemingway wore an unbuttoned pajama coat affording a view of chest that—if Max Eastman still is interested—would have made the eyes of a fur trapper pop.

"I've worked at it solid for seventeen months," said Hemingway of his new novel. "This one had to be all right or I had to get out of line, because my last job, 'To Have and Have Not,' was not so good. For seventeen months I wrote no short stories or articles—nothing to earn a penny. I'm broke."

A friend said: "Ernest, if I am paid $200 for the job I am doing tonight we will have a wonderful time tomorrow." "Don't worry about $200," said Hemingway. "Whether you get it or I get it we'll still have a wonderful time tomorrow. Charley Scribner isn't broke."

The talk was a mixture of Spanish, French and English. Each comment that Hemingway made on his writing he prefaced with an explanatory speech to Gustavo Duran, the former pianist and composer, who had developed as one of the most brilliant of the army corps commanders on the Loyalist side of the civil war in Spain.

"Sorry, Gustavo, but Bob has to ask these questions; it's his job, and I'm supposed to answer them, see?" And then, rapidly: "I start work each morning at seven-thirty and work until about two-thirty. The first thing I do when I'm writing a novel is read back through all that has gone before. That way I break the back of the job. Then I put the words in—like laying bricks. I write in longhand and don't try to make much time. I've tried this speed writing, getting it all down and then going over it, but the trouble is if you speed too much you don't know if you have a book or not when you've finished the first draft."

"About how many words do you write each day?" Duran asked seriously. Hemingway looked at him, not sure whether or not he was being ribbed. "I don't know, Gustavo. Some days a lot, some days a little. I never write to fit a thesis or a plan. I start with blank paper and put all that I know at the time on the blank paper. Most of the time it is tough going. You can't figure any average. Why in hell do you want to know, Gustavo?"

Duran shrugged: "I don't know. It is interesting." He talked of his own job as a commander. He said that in his army regulations the first sentence was the seemingly meaningless one that roughly translated into "The first duty of the commander is to make decisions."

"It seems simple when you read it. You think, 'What is decision? Each day I decide what color shoes to wear, what to eat.' But decision, when the life or death of hundreds of men depends on your decision, that is much else. In Spain I was assigned, as you know, to hold a position. My cowardice told me to draw in my left flank so that if I failed I would be near the French border and the lives of thousands would be saved if we lost. My judgment said perhaps that is right but perhaps it would be better to turn my right flank, though if we lost we would be cut off from safety. That is a decision that hurts all through your body; you cannot sleep, you ache. There is nothing more difficult in life."

"Which flank did you turn?"

"My right flank. But that is not important. The decision is important."

"So you suppose all commanders feel that way? Did Napoleon?"

"Napoleon was a victor. When you are a victor, what can hurt you? But when you must fight a long defensive action with no chance of winning, only of holding the enemy off, then with every decision you are in hell," said Duran. "You ache with wanting—but what you want cannot quite be reached. It is like my sitting in this chair wanting to rip that necktie from your neck. I reach, I almost seize it. It is just beyond my hand. Always in war there are possibilities plain to be seen, but materials are lacking, the men fail, a mistake is made somewhere along the line —and frustration eats your stomach."

It was suggested that perhaps because the military decision is so difficult to make, that is why when it is made rightly it pays off so well. There is nothing in finance, for example, to compare with it, or in internal politics, and perhaps for twenty years the importance of the military decision has been underestimated and aims that are practically inferior have been mistakenly rated above the real pay-off, which still is strength at arms. Hemingway exclaimed: "That's what the new novel is about!" And then another visitor arrived, and the talk took another turn.

Much of the conversation ran to questions of survival or failure to survive. "Where is so-and-so?" "He went back to Russia and was shot." Another Spanish fighter had landed in a German concentration camp. A married pair "tried to get to Chile but were turned away. They finally were admitted to Buenos Aires." Duran himself escaped from Spain aboard a British destroyer, was taken to Marseille, transported across France in a sealed train, and shipped to England.

"The world now is very confusing. It is amazing how sure we once were, Ernest, that our ideas were right."

"The fight in Spain will have to be fought again," Hemingway said. Duran looked at his hands. "I don't know."

Telephone calls, visitors ushered in and out, another rather hesitant question about writing and another apology to Duran.

"The thing wrong with 'To Have and Have Not' is that it is made of short stories. I wrote one, then another when I was in Spain, then I came back and saw Harry Morgan again and that gave me the idea for a third. It came out as a new novel, but it was short stories, and there is a hell of a lot of difference. A novel —when you do a novel—" He couldn't find the phrase he wanted. "I don't know how many more I'll do. But they say that when you're in your forties you ought to know enough and have enough stuff to do one good one. I think this is it."

After his long session of work Hemingway looked elephant-big, enormously healthy. His talk is unevenly paced, a quick spate and then a slow search for a word. His chair keeps hitching across the floor toward the other chairs, and then as he reaches a point, a conclusion, he shoves his chair back to the edge of the group again. While Duran was telephoning in the next room he said that Duran was a character in the new novel, which is set in Spain during the civil war, and that while he was writing the book he badly wanted to see Duran, "to straighten things out, to get information."

"Now that I've finally found him the book is on its way to the printer, can't be changed. But I've questioned him and the stuff I used was all right. You write what should be true as, with what knowledge you have, it seems to you. And that's the best you can do, anyway."

JAMES NORMAN HALL TALKS ABOUT WRITING AND IDLING

"Loafing," he maintains, "is the most productive part of a writer's life"

August 18, 1940

James Norman Hall said that it is wonderful to live in Tahiti if you are a writer, because loafing is so easy to do there and "loafing is the most productive part of a writer's life."

"Of course, you've got to spend a lot of time working. But your most valuable time—it seems to me—is that spent in idleness. Because that is when you get your ideas. The writing is merely the fulfillment of the inspiration drawn from loafing."

Mr. Hall was stopping at the Commodore Hotel for a few days, breaking a journey from Boston to Santa Barbara, where Charles Nordhoff, his writing partner, awaited him. Though he had spent practically all of this year in New England, he had a mahogany tan that looked Tahitian. He is a quite tall, very thin man—so thin that he crosses both legs and ankles at once.

He said that the "Bounty" trilogy had its beginning in Paris during the last war. On a day's leave from the Bleriot School, where he was learning to fly one of those 1916 airplanes, Hall bought an Oxford Classic in the W. H. Smith bookshop that was a report of the Bounty tragedy written in 1832, soon after the discovery of the last of the mutineers on Pitcairn Island.

"The story interested me enormously, as, of course, it would any one." He had plenty of time to think about it, considering that he spent much of the war in a German prison camp. But it wasn't until 1939, after years of living on Tahiti, that he and Nordhoff decided to write the story.

"We communicated with Ellery Sedgwick, an old friend, and he liked the idea, so we asked him to put us in touch with a good sleuth who would do some research work for us. Through him we obtained the services of a retired British naval officer who proved an excellent researcher.

"He dug into the files of Bounty records and photostated those parts that he thought would be of value. The photostats that he sent us in Tahiti made a pile about four feet high. These, of course, were the old hand-written records kept by the Admiralty.

"He even built a model of the Bounty according to exact specifications, sail plans, deck plans, and so forth. As the model was unlikely to survive shipment to Tahiti he photographed it from all angles to show every detail and sent it to us along with copies of the plans.

"We had a great time working on it. Of course, we obtained every book that had been published—all the books we could lay our hands on—and for a year we read. Then we started writing.

"Our writing system is to start work at seven-thirty or eight in the morning, knock off at eleven, start again about two and end the day at four. There is no nervous tension, no sense of hurry. So many people asked how we managed to collaborate that I once wrote a piece about our using a four-handed typewriter and that sort of nonsense. The fact is that we simply work together in a common-sense way.

"We didn't have to imagine much except about the return to Tahiti, after Bligh and his men had been turned loose in the long-boat. The bosun had kept a journal and we used what we could of that, but it hadn't been published in full at that time and we had to get along with what we found extracted from it and used in other books. We didn't need to 'dramatize' any of the story. The facts were more dramatic than any we could have created."

He said that he doesn't know what will happen to Tahiti. "The boat service is knocked to hell by the war and I have had letters telling me that there has been a temporary shortage of flour, sugar and some luxuries that formerly could be obtained there."

He thinks it unlikely that Tahiti will change hands, as it isn't sufficiently valuable to be wanted very much. On the subject of living costs he said that the articles that tell of living in Tahiti on ten dollars a month or so always puzzle him.

"I suppose that I could live on ten a month in New York if I ate nothing but rice and slept in the subway or on a park bench. Living is less expensive than here in the United States, I suppose, but there is so great a range in standards of living, here and there, that it is a difficult subject to be definite on."

He and Mr. Nordhoff intend to stay in California until about October working on a new novel. He has arranged for passage back to the island for either October or November: "It all depends on when the boat is ready to go."

Another reason that he likes Tahiti, he said, is because he's a "great reader," and there is plenty of time there for that.

He is considering making a book of the open-boat voyage of Captain Mitchell—"a tale that even beats Bligh's." Mitchell was forced to leave his ship, the *Hornet*, in the South Atlantic and with his crew in a longboat voyaged on astoundingly short rations to the Hawaiian Islands. It was a journey of 4,000 miles and took two or three more days than did Bligh's famous voyage described in "Men Against the Sea." Mark Twain was in Hawaii when Mitchell and his men arrived and Twain said later that his description of Mitchell's ordeal was his real debut in literature.

Nordhoff and Hall considered writing of Mitchell some years ago, but because the voyage had so much in common with Bligh's experience they have held off.

"But we may do it. We'd certainly like to."

JAN STRUTHER, WHO CREATED MRS. MINIVER

Now in this country, she discusses her heroine's remarkable career

August 25, 1940

JAN STRUTHER, the only woman ever to become a member of the editorial board of the *Times* (of London), is in this country, "not as a visitor but as an immigrant."

"It was obvious that I could do nothing on the land—while I was doing the work necessary to grow one potato any one else could grow hills of them—and I couldn't carry stretchers, and I was another hungry mouth. So I came away."

For about a year her "Mrs. Miniver" sketches in the *Times* had had considerable morale virtue. Mrs. Miniver was an unfrightened woman who faced the war without palpitations and whose general attitude was precisely right in the British tradition, she had been told.

"But the time came when finally I was heartily sick of the woman. She was so popular that I had to stick it, but when one of our papers offered a prize for the best parody on Mrs. Miniver, I wrote much the cruelest parody, sent it in under a pen name and won the prize. I then thought it only fair to admit that the parody of my own work was also my own work and to ask that the two guineas be given to the runner-up. The paper came through with a second prize for the second best parody, but let me keep mine, so I gave the money to an organization for distressed gentlewomen.

"Soon after I came here I gave an interview to a girl reporter and complained that I had been too often taken for the real Mrs. Miniver, that the sketches were thought too often to be autobiographical. She read the book that night and the next day called me to say that she now understood what I meant. 'Mrs. Miniver has more class than you have,' she told me. She was exactly right."

Her membership in the *Times* editorial board was achieved through a free-lance route. Peter Fleming, author of "Brazilian Adventure," "One's Company," and other tales of travel in far places, was temporarily serving as "a sub-sub-editor of the *Times*." He asked Jan Struther to write his bits for the Court Page. "He felt that the page could stand a bit of ginning up and was entirely right." Miss Struther brought a light touch to the Court Page that was widely appreciated and it was through these that she achieved a place as a leader, or editorial writer, on the *Times*.

"At first I continued to do the work at home, but the children were in and out all day, and there always was trouble about the laundry or one thing and another, so finally I asked if I couldn't use the *Times* offices. The chairs and tables there were all built for the accommodation of quite large old men, so I required a footstool to keep my legs from swinging and going to sleep, but such details were arranged and all the old gentlemen became accustomed to me save one, and very nice to me save one. However, it was obvious that my uses to England were limited. So early this Summer I came away."

She brought two of her children with her. One is twelve, the other nine. "My oldest boy is sixteen and he"—She broke off the informal flow of talk and with a careful precision said: "I couldn't bring my oldest boy out. It was not only that the law wouldn't let me bring him; I couldn't have anyway. He is sixteen and strong enough and he happens to be an excellent shot. This Summer he is working on the land in Scotland."

They arrived on the Fourth of July in Canada—a shipload of 1,200-odd mothers and children and only fifty-three men other than the crew. Most of the men passengers were engineers being sent to Canada to take a hand at production.

"I asked our steward how he felt about all these women and children—the children were everywhere, filling all free space with their balls and dolls and themselves, and sprawling on the decks. The men couldn't be free of them anywhere. The steward told me that he'd had 3,000 troops on his last trip and hadn't turned a hair, but these women and children had driven him deaf, blind and silly.

"I'm in a rather hazy frame of mind and almost everything seems symbolic. There was a symbol in the air when we saw our first fine sight, the gleam of the lights of Quebec at night. We all rushed to the ship's rail and looked—a city lighted at night! . . . Not that I'd minded the blackout. It was rather interesting and we'd developed eyes for the dark, like cats. . . . But we crowded together looking at those lights."

The children were sent to Cape Cod to keep cool. Miss Struther has spent the Summer roaming New York: "I spend much of my time riding the elevateds and looking into the second and third story windows of the Bronx. The south end of Central Park reminds me of the great plateau in Spain, the great buildings are like mountains. Of course, the sky-line in general doesn't affect me greatly, or the smart places about town and so on. I've subscribed to *The New Yorker* for fifteen years and know a certain side of the city rather well. But I had looked for something smarter and harder than I find—I had not expected the delight that I have in New York, the interest and liking that I had believed I could find in no city save London.

"My children are delighted when they hear taxi drivers say 'foist' and 'thoid,' just as in the films. They say, 'Gosh, aren't the cops tough!' with the very greatest admiration. It is good, too, to hear European languages freely spoken without people making notes and whispering 'fifth columnists.' The foreign pavilions of the World's Fair are like Europe preserved in ice cubes."

THIS BUSINESS OF WRITING FOR THE MOVIES

Nunnally Johnson who wrote the screen version of "Grapes of Wrath" talks about continuity and the "story line"

Hollywood
September 1, 1940

NUNNALLY JOHNSON'S gestures were restrained. He had just moved into a mogul's office on the Fox-Twentieth Century lot. The office is air-conditioned and, as a result, Mr. Johnson had a stiff neck. He winced as he reached too far in taking a fresh pack of cigarettes from a drawer in his desk in which the contents of at least four cartons of cigarettes were neatly stacked. He moaned as he swooped too fast to answer the hushed bell of his telephone, which, by the way, rang only once in an hour and a half, thus moderating the belief that all movie producers live in telephonic hysteria. He winced again as he snapped his head back while berating the theory that motion pictures are created to entertain a 12-year-old intelligence.

"Some one has said that after you've filtered a story through producers, directors and actors, you've nothing left that is suitable for any one over twelve to look at. But that isn't what we try for. Every picture produced means not stage money or talked-about money, but real money—money taken out of a bank—and any one who thinks we don't try to get the worth of that money in good value is nuts."

Mr. Johnson, thin, nervous, energetic, wrote and produced the screen version of John Steinbeck's "The Grapes of Wrath," and has the most enviable writing job in the movie industry. "The nice thing about it is that since I'm hired as a producer I can go out on a lot where a director is kicking my script around and say, 'Listen, what we want you to do is make this pict-chuh the way it's written heah on this papuh. Jus' you stick to this papuh.'" His Southern accent—he is a Georgian—becomes most pronounced when he is saying something particularly forceful, even if the force is only a memory.

He said that making the continuity for "The Grapes of Wrath" was essentially a simple job. "The story line was clear—the migration of a people forced from their homes. It is old as the Bible. And, of course, the book was beautifully done. The only real change I made—and I had to make it—was in the ending. There had to be some ray of hope—something that would keep the people who saw it from going out and getting so drunk in utter despondency that they couldn't tell other people that it was a good picture to see. Steinbeck agreed on the necessity for a more hopeful ending. Yeah, he liked the script."

When interviewed Mr. Johnson was engaged in a harder task, that of discovering the "story line" of Erskine Caldwell's "Tobacco Road." "When a play runs for seven years there is no use saying the structure is bad, because it couldn't be bad and still run for seven years. But I can't find the story line in the play. I'm huntin' it in the book. It is there, all right—it's got to be."

He said that he had been studying the play with great thoroughness trying to discover the secret of its appeal. "It can't be dirt, because dirt doesn't put plays over. Best explanation I can find is that if you took the lowest outcast and let him see that play he'd feel superior to the people in it. I don't know where Caldwell found those people. I'm from Georgia myself, and I never saw any people there who were too lazy to eat. But Caldwell makes me believe in them anyway."

His writing method is to seek out a story line, "and follow it through, keeping it as clean of unnecessary material as possible. Some stuff that isn't needed is bound to be left in—but that must be kept to a minimum." He rewrites page by page, "until every word is the word I want. Sometimes a page needs only three or four rewritings, sometimes twenty."

Johnson quit newspaper work to write for *The Saturday Evening Post,* came to Hollywood when the depression made the sale of short stories difficult. "They told me I could have a job at Paramount if I would pay my own fare from New York. It was humiliating to be so little wanted and—what was worse—I had to borrow the money to pay the railroad." He had been a humorous writer, but the lack of sales had tended to scare the humor out of him. "Especially when you are writing humor, a main thing you need is confidence—you must be sure that your little jokes are funny or you can't keep on thinking up little jokes. My jokes hadn't sold, so how could I be sure of them? I was a real worried would-be humorist when I hit this town."

He said that writers for the movies suffer a great deal because there are still geniuses in high places who, though they are unable to write anything that makes sense or even spell, are continually becoming inspired. "They'll yell, 'Somebody sharp me a pencil!' and then they'll slit hell out of a script that a competent writer has worked on for weeks. But most of these guys are leftovers from the old silent days, and they are gradually moving on. The 'idea men'—most of them phonies—don't get the attention they once had. The idea men used to come busting into an office with some such remark as 'San Francisco! Make a picture about the earthquake. Put a word man on it.' And for that they'd be paid a lot of dough. But dough isn't so easy to get any more.

"Respect for trained writers is increasing. I think that pictures are a whole lot better as a result. The reason there still are so many bad movies is because there aren't enough good writers to go 'round. After all, with three hundred pictures made each year, you can't find good men for all of them. We hunt for good men, and when we find them we ask for the best they've got. Because, in general, it is the best pictures that pay off. And, like everybody else, we all want our names on stuff we are not ashamed of."

SIGRID UNDSET SPEAKS OF WRITING AND WAR

An interview with the Distinguished Novelist who Recently Arrived from Norway

San Francisco
September 8, 1940

SIGRID UNDSET said that she had nothing to say about literature. "While the war is on literature is not a thing to talk about." Would the war tend to make the literature of the immediate future reportorial, as Stefan Zweig believes? Mme. Undset shrugged her shoulders. "I do not make prophecies." What of her technique for writing? "If you knew anything at all about writing you would not ask that question. How can I tell how I write? I write! As every writer knows, one must discover one's method for one's self. In any event, I do not give advice."

The author of "Kristin Lavransdatter" is a tall woman—almost six feet in height—heavy, with wide shoulders and hips. Her face is broad and flat and the skin red. She was utterly disdainful of what she considered an inevitable reportorial sentimentality. Interviewers in newspapers here had spoken of her "grief too great for tears" and of her being a "wanderer on the face of the earth, homeless, hopeless."

"You reporters," said Mme. Undset, "have a German sentimentality for which I have no use. I do not care for the German traits."

She took a humorous pleasure in making such frontal attacks and it was in that pleasure that she was best revealed, for it was only then that her chill, utter impersonality was warmed, that the massive solidity of her mere will to endure gave way to a sparkle of life.

She said that her recently published "Madame Dorothea" had been intended as the first volume of a long book, but she did not know whether she would go on with the work. "I left all my notes, all my preparations, in Norway. You see I left the country with only a traveling bag and in a great hurry. I doubt that I can continue writing while the war goes on. I shall lecture this Fall and Winter. After that I don't know."

She said that the young men of Norway "were infuriated that their country was so badly prepared, that their elders had put their trust in so weak a thing as neutrality."

"The Germans did not succeed because of numerical superiority, but because they had better weapons. All the young men of Norway who were worth anything went to fight, and 40,000 of them lost their lives. Had we been prepared they could have fought as the Finns did, but all we had were machine guns and shotguns.

"Our men are good shots and they are not frightened. I know of men out alone who took on 200 Germans at once. Yes. They would hide on hillsides and fire with shotguns at German columns. They fired carefully, making each shot account for one German, and they were very good ski-runners—they could fight a long time and then get away.

"I know of one who brought down a German plane from a hillside. He shot at the aviator's hands and crushed them."

She said that she had seen considerable fighting. "I watched bombing raids and saw machine-gun fights."

Mme. Undset came here a few days ago aboard the steamship President Cleveland from Japan. After her flight to Sweden she traversed Russia on the Trans-Siberian Railway, and it was during that trip that she learned of the fall of France. She said that this was the worst blow. "France always has been the brains of Europe. If she is smashed permanently I fear it will be the end of Europe."

She said that the people of Russia seemed very poor; that most of the shops were closed and that the window displays were usually of papier-mâché, as there were not enough goods for sale, certainly not enough for display.

"In Vladivostok in a pouring rain I saw a line of hundreds of people waiting to buy some printed cotton goods that were so shoddy that if I had offered some to one of my servants in Norway she would have said that they were not worth the trouble of making into clothing. Of the hundreds of people one man had an umbrella. But they waited patiently enough.

"It is the dirtiest country I have seen, filth everywhere. And they cannot buy goods—I know that. A young man on the train with us sold his winter overcoat. It brought him 800 rubles."

Mme. Undset lost her son Anders, 27 years old, in the fight against the German invaders. She is accompanied by her 21 year old son, Hans.

After not more than ten minutes' talk in the lobby of Nob Hill's best hotel she stood up.

"Now you must excuse me. Some people of importance, literary people, are giving a luncheon for me on—I believe it is called Treasure Island. I must see that my son is ready to leave when the car comes for us. And please, whatever else you must do, don't be sentimental about me, if you can help it. I know that is a great deal to ask. But, for once, try to be a writer and not a sentimentalist, and simply tell the truth."

GENE FOWLER TELLS OF HIS WRITING PLANS

Interviewed on Hollywood, He Discusses Anecdotes, Failures and His Next Book

Hollywood
September 15, 1940

GENE FOWLER said that the book he wanted to write told of the life of the greatest failure he ever had heard about. "He's an old fellow now, utterly bedraggled, looks sort of like a stale ladyfinger around the mouth because he hasn't any teeth and his hair is sort of like he wore a pomeranian on top of his head. The government thinks that he is an Indian and lets him live on a reservation. But he's no Indian. He is half Jap and half German. His name is Sadakichi Hartmann and he is one of the greatest men—as well as the greatest failure—I ever have met."

Mr. Fowler said that he realized that most people did not enjoy reading about failures. "They like to know about successes because in any such story there may be a clue, an unveiling of the secret—something that will help themselves." But he said that he was very near death in an automobile accident not long ago and when he thought that he was going to die he looked back over his life and made a quick estimate of what he should have done that he hadn't done.

"And I decided that the great waste had been the time I had put in writing things that I didn't want to write. The time gained was that time that I'd spent writing to suit myself. And I like to write books. The last one, 'Illusion in Java,' cost me eighteen months of work, $25,000 in travel expenses and contracts for $90,000 worth of movie work that I turned down. It brought me in just two weeks' salary—$4,000."

He said that he didn't know, maybe it was selfish of him to go on writing books, "making a lot of work for publishers' salesmen and bothering booksellers and the public and you fellows who have to read them in order to review them. But, of course, I'm prejudiced. They seem all right to me, real interesting. I suppose the trouble is that they are so full of anecdotes. They don't follow a straight line to a set conclusion. Well, when you go for a walk you don't necessarily race to get to some particular point. If you turn a corner and there's a street that interests you, you go down it. That's the way I like books. I have what may be an old-fashioned love for anecdotes, stories that show many sides of a person, not just one side. One of my favorite sports is to sit around having a few drinks—not so many now as once upon a time—and exchange stories about copy-readers and actors and cops and so on." He named a few of his intimates: Ben Hecht, John Barrymore, W. C. Fields, Roland Young, Frank Condon, the directors Leo McCarey, John Ford, La Cava and Capra, and half a dozen more. "That's how we spend a lot of our time. We don't talk ideas because we don't care so much for them. We tell anecdotes."

It was a Saturday afternoon, but Fowler expected to stay in his office all day and most of the evening, working. "They appreciate industry out here. A lot of writers who come to Hollywood don't realize that and hold up pictures that should be made fast. Of course, work doesn't come quite as easy here because it is siesta country, and then there are all the Christmas tree ornaments of the life here that are likely to fool you—the servants, the big houses, the fancy automobiles, the afternoons on the golf course and at the races, the long week-ends in the mountains or on the desert or in boats. When you get believing that you have to have these ornaments they become too important and it hurts your work."

He returned to talk of Sadakichi Hartmann, who "started with all that it takes to be a great man—apparently all that it takes. For instance, when he was 15 or so he realized Walt Whitman's stature as a poet—as few others did then—and insinuated himself into Whitman's Camden home as a secretary and general helper.

Whitman was broke and Hartmann organized a campaign to raise funds for him. Every one denounced him for this—even Whitman did. Whitman wrote letters calling Hartmann practically a fake, but Hartmann raised money and it was used.

"In the course of the campaign he went to Whittier, who said that he would contribute but that he didn't want his name linked with Whitman's because he not only considered that Whitman was not a good poet but he considered his poetry indecent. 'I cannot allow my name to be linked with his,' said Whittier, and as Hartmann says, he has had his wish. His name wasn't linked with Whitman's then and it hasn't been since.

"Hartmann knew them all—the great writers of his youth. And for me he has been a kind of bridge to them. But everything, always, that he has tried to do has gone wrong. For instance, once he had a newspaper job interviewing writers. He went to France and saw Zola and wrote a marvelous piece. But when he turned it in they wouldn't print it—said that it lacked the dramatic qualities of his other interviews. So he rewrote it—placed it in the mouth of a coal mine and faked every word. They printed that and said it was wonderful.

"Nothing he has tried has been right. And he has tried the works because, as I said, he was potentially a great man, a very great one, a genius. Maybe no one will read my book about him—that would fit into his life pattern. But, anyway, I'm going to start writing it in a week or so, and maybe I'll do it fast, the way I did my early books when the Sheriff was always at the door. It is very odd and I don't understand it, but the books I write fast and am not satisfied with seem to sell a lot better than the books I slave over."

THOMAS WOLFE AS FRIENDS REMEMBER HIM

Anecdotes and Tentative Estimates of a Man who Lived Triumphantly as a Free Artist

September 29, 1940

Thomas Wolfe lived without mental or physical comfort and so reached into that wider freedom that makes dead artists envied and living artists disliked. He tortured himself, grossly insulted most of his friends, delighted his acquaintances. He was entirely certain that the universe held nothing so important as his work and was utterly ruthless in the advancement of that work. It is said, however, that he made wonderful apologies: "No man in the world could be more humble than Tom when he came to you and told you all about some horrible thing that he had done and that he hoped you would forgive. You see, there were two Wolfes—one the Wolfe with the gift that was like a possession, the gift that had to be guarded by every weapon, even gross cruelty. The other Wolfe was—well, humble and amazed, eager and sensitive, generous, humorous. I've never known a finer man, a better companion."

Wolfe was very tall—six inches over six feet. And he was built in proportion. There are those who say that his great size was simply glandular, that he lacked the strength that his appearance promised, and that it was his attempt to live up to that appearance, to behave like a giant, a superman, that killed him. There seems to be no evidence to support this view. For years Wolfe thrived on sixteen-hour working days—often without even breaking off for food. His muscles were sound: in barroom frolics he handled normal-sized men as though they were children. His appetite was the kind of thing that entrances good cooks, and his capacity for drinks made him a favorite with the most critical class—bartenders. Even at those steak houses where, for two dollars and a half or so you could get a real thick slab of meat of a size that women wince away from, Tom often wasn't satisfied with one order—he'd eat three steaks. And it is said that he could start drinking at noon, keep at it steadily, and at midnight be really—not drunkenly—entertaining.

The accidental or glandular giant requires extraordinary amounts of sleep as a usual thing and has very little physical endurance. Wolfe could get by on little sleep and could work almost endlessly. Most successful writers have convinced themselves that they can do good work for only four or five hours a day. For Wolfe a stretch like that was merely a warm-up period. Nancy Hale has told of hearing a curious noise on Forty-ninth Street very late one night. She went to her window and saw Wolfe swinging by, and heard his chant: "I wrote ten thousand words today. I wrote ten thousand words today."

It was his habit to prowl the streets late at night after his work was done. He was too keyed up to go to sleep, commonly was hungry and there never was anything very inviting about his quarters. The rooms in which Wolfe lived, says Maxwell Perkins (editor for Charles Scribner's Sons, Wolfe's executor, and through Wolfe's life his nearest friend) "always looked as though he had moved in a few hours before and intended to move out a few hours later."

Sanderson Vanderbilt, assigned to write a newspaper interview with Wolfe in 1935, went to see him on the fourth floor of a brownstone house on Brooklyn Heights, where Wolfe was then living. "An icebox stood in the bathroom," Vanderbilt reported next day in *The Herald Tribune,* "but it evidently was not used, for Mr. Wolfe had placed a bottle of milk, half a dozen eggs and some sliced bacon out on the window sill. There was a bridge lamp in the corner, but it lacked both shade and bulbs. A telephone on the mantel proved simply an ornament and near by rested an unpaid $17.18 bill for its services. The bed in the adjoining room had been hastily made and beside it was an old green alarm clock that operates only when flat on its face. . . . A clay jug was filled with stubs of pencils with which Mr. Wolfe writes."

Mr. Vanderbilt didn't know it but there was a perfectly good reason why that icebox was not connected up and used as a food storage place. The icebox wasn't kept cold because Wolfe used it to write on, instead of a desk. The entire enormous manuscript of "Of Time and the River" came into being atop that icebox.

Through most of his life Wolfe was suspicious of people; only after he became assured that he was famous, that he was not laughed at but admired, did this generalized suspicion relax. Mr. Perkins has a theory that his early questioning of the motives of all strangers was merely "because Tom was a mountaineer." Wolfe was born in Asheville on Oct. 3, 1900, and during his boyhood Asheville was still, in a sense, trapped by mountains.

Mr. Perkins quotes Wolfe as having told him that in his boyhood, before motors were common and when there were no planes, Asheville was like a separate and little world, and he felt imprisoned there, cut off. His imagination was intensified; he saw the world beyond in most vivid colors. "His desire for experience, by being pent up, was increased and sharpened," Mr. Perkins said. "It was not this that made him what he was, of course, but the character of what he did and wrote was qualified by it. This gave his writings their particular intensity and violence, and later increased his sense, as with one released from a prison, that there was not enough time, and so made him wild to see, read, taste, feel and record everything."

"Tom was on the rack almost always," Mr. Perkins said. "And almost always would have been—and for one reason. He was wrestling as no artist in Europe would have to do with the material of literature—a great country not yet revealed to its own people." He feels that Wolfe blazed a trail in interpreting America and Americans to Americans and that although no one can say how long his books will last, the trail is there and other writers will follow it.

Mr. Perkins talked of his own work with Wolfe on the immense manuscripts that always had to be cut down. Every night for a solid year they worked to cut and fill the gaps in the manuscript of "Of Time and the River," which was two feet high.

"It was stuff dangerous to monkey with—but Tom knew more than I knew, or than he thought he knew. For instance, when in 'Of Time and the River' we came to the point where Eugene's father died, there was a gap, and I said that we needed something to fill it in, but that since Eugene was away at Harvard Tom need only tell of the shock of the news, and of Eugene's return for the funeral—a matter of perhaps five thousand words. Tom agreed.

"The next night he came in with some thousands of words about the life of the doctor who had attended Gant. I said, 'This is good, Tom, but what has it to do with the book? You are telling the story of Eugene, of what *he* saw and experienced. We can't waste time with all this that is outside it.' Tom fully accepted this, but still, the next night, he brought in a long passage about Eugene's sister, Helen, and her thoughts while shopping in Altamont, and then at night in bed when she heard the whistle of a train. I said, 'How in God's name will we get this book done this way, Tom? You have wasted two days already, and instead of reducing the length and doing what is essential, you are increasing it and adding what doesn't belong here.'

"Tom was penitent. He did not argue back as he almost always had done. He promised that he would write only what was needed—and yet the next night he brought in thousands of words about Gant's illness, all outside of what I thought was wanted. But it was too good to let go. I said so. It was wrong but it was right, and Tom went on and the death of Gant is one of the finest things he ever wrote."

Mr. Perkins poked at his hat—which he always wears in his office—and ran his fingers across his forehead as though to bless the luck.

"Thank God I had sense enough to see it that early, even though it seemed to me to violate the principles of form. But I do not think I could have stopped Tom anyway. He had agreed that I was right but underneath he knew what he was doing and had to do it."

Wolfe had a habit of calling Mr. Perkins at improbable hours to ask him to come out and have something to eat. At other times he wouldn't telephone, would just drop around. One night he came by and found the house dark. Next day Mrs. Perkins said that a flower pot was missing from a window box and that she didn't understand it.

"You would think," said Mr. Perkins, telling this story, "that that flower box was too high for anyone to reach—and who would want a geranium? But long afterward Tom said: "I meant to tell you, I took one of your geraniums. A cop saw me, and he said, 'What are you doing?' I said, 'I'm taking it home to water it.' He just laughed.' "

Despite all the probing into himself that he did—all of his books were, of course, autobiographical—Wolfe was not entirely devoted to the whole truth, he had a way of favoring some facts, slurring others over. For example, he always made much of the fact that his father was "a working man, a stone cutter." And the added fact that his father, through good judgment and good fortune in real estate deals, had amassed a fortune of $100,000, impressed him much less. It was always someone else who had the silver spoon.

His own three years at Harvard became, in his mind, a kind of accident, merely a part of the miracle that embraced all life. And he'd tell of how his first novel, "Look Homeward, Angel," was begun in an attic. It was true that the vast room in which he then lived was on the top floor of a building, but it seemed most comfortable to persons who visited him, and the building had an excellent location—Tenth Street near Fifth Avenue.

When these contrasts between reality and his thought were pointed out to him, Wolfe accepted the truth casually. He was under no suspicion of a pose, no possible suspicion, because he could not even suspect himself of so picayune a fault as posing.

Edward C. Aswell, who edited Mr. Wolfe's last two books on behalf of Harpers, and was with him through much of the last years of his life, spoke of Wolfe's utter disregard of time—a subject on which most of the people who knew Wolfe grow eloquent.

"I live in Chapaqua," said Mr. Aswell, "and I suppose that Tom and I agreed to meet at the Grand Central and go to my house at least twenty times. We never once made the journey together. Always in making the arrangements Tom would say that of course he would be at the train, but that if something *did* come up and he *did* miss it, then he'd be on the next train. Actually, he was always on the next train, or the one after, or the one after that. One Christmas Eve he said that he would meet me at the station at 3 in the afternoon and come home with me for dinner. He wasn't at the train, but I went on out because we had a number of guests, and I thought that possibly he'd be along by the next train. I met trains for a while, then started telephoning and called everywhere that he might possibly be. Finally, at about dinner time, I called a bar located near the home of Tom's agent. He was there.

"Well, I went to the station to wait for him. He wasn't on the train I expected, or the next. He finally caught the last train that night. And you'd think, wouldn't you, that he'd be in bad shape. He wasn't. He got off the train talking a mile a minute, and talking well, perfectly steady on his feet, and the only way that I could have told that he'd been—well, having a few—was that the enormous woolly toy dog that he had bought for my son had somehow lost its wrappings, evidently had lost them hours before. He clutched the dog in his big fist and gesticulated with it while he told me, with the greatest gusto, of his adventures."

Wolfe often said, and meant it, that more than anything else he wanted a home and children. At the question: "Why didn't he marry, then, and have a home and children?" his friends look pained. "Oh no," they say, "not Tom." "But why?" "No woman possibly could have lived with him—not possibly." "Did he realize that—that no woman could live with him?" "Possibly. But, anyway, his work meant too much. Also, women made him mad. Too soft, too devious rather than direct. It is doubtful that he'd have even tried it."

VAN WYCK BROOKS ON CONFIDENT WRITING

America's Foremost Literary Historian Discusses the Writers of Early New England

October 6, 1940

"THEY SOMETIMES WROTE one draft—and sent it to the printers!" said Van Wyck Brooks, almost despairingly.

He was talking of the writers of New England to the study of whose works and lives he had devoted at least a decade of his own life.

"Many of the Victorian writers did the same thing. Look at a Dickens manuscript, for instance. Not a word crossed out; hardly a moment, it would seem, when the pen wasn't racing down the page! They were so wonderfully sure of themselves, so certain that when they had once turned their minds to a topic they had disposed of it completely."

What was behind this confidence? "For one thing, they were strictly disciplined in childhood—at home and in grammar school. And that discipline held." Their minds were clear. They focused them on an object, a subject, and were filled with interest in that, not concentrated on themselves, on what their own minds were doing. Good writing and self-consciousness do not mix. All great writing comes from the subconscious, unimpeded by the mechanical surface mind."

And they were aided, too, by a simplicity of viewpoint. "To them a bad man was as obviously bad as a bad egg. They weren't confused by the notion that character is gray—part black, part white."

Emerson—the greatest of all the New England writers, in Mr. Brooks' view—had a less simple approach. And he rewrote. "When he wanted to do an essay—on manners, for example—he looked through his notebooks until he found a half dozen or so observations on manners and then strung them together. But not easily or casually. He rewrote, almost as moderns do."

He spoke of "mechanical" and "intuitive" biography and history. He feels that the mistake he made in writing "The Ordeal of Mark Twain"—"Though don't misunderstand; I don't go back on the book"—was in making use of the "mechanical process" of psychoanalysis to get at Twain. "No man fits in the categories of psychoanalysis; it may do for the study of types but not for individuals. Bernard DeVoto attacked the book on the ground that the West as I pictured it was not true West. But his picture of the 'true West' is much like mine. It is just as disorderly and primitive, only he does not seem to feel that this would have any effect on a sensitive boy. Yet I do feel that my method was mistaken; that psychoanalysis is not a proper method for biography."

Mr. Brooks gives the impression of being a stubborn man. He is also very kindly and, despite enough awards and praise to stuff at least a dozen shirts, is shy, and strongly human. He is of medium height. His mustache is straw-colored, though his close-cropped hair is brown. A rather tweedy manner at first meeting relaxes into easy understanding. He has written the literary history of New England in two volumes. He is now starting on what he sees as a sixteen-year job of examining the writers of all America. This new history is planned to fill four books and he intends to give himself four years for each book.

His method of work is "to dig." Before writing of a period "I make a list of all the authors of the time and place and then read all that they have written; simply go through them."

He reads for six hours each day and went through about 900 books as preparation for each of his New England histories: "The Flowering of New England," and "New England: Indian Summer." He lives in Westport, Conn. and obtains a good share of the books he requires for research from the Bridgeport Public

Library. "For the rest I go to the Yale Library—they have everything." He doesn't bother with unpublished letters or manuscripts, "but the task of reading some of the forgotten authors is quite as wearying. The lesser writers are utterly unreadable now for any purpose except study. Yet they often give me the significant detail that brings a place and period to life."

He mentioned Elizabeth Stuart Phelps as one such—a once popular novelist now entirely out of date. "But in the work of such minor figures, so closely linked with their own times, the sound, manner and instinct of the times may, by the diligent searcher, be discovered."

His writing method is this. As he reads he makes notes on the margins of the pages—"notes of facts as I find them and ideas as they come to me." He then copies these notes. Browsing through them when the reading is finished he comes to a few that fit together and makes these the foundation for the sketch of an incident, a character, a scene. Only after he has made about fifty such sketches does he plan his book, "following my nose through to an outline," and by then much of the basic work has been done.

He then starts rewriting, going ahead very slowly, "only about a page a day." "I take everything from my notes; consult them constantly."

He said that "there is nothing more discouraging than to face a blank sheet of paper at the start of a day's work." So each morning he rewrites the work of the day before and thus has a warm-up start—a confidence based in fairly easy accomplishment—that carries him on into another day's work. He said that he never is really content with his work, that he goes on cutting and polishing, welding the facts into as closely concentrated a form as possible, until finally the galley proofs must be sent in and the pages sent to the bindery.

He spoke frequently of the money difficulties that writers today face and contrasted the situation now in that respect with the situation of the men who wrote a hundred years ago in Boston. "They had no wolves at their doors; in the America of even fifty years ago the problem of subsistence could be handled easily by a man who would really work. Money was of small moment."

He said that in Maine, where he spent last Summer, the average income along the coast is $800 a year per family and that this is held sufficient because in Maine "the drive to gadgetry has not yet gathered force." He told of a friend who tried to pay a fisherman for a lobster pot and was met by "the cavalier attitude that money simply had nothing to do with his taking and keeping an extra lobster pot. When my friend hinted at payment the fisherman was puzzled and kept repeating that as he wasn't using the lobster pot there was no possible reason why my friend shouldn't take it."

"In Maine society has been so long stabilized that every one behaves like a gentleman, money is in its proper place and every one is respected who is not a dirty loafer. That is democracy."

MR. LION FEUCHTWANGER TALKS OF HIS WORK

The Author of "Power" Arrives Here After an Escape from a Concentration Camp

October 20, 1940

IN THE 1920's—from 1925 to 1929—Lion Feuchtwanger translated his name into J. L. Wetcheek and contributed to the *Berliner Tageblatt* a series of not very gentle satires on American attitudes. One trifle of a lyric ran:

The quota law keeps out the undesirables effectively.
        Oh! Boy!
The Nordic strain is organized, and sells ideals collectively.
        Sweet Mama!

The Wetcheek squibs were translated by Dorothy Thompson and published under the title "Pep," in the Summer of 1929.

Mr. Feuchtwanger was again Mr. Wetcheek when he arrived in this country a week ago Saturday aboard the American Export liner "Excalibur." It had not been considered safe for him to travel under his own name. Americans had snatched him from the bathing place of a huge French concentration camp, dressed him in woman's clothing, and by various ruses had helped him across frontiers to Lisbon. There an American woman had given up her passage so that he might escape to this country. So it was as Mr. Wetcheek that he smiled from the promenade deck of the "Excalibur" and watched the customs cutter draw alongside.

Many of the passengers aboard the "Excalibur" had slept on iron and wire cots so close to the floor as to be practically pallets, very narrow and quite short. These contrivances still crowded the floor space in most of the public rooms. Mr. Feuchtwanger received the press in the gloomy ship's bar. He went twice over the story of his escape. Several times he was asked which side, in his opinion, would win the war. He invariably made answer with: "Hitler has already lost it." And a representative of the League of American Writers, who had come down on the cutter, would hastily interpose with: "That's all he'll say on that subject. He prefers to leave his statement enigmatic."

Out on the deck a pair of small children gamboled around to express their recognition of the Statue of Liberty, which they had seen in pictures.

When the news interviews were over Mr. Feuchtwanger talked of his work. "I have to write fourteen more books," he said. "Yes, I must. It is necessary to write fourteen more books before I die." He said that he believes that he has evolved a new method for writing the historical romance.

"My historical novels are essentially political novels. I am not interested in history for itself. I am a pedant, and when I need to describe a chair of the eighteenth century or a costume of the second century I make my description accurate. But the pageantry and costume of older days reach my books only by accident. It is my attempt to use only those aspects of history that have meaning for us today, that are alive today, and that may help us in our modern course. It is my belief that the psychology of people has not changed in 2,000 years, and that the men of yesterday were no more or less cruel and no more or less greedy than are men today.

"So it is of the tides in their affairs that have meaning to us today, because they resemble or point up the tides of our affairs, that I write in my historical romances.

"On the other hand, when I write of contemporary scenes I employ the historical technique. I look at the present as one might from the vantage of a hundred years from now, and I try to show the great movements of this time as they might look to a watcher in the future."

He said that he plans a book "like an architect." "It is ever my effort to approach the ideal, and the ideal novel is one in which every word performs three duties—it advances the expression of the idea, the theme; it makes for action, for situation; it puts a light on psychology, character." As preparation he dictates an essay in which the theme of the book is expressed. He then dictates an outline of action, all of which will, so far as he is able, give expression to the book's central idea—"I want to keep the episodes that do not advance the novel's idea as few as possible." And then he goes to work on the characters.

"I always do too many characters, so that there comes a time, in about the fourth or fifth month of preparation, when I must conduct a mass slaughtering of about half the people I had hoped to find room for."

He seeks to keep the central idea of the book imbued in the characters and implicit in all the action, and works to that end, chopping and piecing together the various sections of his preliminary plan. He says that even after his careful plan has been completed his progress is slow.

"I dictate for the double reason that in so doing I may see my words as they are put down, and also can hear them. The sound of words is important. But I cannot dictate with speed. I am a writer, not a speaker."

He believes that it is possible to understand the world today only if one is thoroughly familiar with the thought of Darwin, "who invented the theory of evolution"; of Marx, "who invented the process of understanding our economic world"; of Freud, "who invented the process by which we can understand psychology"; and Einstein, "who invented the theory of relativity."

He considers that Hitlerism is only a by-pass to a better future. "He has seized upon the wonders of the machine age, and upon the inventions of Freud and of Marx. We must and will learn the greater values still in the machine, the greater wisdom of cooperation, and so will defeat him."

H. G. WELLS DISCUSSES HIMSELF AND HIS WORK

He insists on being thought of as a journalist, not a "literary" writer

October 27, 1940

H. G. Wells was calling into a telephone vigorously enough, but when he came into the pleasant study that had been set aside for him in the home of his host, Thomas W. Lamont, his voice had died to a husky murmur. He said that he was tired, that he had just come from the World's Fair, where he had gone to see the British Empire exhibit. "It is disgusting!" Why disgusting? "Becauses it very stupidly appeals to the worst traits in your people. Snobbery. All that nonsense tracing George Washington's genealogy to King John. Of course he was a descendant of King John. So am I. I am also a descendant of William the Conqueror. So was he. Simple mathematics! The entire population of England—two parents, four grandparents, eight great-grandparents, sixteen—but I'm sure you can carry it on yourself. The entire population must, on a simple mathematical basis, have great chunks of notable old ancestors. The genealogy table is stupid and disgusting!"

He smiled very pleasantly and dismissed the British Empire exhibit. I had always pictured Mr. Wells as a rather large, stocky man. In fact, he is somewhat less than medium height and his fine features and small hands and feet indicate that "stocky" never could have been the word despite the impression gained from photographs. His voice has a thin quality; emphasis sends the pitch higher. His talk is humorous and mildly self-deprecatory.

He said that he is amused by the fact that critics are continually discovering that he repeats himself from book to book. "I should think that it would be clear by this time that I am not primarily a 'literary' writer. I seek, in fiction, to advance ideas and naturally I repeat the ideas in which I believe. I have been repeating some of them continually for more than forty years. I am in much the position of a man who has devoted his life to, say, the study of magnesium salts. In his youth he has written a book about magnesium salts that is just as complete and as clear a statement of his knowledge in regard to magnesium salts as he was capable of writing at the time. But with the years, devoting himself tirelessly to magnesium salts, he learns more and more about his subject, rejects some of his old theories, develops new ones, and so writes another book that repeats many of his fundamental theories, changes others, and discards others. That would be understandable in his case, wouldn't it? Then why not in mine?"

But surely his short stories were "literary" in their effects? "Yes, because the short story must aim clearly at a certain point, a certain effect, reach that effect, and stop. The form is inevitable. I wrote most of my short stories when I was quite young and I wrote them to earn a living. Five guineas each, they brought me, the early ones."

Had five guineas been the standard pay? "For an unknown it was quite good pay. And I was very fortunate for something told me when the checks came in with that little space alongside that is the receipt to write in a line above my signature, 'for first serial rights only.'" Mr. Wells chuckled. "That was very intelligent, for you see, it gave the magazines no further rights in the stories, and I've sold them many, many times over ever since. And for much better pay."

When and why had he stopped writing the short stories? "When they interested me only if they were unusual, well off the beaten path. You see, editors cannot afford to interrupt their formula tales of young love and so forth—the tales that month in and month out sell their magazines—with anything that is too unusual. Because there were two reader reactions, neither of them particularly favorable. In one case the reader says, 'What the devil is he printing this stuff for? I don't understand it and I want young love.' In the other case the reader says, 'That was excellent. We want more such stories. We must have more such stories or we won't read your magazine.' But there aren't enough such stories, there simply aren't, you know. 'The Lady or the Tiger,' you remember, who was it who wrote that? Yes, Frank R. Stockton. I suppose a great many people said, 'We want another Lady or Tiger.' But how could he? He couldn't repeat that story possibly. And when you talk of my stories it is probable that you are thinking of 'The Country of the Blind,' and that other one. What is its name? It was rather good, I think. About the Taj Mahal . . . Love. 'The Pearl of Love.' I could hardly do them again."

He talked of the novel of ideas, repeating some of the material in his introduction to "Babes in the Darkling Wood," which was recently published. ("You might mention that title if you will. I'm keenly interested in the book and believe that it has a good chance if only enough people talk about it. But it is a gamble. It could be a best seller and it could stop at 3,000 copies.")

He said that he has had faith in books of ideas since in 1901 he published a collection of articles called "Anticipations."

"At that time it was taken for granted in publishing that the public would endure ideas, but would buy fiction. 'Anticipations' was a book of ideas, so only a couple of thousand copies were printed and they were snapped up at once. Yes, in fiction form, and yes, there were love stories in them. . . . No, I doubt that love sold them. I've never thought that love should be carried too far to the point of inconvenience. Have you? More aptly, there is something abject about the man or woman who is too deep in love. This thing of being rejected time after time and standing through the night under a beloved's window—I read a story by Stefan Zweig that had something of that sort in it—I hardly think it is normal. No. The normal man becomes interested in a woman, makes a few tentative advances, gets nowhere with them, makes more definite advances, is refused, and then refused again and still again. Well, what does the normal man do? He picks up his hat, doesn't he, and moves along? The normal woman, too often discouraged, does, in effect, the same thing. That is natural. Love carried to great sacrifice is abject. Love is hardly primary in my books. It has its place. But I am a journalist. I appeal to the mind."

Of his method of work he said that he writes a first draft that is full of gaps and has that draft typed. He then goes over the typed copy, writing inserts and additions between the lines and on the margins.

"The second draft is then typed, and I go through that again, always adding considerable amounts and taking away lesser amounts. I repeat this process four, five, six or seven times, and in these continual revisions the book takes shape and form. This is an effective means, I think, of giving a book shape, of proportioning it correctly. The invention of the typewriter has had an excellent effect upon the proportioning of books. One hardly dares say it but I believe that 'Gone With the Wind,' for example, was better shaped than many of the revered classics."

He commented that one difficulty in writing is one's conception of the "blank face" of the reader. "When you talk you make a quick estimate of how much your listener can take, and talk in shorthand or longhand with daring or without it, as the face of your listener seems to require. But in writing there is the blank face—what will they understand, what must be explained, and repeated, what is too difficult for them to believe?"

He spoke, in passing, of cheap books and offered two Penguin editions of work by himself. "The best read men in England for some years, taken all in all, have been the men on the dole. Really. They read everything and they understand what they read. They have time to think about it."

Another comment had to do with the essential anonymity of writers in this country, this developing out of a description of the plight of a great European writer who seems uncomfortable here because he is accustomed to daily recognition even by passers-by. "Yes, I can believe that. But he must become accustomed to it," said Mr. Wells. "The writer visiting America is a celebrity for about a week. At the end of two weeks the very ship news reporters who put down his every word when he arrived cut him dead on the street."

He was leaving New York for a lecture tour. "I'll deliver the same lecture twelve times. The title is 'Two Hemispheres—One World.' It will result in a great deal of correspondence, all of which will sum up, I suppose, into, 'You filthy toad, why don't you pay your debts?'—Afterward? Back to England, of course. We're in the front line there, you see. I'm merely on furlough."

SOME DIFFICULTIES CONFRONTING THE SATIRIST

Dawn Powell, Whose Witty Novels Find Too Small a Public, Discusses Her Trade

November 3, 1940

DAWN POWELL said that for a number of years she did most of her writing in the children's room of the Public Library at Fifth Avenue and Forty-second Street.

"They have those low little tables in there that are just the right height for me. And it is always quiet in the children's room. Children aren't allowed there, so far as I know. Of course, you're not supposed to write in the library, but you always can take down a book and make out you are copying something from it. Another advantage of the children's room is that you don't come up against the eye-twitchers and ear-twiggers of the third floor reference rooms. You know the people across the table from you who keep twigging their ears or screwing up their faces, and each time they do it you can't avoid looking up?"

Miss Powell's books come oddly from the children's room. They are very witty satires that, perhaps unfortunately, satirize those people who, to the bulk of the public, must seem the stuff that dreams are made of—fashionable chanteuses, radio big names, advertising contact men, successful commercial artists, popular playwrights, mistresses who have attained Park Avenue addresses.

The novels are based in the satires of the Greeks and Romans. Miss Powell's "Turn Magic Wheel" of several seasons ago faithfully followed the structure and points of "Turn Magic Wheel" by Theocritus.

The books make a stir on publication but don't get much of anywhere in sales. Miss Powell said that she guessed she had better make her next book long and dull. "It must be good to have your work respected, to pick up the reviews and find that at last you have been accepted as solid and worthwhile and to be recommended. There is so great a premium on dullness that it seems stupid to pass it up."

She told of a friend who came in to see her one day just after completing a new book. "He was rubbing his hands together and exclaiming that his new book was amazingly dull. 'I have it chock full of Hegel and such fellows,' he said. 'Dawn, it is so dull that even I wonder how I did it. Thank God, I won't have to read the proofs—my wife will read them.' And, of course, every one said that it was a wonderfully thoughtful job—so intelligent," said Miss Powell, her voice falling away.

She believes that the way of the satirist is made difficult by the fact that "you both confuse and anger people if you satirize the middle class."

"It is considered jolly and good-humored to point out the oddities of the poor or of the rich. The frailties of millionaires or garbage collectors can be made to seem amusing to persons who are not millionaires or garbage collectors. Their ways of speech, their personal habits, the peculiarities of their thinking are considered fair game. I go outside the rules with my stuff because I can't help believing that the middle class is funny, too."

Her most recent novel, "Angels on Toast," is concerned with the business men who may have homes but don't want them and spend most of their time in train drawing rooms and in hotels. In her view these are the lively people who are farthest away from puritanism, who can enjoy life to the full and without regret, and so are the proper subjects for lively books. Since she has shown them as selfish, tricky and drunken, unfaithful to wives and mistresses and friends, she said that she had worried quite a bit as to what the reactions of the persons on whom her characters are based would be, and had found comfort only in the hope that the models (being no great readers) never would get around to the book.

"It was a relief when one of the men who had supplied me with a bit of material telephoned that he was buying the book in quantity lots to give to his friends. He liked the picture of himself that he had found in it and was grateful that I hadn't made use of the fact that he is supporting several people simply out of the goodness of his heart. He has an uncomfortable feeling that such facts would have labeled him as a sucker."

To the observation that, though amusing, most of the characters in her novels seem pointless, Miss Powell wondered how many people out of an odd lot of a hundred wouldn't be rather pointless.

"I'll bet if you walked through an office at 5 in the afternoon and asked people working there, 'What is your aim in life?' most of them would be up against it to give you an answer. There is the eternal aim of getting to dinner on time, and of remembering to buy toothpaste, but in general I doubt that aims are very clear and I believe that writers who supply major aims for characters who essentially are commonplace and minor are faking. When you get down to the subject of life aims you are very likely to find yourself on the level of a fan magazine interview with a movie star."

STUART CLOETE DISCUSSES HIS WORK METHODS: HE TURNED TO WRITING AFTER FIFTEEN YEARS OF RANCHING WHEN HE DECIDED THERE WAS JUST SO MUCH YOU COULD DO FOR COWS

November 17, 1940

THE FIRST LAND grant in South Africa was given to a Cloete. The first Cloete was pure Hollander. But the family soon became Anglicized. Stuart Cloete whose new book, "Yesterday is Dead," a best-selling novel of the African veldt, was an officer in the Guards during the last War. He has been in this country for some months but plans to return to England in December. "Not that there's much for me to do there. But I don't feel quite comfortable being away. For that matter, I hardly suppose I shall feel very comfortable when I go back."

He is a tall man, built for action. After fighting in the last War he went back to South Africa and was a rancher for fifteen years. "It isn't a bad life, ranching. But after a while you begin to think. One day it occurred to me that I had spent enough of my life at the job of looking after cows. There is just so much you can do with cows. I had a lot of good ones and if I'd stick at it for thirty years more I'd have better ones. The trees I had planted were six feet high. In thirty years they'd be twenty feet high. But it seemed to me that nothing else would change much whether I stayed on the ranch or not. So I chucked it and went up to London. That's when I decided to have a shot at writing."

He spent about two years working on "The Turning Wheel." "It was historical, you see, and I'd have to plow through long books to find a fact—a fact or an incident that I could use. Also, I have cycles of writing. I work like hell for three months and then for a month or more I'm certain that I'll never have another word to say—not a word. So I suffer. And then resign myself. And then the month is up and I start to make a little headway again. A couple of weeks more of trying before suddenly I'm back in the groove."

He has written two South African novels and expects to turn out three more. The second one, "Watch for the Dawn," didn't do so well. Probably because it was published on the day that war was declared and no one was paying much attention to the book news. He was in the middle of his third novel when he broke off to write "Yesterday Is Dead." "The new book started as an effort to clarify my own thoughts—and my own thoughts required a great deal of clarification. I wrote every day at an unprecedented pace for me—80,000 words in six weeks. I take a fall out of so many things that people believe in that I've left myself open to attack from all sides. But that is all right too. There are no shells to crawl into, no places to hide. We are all open to attack and might as well realize it."

He said that he probably would do a few short stories before returning to his novel. "Though I'm not very happy doing them. They are so circumscribed. You must start exactly here and move at a precise pace to there. The bad thing with me is that before I've gone many pages my characters have a way of getting in bed together. I don't know. Maybe there's something wrong with the way I think but if characters are real to me I like them to act like real people. In fact, I find it very hard to keep them behaving in any other way."

He is convinced that all fiction writing, if it be well done, is done by the subconscious. "The front of your mind is continually drifting about—prying into what your intentions are toward unpaid bills and deciding whether you're hungry or not hungry and thinking up clever lines to answer the argument that was ended last night. Meanwhile, your subconscious is slogging along trying to complete the job that your conscious mind is hindering."

Early in his writing career he discovered a method of unblocking the channel. The method works for him and he says that there are other writers who use it. "I used to go to a Lyon's—a London restaurant—where they had an all-girl orchestra. I'd get up as near the orchestra as possible and let the music beat at me. Within ten minutes I'd be at work on a story. So when I'm writing fiction what I do is to put a record on a gramophone and play it over and over until I've worn it through. This is guaranteed to drive your wife and your neighbors crazy but it is an enormous help. You get into the rhythm of that record it drowns out the wandering thoughts of your conscious mind and you go to town. My taste in music is not all extreme. I like quite cheap music so I suppose that means more suffering for others than good music would cause them. But what I'm after is the underlying beat, the rhythm that fits the workings of my own mind."

His home in New York is an apartment in a made-over private house just north of Rockefeller Center. Mrs. Cloete is an American and for some years they have spent much of their time in this country. "We like this place because it is central, because it is quiet, because we didn't have to sign a lease and because it is cheap. I never stay in the same place very long because when they insist upon my signing a lease I move. Might as well. I'd move soon after signing. After fifteen years on an African ranch I feel that I've stayed put long enough. We own a ranch in Africa and a place in the Bahamas but for some time to come our trunks will be home enough for us."

MR. MAUGHAM ON THE ESSENTIALS OF WRITING: THE AUTHOR OF "OF HUMAN BONDAGE" HAS TEMPORARILY QUIT FICTION

November 24, 1940

W. Somerset Maugham is in this country as a British agent. He glanced about the grill room of the Ritz Carlton Hotel—the grill room is below street level—and with an air of semi-professionalism commented that it would make a middling good air raid shelter. He ordered corned beef hash and a poached egg. "Not long ago I was extremely hungry, and had been hungry for days and had the chance to eat bully beef with a sauce over it. Delicious. I hope to recapture the flavour with corned beef hash."

The hunger and the bully beef were part of 67-year-old Mr. Maugham's second World War adventure. When the blitzkrieg started last Spring he was at his home on the Riviera. "We were evacuated in two British colliers about 1,300 of us. There were 500 aboard the collier on which I was a passenger, 538 including the crew. And when I tell you that the lavatories had been planned only for the thirty-eight crew members you will understand that conditions were not ideal. We had been told to bring three days provisions and one small suitcase each. More than a week elapsed before we touched at our first port, Gibraltar, and as many of us had brought most of our provisions in bottles, on the theory that food was less important than good cheer, we were hungry. That bully beef was a God-send."

He left England at the beginning of October and has spent the time since then in and about New York, lecturing, giving interviews, writing articles. He will go to Chicago in December and will spend January on the Pacific Coast. "After that I don't know. But I hope that when I return to England the clipper will make a direct flight."

Like H. G. Wells he believes that entry into the war by the United States is against England's advantage. England is safe from invasion, he said, as long as the R. A. F. can stay in the sky and the R. A. F. cannot be knocked out. "The Germans are losing three planes to our one and even that figure does not indicate our advantage in pilots. Often our pilots can bail out of a doomed plane, return to the airport and take up another machine. Every German pilot shot down is out of the war."

Mr. Maugham says that he has sworn off fiction for the war's duration. He spends his mornings writing letters and articles. The articles he says, come hard; he is not accustomed to marshalling arguments with facts to hinder the flow and he prefers to write about the people of his imagination. A story comes to him "in a straight clear line"; an article may be written only by taking conscious thought. He enjoys writing fiction. "I am convinced that the subconscious does the really difficult work. I sit down with fountain pen and paper and the story pours out. However lousy a section is I let it go. I write on to the end. Then the subconscious mind had done what it can; what is to be created is there. And the rest—the rest is simply effort. You may go over and over, polishing, rewriting the lousy parts, sometimes rewriting a page for the whole day, going over a chapter time and time again, until, though you know it isn't right, it is the best you can do. But that is the labor of the conscious mind, the effort of a craftsman. It is the first draft, the creative draft, that is basic."

He said that as soon as the war is over he would hurry to England. "I have an idea for a book, a book and a half, that I am most anxious to write."

Why has he, after "Of Human Bondage," so rarely returned to the English scene for his characters and backgrounds?

"In England, you know, civilization goes fairly deep, and it is an old civilization. This makes for an apparent sameness in the people—one must go through many layers to discover what it is that sets each man apart, to discover the unique and the natural man. Every man is unique, of course, but the strangeness that makes a man a story, the oddity within him, is not easy to find in a man who wears his civilization thickly. During the first World War I traveled, and after it my travels became extensive. In those parts of the world where civilization is worn thinner I found that the unique man is far easier to recognize. Material leaped at me—I handled it as well as I could."

On writing in general he said that it is the personality of the author, the free range of his mind, that determines the value of his work.

"The four greatest novelists who ever lived—Tolstoy, Dostoevski, Dickens and Balzac—none of them could write; that is, none were good craftsmen. But they saw deeply into people, and they saw people the right way; they were the right men in their handling of people. That is why they are great."

"Mr. Maugham, do you believe that Dickens liked people?"

"The books indicate that he did—the biographies make it appear doubtful.

"I think it is unimportant whether he liked people or not. What is important is to understand them. For myself, I like very few people. But I believe that I understand because, though I cannot say that I like them, I can be interested. I am interested in almost every one I meet. If your interest is sufficient, likes and dislikes are rather beside the point. It is not the business of a novelist to judge. He observes."

"Do you, Mr. Maugham—do you have any moral standards?"

"Just now I have. In fact I am quite hot on moral standards just now. Because I believe that France fell not because of rotten politicians, not for any of the causes usually given, but because the people of France were morally confused. They had no moral standards. I hate to talk this way, I hate to preach, but I truly and honestly and warmly believe that we can defeat Hitler only if we keep our standards very high, if we are not soft with ourselves."

"But did you, through most of your life, have moral standards?"

"Oh, no," said Mr. Maughan. "Not at all. I've met so many people, often the scum of the earth, and found them, you know, quite decent. I am an uncomfortable stranger to moral indignation. I feel it now because I believe that it is the great necessity of the present. We must set up standards now and live up to them. In England, I don't know whether you have heard, every one in the country is working—all out—for the country. Labor has given up gains that were the result of years of struggle. They have given up these gains overnight and under no more pressure than the advice of their leaders that the sacrifices were necessary for the country's good. Every one is making sacrifices; that must be. We have set standards for ourselves to save ourselves, to win; and we will live up to them."

AN INTERVIEW WITH BRUCE LANCASTER

He talks on the labors and pleasures of writing historical fiction

December 1, 1940

BRUCE LANCASTER, author of "For Us the Living" and "Guns of Burgoyne," is one of the happier writers in that he did not approach his career when very young and so spend years of frustration when his hopes were greater than his possibilities, but in maturity when, coming fresh to the work, he could bring to it both confidence and experience in effort. Ask most authors what they do when ideas bog down and the words don't come, and you touch a vein of ready eloquence. Ask Mr. Lancaster the same question and he looks rather surprised. It becomes apparent that he brings to his work much of the freedom and assurance that marked the authors of the past. He speaks of fiction as an opportunity "to put one's ideas into circulation," and, with an enviable simplicity, makes his points in story form.

Mr. Lancaster is a large man who played tackle on the Harvard football team for several seasons, though his college career was considerably interrupted by service as a soldier. He quit Harvard in his sophomore year, 1916, to enlist for the Mexican trouble and again in 1917 to go to France with the Twenty-sixth Division, 101st Field Artillery. He was graduated as of the class of '19, spent the next eight years in business in his native Worcester, and then joined the United States Consular Service. He was vice consul at Kobe, Japan, until 1933.

He married Miss Jessie Bancroft Payne, a relative of Sir

Henry Fielding Dickens, son of Charles Dickens, and a descendant of George Bancroft, the historian. He turned to writing partly because "my wife wouldn't stand for anything else," and partly because he happened to read a rare volume on Japan, a report by Engelbert Kaempfer, a Dutch physician, on life in Japan in 1690.

"Kaempfer was the first trained European observer to write of Japan. Living with the small Dutch colony of traders who were allowed to exist as virtual prisoners on an artificial island, Deshima, in the harbor of Nagasaki, he learned a great deal about Japanese ways of life, and when I read his book I decided at once that, contrary to general opinion, the life of Japan had changed very little in 250 years. To show how few changes there had been I wrote my first novel, 'Wide Sleeve of Kwannon.'"

Out of this novel grew his fundamental technique, which is that of writing about one facet of a time while seeming to write of another; that is, reporting by reflection. His main character in "Guns of Burgoyne," a novel of the American Revolution, was a Hessian soldier. "I wanted to show free men—the free men of the colonies—and it seemed to me that the best way to do that was to let them be discovered by a man who never had been free, who had, when he came here, no conception of freedom."

Similarly, his "For Us the Living" purports to be the story of Hugh Bruce, a rough young frontiersman in Illinois in the early part of the nineteenth century. Actually the novel is dominated by the young Abe Lincoln, who comes into the book as Bruce's closest friend. "I wanted to show democracy actually at work in the environment from which the greatest figure of democracy came."

He said that his system of work is based on an old New England recipe which advised "stir until tired." He starts work at about mid-morning and keeps going until late afternoon or early evening. "I stoke myself with lunch of lettuce sandwiches and tea, eating with one hand and typing with the other, because I've found that if I knock off for lunch it is difficult to get going again." He tries to cover one incident of importance to the story each day. After work Mrs. Lancaster takes the pages and a pencil and reads aloud what he has written. "When she comes to something that won't do at all she jabs at it with her pencil and says it is terrible. Usually she realizes this only a split second before I do. We find it fairly easy to agree on what is to come out. Then we talk over the gaps and decide together how best to fill them."

They have pretty much "dug in," he said, in their house in Cambridge. They have the freedom of the stacks at the Widener Library and do most of their research there. "We enjoy the work and keep at it just about all the time—neglect week-ends and holidays, and so on. The research for a novel never is finished; there are always historical facts to be checked. We spent eleven months on 'For Us the Living' and, in our reading, studied not only the few years and the region with which we dealt but the twenty or thirty years before and the twenty or thirty years afterward. You see, several of the characters were old people who had come to Illinois over the Wilderness Road. To get all possible light on them we studied the Wilderness Road from its beginnings, the means of transport, the farm and household implements they had carried with them, the colorful stories that they might have to tell of their early adventures. Then we went on ahead to find out what would become of the younger people in the book, what would shape their lives in the future.

"We are very careful never to distort history—though sometimes the temptation is there. You'll find a good incident, you know, that is only a few years out of your period and you'll want very much to work it in. But we couldn't defend that, so we don't do it. Then, too, you'll frequently find an actual circumstance that you legitimately could use but that, no matter how hard you try, you can't make fit. Do you know, a piano was hauled over that Wilderness Road to the early frontier. They cut the legs off and hauled it in a wagon. I tried three or four times to work that piano into my story, but it always read as though it had been dragged in, dragged in almost as laboriously as the original piano. Finally we gave up."

AN INTERVIEW WITH MARY ROBERTS RINEHART

Who feels that her present life is "too much a bed of ease" and plans to visit London

December 15, 1940

Mary Roberts Rinehart in her Park Avenue apartment—which is about as big as a park—commented that she wasn't sure that the life there was good for her. "Not good for me, that is, as a writer; perhaps it is too much a bed of ease." The Filipino cook, who is a wizard with mashed potatoes and chicken, and undoubtedly equally skilled with many other foods, as no one who beats up potatoes as he does could be a slouch; the solicitous maid who says: "You have worked long enough, Madam. Your bed is turned down"; the glowing fire in the library that tempts to idleness; the closets that are, individually, as large as the living rooms in cheap houses—"but where do the stories come from?"

The storyteller who is freed of conflict and action must reach far back for material. There is, Mrs. Rinehart said, a kind of inspiration in change, if the change is drastic. But when you no longer are young and have fitted your life into a pattern that is the most pleasant you know how to attain, change comes hard. In thirty-six years of writing Mrs. Rinehart feels that she has served the equivalent of a twenty-year penitentiary sentence. "Most of it in solitary confinement. You can't write at a party; you can't write and talk to friends at the same time. You can live on coffee and cigarettes instead of bread and water." Naturally, she has made the prison a mighty pretty one, a place of luxury difficult to discard.

"To go to Hawaii and lie on the beach once would have seemed too much to hope for. Now it would be no change at all. But if I could fly over bombed London, then I know that—well, that my imagination would flare up, that my mind would again be filled with stories almost as it was during those years when I hardly could take time to write a story because there were so many more crowding at it, pressing for their turn to be written."

Two bloodclots, Mrs. Rinehart said, have damaged her heart. The Clippers to Europe fly high but are not fitted with oxygen tanks—"So I don't know. Perhaps it is foolish to go. Yet I hope to go to England in the Spring, or perhaps before. I reached the Belgian front lines early in 1915, and I want to report again. Of course, there may be some small difficulties, as I am not allowed to walk upstairs. My son Stanley made, I think, the most pointed comment: 'I'm sure you'd be magnificent, Mother, going down into a dugout, but how would you get up again?' But I'll worry about those stairs when I'm at the foot of them. I want to go to England."

Mrs. Rinehart has written fifty-six books, seven plays, uncounted articles, short stories, travel pieces. She had intended to be a doctor and took training as a nurse; the course was supposed to be a preliminary to entrance in a medical school. "But of course I married a handsome young surgeon on the hospital staff." She started her nurse training when she had been 17 years old for only six days. "In those days the girls who were my friends did not know that prostitutes existed; I took care of prostitutes. I watched men and women die of knife and gun wounds, assisted at births, helped look after alcoholics and maniacs. That period of training was of incalculable value to me as a writer."

Mrs. Rinehart said that she never has thought of herself as a "literary figure." "I am a storyteller." When she writes, the picture of the scene she is describing is very clear. "I have a strong visual memory that is not unusual, but certainly is useful. I have no memory at all for names, remember only briefly what people say, but retain always a sharp image of how they looked, what they wore, what gestures they used, and what their surroundings were—to the last detail. At my desk writing a scene, the externals of action are all before me and I need simply to select what details to put down. Of course, finding the reason for putting them down, the point, is not simple at all."

She has trained herself to pick up a pen and start writing the moment she sits down at her desk. "This is the one way to do it. The word 'inspiration,' when examined, means, I suppose, writing above your head. I have written above my head on occasion, but the ability to do so comes not anywhere but at the desk, or from anything but long exercise in effort."

Stories rarely come full-formed to the mind of even a natural storyteller. "I usually build them by plugging, though about three years ago on a Monday I woke with a new story that apparently had come from nowhere. I was scheduled for a serious operation on the Thursday of that week, and had been ordered to stay in bed. So I sent for yellow paper, a pen and a writing board, and at 11 o'clock that night had completed the first draft of the story. The next day my secretary typed it, and on Wednesday I revised it. While the operation was going on a magazine editor bought the story. No, it had nothing to do with my own circumstances. It was about a man who hated his wife and wanted to kill her."

Mrs. Rinehart wrote three short stories when she was 14 years old. They were sold to a Pittsburgh newspaper for a dollar each, and printed. She made a fresh start in 1904 when her three sons were small children and went early to bed and when Dr. Rinehart was out of the house on night calls. In an old handbook that she recently found among her papers she kept an account of her work and what it brought, in those first years. Item No. 1 in the book is analysis in light verse of the components of a mystery novel—the analysis still is sound—and it sold to *Munsey's* for twelve dollars. The next bit of verse brought ten dollars. Then there were short-story sales at prices that crept up to forty dollars, wavered back to twenty-five and thirty, and then soared to $125 on a story that had been rejected thirteen times, and sold to *Scribner's* on its fourteenth journey out. "The Man in Lower Ten" and "The Circular Staircase," which as books brought in thousands of dollars in royalties, were serialized at $400 and $500 respectively.

Mrs. Rinehart had been climbing toward the "quality" magazines, once a pulp market had been fairly well established. It was a great day when the editor of *Harper's* wrote to ask her to submit a story. She wrote one—it was returned with an ordinary printed rejection slip. She learned later that a manuscript reader was responsible for this, that the editor never had seen it. But meantime she had sent the story to *The Saturday Evening Post* and George Horace Lorimer had read it and dispatched not a letter but an editor to Pittsburgh. The story was concerned with a woman named Tish, and Mr. Lorimer wanted not only that but all other stories about Tish. Tish has been a *Saturday Evening Post* character for thirty years.

THE CURIOUS RETIREMENT OF MR. HERGESHEIMER

Who feels that, having written ten good books, it is folly to work more

December 22, 1940

"MR. VAN DE WATER!" Joseph Hergesheimer bellowed. The interview was over, the Hotel Algonquin elevator on its way up. Mr. Hergesheimer came slapping along the hotel corridor in his slippers. There was one point, he said, that he wanted to make absolutely clear. This was that he had retired as "a serious novelist." He continued to write, he said, wagging his finger, commercially. And in no other way save as a serious novelist had he retired. The fact that he sees very few people nowadays is no indication of retirement. It is due simply to his conviction, he explained, that there are very few people who are able to afford him the smallest amusement.

Actually (to continue in the Hergesheimer rhythm), the point had not been obscure. Mr. Hergesheimer had stated, emphatically, that he had written ten books that he believed to be good, "and if they are not good certainly there is nothing that any one can do about them now." The books (and listening to him you remember the barge in "Balisand," and the girl falling downstairs; remember "Java Head," "The Bright Shawl," "The Three Black Pennys," and that atmospheric masterpiece, "Wild Oranges") were written during the best years of his life. Every one of them, he said, represented the greatest effort of which he was capable. He would merely be stupid and unreasonable, he pointed out, if now, a man past sixty, he attempted to surpass or even equal the difficult and demanding labors of his prime.

Any novels that he wrote from now on would, he was sure, be "empty." "I wrote one empty novel and it slipped by; I was not called for it; I will not do that again." His living—"and I live well"—now comes, in part at least, from the proceeds of short stories. "Any one who says that commercial short stories are difficult to write is simple minded or a liar," he declared, adding, however, a moment later, that he had spent four months analyzing the meaning of the word "honor." Certain questions of honor made the theme of the most recent short story by Mr. Hergesheimer to appear in print. His answer to that, in argument, unquestionably would be that the story was the by-product rather than the aim of his analysis.

A suspicion had developed when reading the story that some sections had been cut from it. Yes, Mr. Hergesheimer agreed, it had been cut—and what of that? "At the rate of payment that I received I could have taken no umbrage had they printed nothing but the title and the first paragraph. You see, one has a choice. It is possible to write for certain magazines that carry practically no advertising but that print every word precisely as you wrote it, and pay twenty dollars. Other magazines which keep advertising separated from reading matter will pay three or four hundred dollars and print every word. The magazines that pay $3,000 and up will cut anything out of anything to make room for a Pepsodent ad. I respect their judgment. If it were not for the Pepsodent ad they could not possibly pay $3,000 and I, personally, should be the poorer for it."

And in any event, he continued, he is not one of the "velvet-jacket boys" who are wrought to the point of hysteria if a line in their copy is changed. What is important in a story is structure, and if the structure is sound mere changes in phraseology do no great damage. "The word Art never has been adequately defined."

The thought of the velvet jackets brought him to reminiscence on the literary life. He never, he said, felt at home in it. Most of the classics that performers in literature speak of with such easy familiarity he never read. "And most of those that I did read I did not like."

He was able to endure very little of "Don Quixote," Dickens, and so on. "I started, you see, as an artist and came to literature late."

The so-called rewards of literary fame were not attractive, he found. He recalled an invitation that he had received to address the student body of a college for women. His friend H. L. Mencken had a similar invitation and they responded that they would accept only if they were allowed to speak together. " 'You mean in a debate?' No, we said, we want to talk together. They said, 'All right.' Both advanced to the edge of the platform and talked. This seemed to us an excellent comment on the futility of such affairs."

Age is the primary reason for his retirement as a serious novelist, but of almost equal importance is the fact that "no man deeply engaged in serious work has time to learn." As he sees it, novelists are men who know very little about many things, are forced to fake their way in conversation because of lack of knowledge where deep knowledge is presumed, and must suffer fools if not gladly at least courteously because they themselves are for all they know making fools of themselves every time they open their mouths. Weary of slight learning, Mr. Hergesheimer engrosses himself in the task of attaining a true familiarity in fields of learning that attract him. For example, he is now a student in the history of the Christian Church.

LOUIS ADAMIC ON HIS NEW SERIES OF BOOKS

He is engaged in a crusade to make immigrants feel they "belong"

December 29, 1940

Louis Adamic is tall, thin, serious and tired. He asked, concernedly, if he sounded "too damned idealistic." Essentially a crusader, he is wary of his own fervor. "This thing is costing a thousand dollars a month; even with the Carnegie grant it isn't easy to swing." And of his working time, "I get up every morning at 6 and most nights don't turn out my light until 12." Yet it is fairly obvious that his interest in the cost of his crusade is not great, that his talk on these matters of money and working time is a kind of cloak of practicality worn in way of proof that he is no fanatic, but simply a calm man trying to deal reasonably and intelligently with a major problem, and cussing out the minor difficulties just as business men do.

That problem is the "psychological civil war" that Mr. Adamic believes is an outgrowth of our "melting pot." "The melting pot," he says, "is used to fry the good out of a lot of people who get in it." The possession of the name Starzinski instead of Hamilton, an inherited taste for pigs' knuckles rather than prime ribs of beef, is a source of "feelings of inferiority" that millions suffer, Mr. Adamic is convinced. These feelings may result in "negative personalities, the limp handshake, the stutter," or in "bumptious blah-blahing by people who pretend to be sure of themselves when they are not." Either reaction is dangerous.

Goebbels is quoted as saying: "The America of today will never again be a danger to us. Nothing will be easier than to produce a bloody revolution in the United States. No other country has so many social and racial tensions. We shall be able to play on many strings there." The tensions, says Mr. Adamic, must be eased or our defense effort never can be total. "People without a firm sense of 'belonging' cannot properly develop, cannot play their full parts in the American scene."

He is devoting six books and about six years to the task of propagandizing the need for "fraternity" in America, to breaking down, at least in the minds of immigrants and their children, the belief that Ellis Island puts a mark of inferiority upon those who pass through it. In a quarter of a million broadsides, a hundred lectures and his books he makes such points as these: that in the last hundred years more immigrants died in industrial accidents than early American colonists were killed in subduing the wilderness and in the Revolution; that the labor and genius of immigrants had as much to do with creating present-day America as the labor and genius of the descendants of early citizens; that now with the presence of nearly 50,000,000 non-Anglo-Saxons in America a new conception of America is necessary; "that the presence in the United States of this vast new-immigrant element is an unprecedented opportunity for creating on this continent an extraordinarily rich culture and civilization, at the same time that it immensely complicates American social, economic, political, cultural and spiritual forces and problems; that inherent in our present population are certain dangers . . . and lest these dangers increase and intensify, all of us—new-and-old stock Americans—must begin to become intelligently, patriotically, actively, critically interested in this entire situation, now generally wrapped in darkness and shot through with fear and sentimentality."

He believes that Hitler has done much to ease tensions; each of his attacks on various countries has added a new bloc of people proud rather than ashamed of their family origins. "The Greeks are blooming in these last few weeks, for example." The first generation of immigrants, he said, never have been so "lost" as has the second generation. Those coming direct from other countries have their own culture to live by, to respect and remember. The second generation, made up so largely of men and women who are troubled by the "differentness" of their parents, suffer most.

Louis Adamic is himself an immigrant. He came here from Slovenia in 1913 when he was 15 years old, fought in the World War, worked at many jobs, and then found himself as a writer. After the publication of his book "My America" he traveled around the country talking to people who had written him about the book, and out of these talks found realization of the problem that the "melting pot" theory fails to resolve. He has founded a magazine, *Common Ground,* which he hopes may be useful in calling attention to this problem, and is engaged in a long series of books.

"One result of all this is that I am filling so many filing cabinets with material for stories and novels that the cabinets are pushing us out of our home. I am building an organization, as best I can, that will carry on this job. When that organization is established I'll drop out and write some of the stories that beg to be written. There is enough material in those filing cases to keep three or four writers busy all their lives."

He remarked on the oddity of the fact that so many writers, once established, seem determined to spend all their lives not only in New York but in the East Fifties of New York. Brooklyn is filled with stories, but of course they never get there. "Broadway, Park Avenue and Hollywood really do not supply the best material in the world."

He told anecdotes illustrating recent changes in America that are the result of strife in Europe. As the Greeks have grown in confidence—"and they were among the unhappiest groups in America," he said that the Italians and Germans in America have been greatly depressed. "The 14-year-old son of an Italian friend of mine recently attempted suicide. You see, his classmates in school were kidding him about the Italian defeats."

But on the other side was the old farmer in the Middle West, a Norwegian, who, through fifty years of residence in this country, had attempted to keep alive the best of the culture that he had brought with him from his home. He told Mr. Adamic: "For many years our children were ashamed of us, because we were different, we were not fully American, as the Yankee stock was. We had no communication with our children. 'Ma, what you got to eat?' That was all they asked when they came to see us—all they asked, and meant. Now there is something new in their feeling. They say, 'You come from Norway. Where?' We get out the old atlas and show them. Then we talk of our memories, and they are interested. They want to know. It is not that they are less American—but they are not ashamed of what we were. They talk to us and are nice to us. They are so nice that sometimes when we are alone, my wife and I, we cry."

JOSEPHINE LAWRENCE TALKS OF HER WORK

She discusses some difficulties of writing honestly when one's outlook is gloomy

January 12, 1941

REVIEWERS HAVE consistently taken it for granted that Josephine Lawrence is a "popular" novelist. Actually, Miss Lawrence said, her books are not particularly popular. "They have a pretty good rental-library circulation and I'm told that sometimes some one comes along who likes one and reads back through the list." The trouble was, she continued, that her view of the world was insufficiently rosy. "I don't know why, I have been quite happy, personally. But for some reason I can't seem to see much happiness around me. When I take a theme and dig in to work on it, it has a remarkable and inescapable tendency to go twisting away into gloom."

It was suggested that much of the optimism—between book covers—of the present comes from recalling the overcoming of the hardships and misfortunes of the past. Miss Lawrence objected that she found it impossible to become interested in the past. "I never read a novel about the Civil War or the Revolution. I believe that our time, today, holds enough to fill any one's mind. I heard a man preach awhile ago and that preacher said that he believed that no one could write well about his own time because he was too close to it. But aren't the historical periods too far away? And in writing of them in fiction, what is to be done except to draw parallels between earlier times and these? That is, show how people in the past handled problems similar to those today. But what's the use of doing all that translating into other times? Particularly when conditions simply are not the same?"

A mass of greenery on the coffee table made a kind of Turkish screen between Miss Lawrence and her interviewer. Miss Lawrence's publishers believe that she lives in Newark; actually her apartment is in New York. Attempts to telephone her at her desk in a Newark newspaper office are discouraged. The standard answer is "Miss Lawrence is away." It is a curious fact that although Miss Lawrence's novels dissect, in a very intimate way, her contemporaries, the meat of them being made up of money troubles and those family problems and relationships that are least mentioned and most deeply felt, she has managed to maintain for herself an extraordinary privacy.

"I always have found it impossible to let people know things about myself, even what can only be regarded as perfectly harmless bits of information. I am extremely interested in others and supremely uncomfortable when they become interested in me. I don't try to explain it. I do believe, though, that the result is good for me as a writer. My contacts are not narrow. They are simply, in general, one-sided. And though I can't express myself in talk, it is a luxury to express myself in writing."

Miss Lawrence has been writing for about ten years and during the last seven has produced seven books. Her first three novels did not find a publisher. A thoroughly conscientious worker, she spends about four months gathering material for a novel and making a complete outline. Then she writes it in two drafts, typing three hours each night. "I married in October and find it much harder to get down to work. When I lived alone I came direct from the office to my work, didn't even bother about dinner. But, of course, you can't behave in that way when some one else's dinner is at stake."

She believes that her hardest work was done on her three unpublished manuscripts. "I hardly missed a night of work for three years and never a Sunday or a holiday. But you can't work as frantically as that more than once in your life. After acceptance there is bound to be a kind of let-down. Always afterward, though, you are bolstered by the thought that if you could work that way once, you could, in emergency, do it again."

Miss Lawrence usually deals with a specific problem in each novel. Her latest book, "No Stone Unturned," is concerned with a business man who has "escaped" from the business world because that world is too much for him. Difficulties of maintaining a family budget; the idiocy of making too many installment purchases; the financial and emotional responsibilities of caring for aging parents—all these have made novels for her. She is editor of the household pages of the *Newark Sunday Call* and one of her departments is made up of letters which frank but puzzled readers write to the paper asking for aid in the solution of their problems. These letters, she said, open up for her fields of inquiry, keep her in touch with what is bothering people.

She believes that her books have been rather too rough on women—to please women. "They are not very kind to women—certainly they are not flattering." The last one, with a man as the chief object of study, "may help bring the list back into balance; I can see plenty of things wrong with men, too."

As a writer, she said, the greatest compliment she could hope for was the comment that her books were written honestly. "Talk of such matters as my writing style doesn't seem to me to help any one. I'm no Shakespeare; I can't write brilliant, beautiful phrases, open up a world with a sentence, and I know I can't and never try. Stylistically I want only to be clear, to be understandable. My real job is to tell, as ably as I can, the truth about some aspects of my own time. After all, I am capable of honesty. And if what I write is honest, that is enough."

A TALK WITH THE AUTHOR OF "OUT OF THE NIGHT"

who found San Quentin Prison the "friendliest place" of his experience

February 9, 1941

Jan Valtin's right ear isn't much good. He was slugged on that side, he explained, with a loaded club. He illustrated by slapping his knife against his head. "Cr-rack!" he said, and laughed. The ear looks all right but in order to listen efficiently to an ordinary conversational tone he must turn his head so that his left ear will be in range.

The upper teeth on the right side of his jaw are missing. Fortunately his front teeth are in place and sound and the wide gap is only evident when he laughs. He laughs fairly frequently because he considers that he is very lucky and that the period he is now living through resembles in many ways the second-act curtain of a musical comedy.

Valtin is the author of "Out of the Night," which is an autobiographical account of his years of service as an "activist" in the Communist party. He is 36 years old, 6 feet 2 inches tall, weighs 190 pounds, has a good, straight nose, a high forehead and, in general, excellent features. He is extremely shy about having his pictures shown in any publicity for the book because either Communists or Hitler's Gestapo might conceivably be looking around for him.

The interview took place in a midtown German restaurant, a locale that he had selected. "If the Gestapo really are after you why do you come to a German place?" "You never will find a real

Gestapo worker in a German restaurant. If you want to find one go to the better hotels, the most typically American places, or to the Jewish restaurants on upper Broadway. And, in any event, I am not so sure they want me—enough, that is, to do anything about it. There has been only one attack, and that was amateurish, an attempt to crowd my car into a railing when I was traveling at high speed. And the men who did that were Stalinists, I am fairly sure.

"Of course, I take precautions." He wolfed the last of his ham, eggs and pickles in one giant mouthful. "I live in the country several hours' drive from here, and the driveway to my house is long and winding, three hundred yards in length. Any one approaching can easily be spotted from the house windows. Then, too, I have a great beast of a dog, a Great Dane with some mutt in him. He weighs 200 pounds and when he stands can put his paws on my shoulders. I have trained him to bark at strangers and to go for the throat at a word."

"Valtin" is a name that he created for himself in a Nazi concentration camp. "It was a most dreary life. We would hear shots in the night and the next morning learn who had been taken out and killed; and would be happy—glad that we were not them, glad that we were still alive. There were no other pleasures. I'd walk about occupying myself with word games—making little words out of big ones; or thinking of 100 words of five syllables each, or figuring out chess problems. And one day I got thinking, 'What name will I use when I get out of this place?' There was a new game, a good one. And other games—what country would I go to? To the new name I gave many hours of thought, and it came to me that the name 'Valentine' is international, with only slight differences in forms. I thought over these forms and it became part of the game to discover that form that would seem fairly familiar in every major country and yet would not be definitely national. It came to me, 'Monsieur Valtin,' I could be in France, 'Herr Valtin' if I were foolish enough to stay in Germany. 'Mr. Valtin'—I wondered about that. I wrote to my sister on the outside and asked her to look in a London telephone book and see if she could find a Valtin. There were none there but two were listed in the Copenhagen book. That is how I acquired my international name."

His real name is known to the Communists. When he left the party in 1938 his picture and his real name were prominently displayed in *The Daily Workers* of many cities and in Communist-dominated trade papers, accompanied by articles branding him a traitor to the cause. Several persons have made telephone calls to the Alliance Books and even personal visits asking for him under his real name. He has received many letters making requests for appointments; a number of the writers of these letters describe themselves as young women who say they want him to "come to see them and have drinks in front of a roaring fire." Some well-known writers have written him. "I have not answered their letters because I am not sure enough of their political connections. I have nothing to fear, of course, from the writers themselves. They would not be more than fellow-travelers, idealistic fronts. But they talk. And at any time when they were talking there might very well be, little noticed, a tough young activist making notes."

Valtin says that he has written all the "politics" that he is of a mind to write. He intends to have a new book ready in September for Fall publication. This will deal with his experiences in San Quentin, the California State Prison, from 1926 to 1929. He was sentenced for assault with a deadly weapon while working as a Communist agent along the California waterfronts.

Trained as a revolutionist by his German father, he had lived the hard life of a trouble-making sailor through his early youth. Sentenced to prison, he found, he said, that San Quentin was "a friendly place; every one was very kind to me there."

"I was 21 years old, but I had not read a book since my fourteenth birthday. San Quentin opened up a new world for me. The food was better than the food had been on most of the ships on which I had sailed; the work was a joke—I never worked more than two hours a day, and never very hard. The Party sent me money, I was allowed to write and receive letters, we had quiet little courses in Marxism and so forth that the authorities knew nothing about.

"But best of all I discovered books. The only English I knew was the waterfront brand; but the books in the prison were in English, so I started to read in that language. By great good luck my primer was Jack London's 'Call of the Wild.' What a wonderful book, I thought. One after another, hardly taking time to eat, I read every book of London's that they had. Then I went to the librarian. 'What next?' I asked. He smiled and gave me Conrad's 'Victory.' I went all through Conrad, not understanding some of what he wrote, but admiring, delighting, in what I understood. Then I took courses, in English, in navigation. I learned a little French and Spanish.

"My first writing was done in San Quentin. A newspaper man to whom I always shall be grateful read a little article I wrote and gave me courses in feature writing. Tasker, the Hollywood scenarist, was editor of the *San Quentin Bulletin* then. Mencken had encouraged him and he was writing his way up in the world, even while still in prison. He needed material, I was eager to write, and he published thirty of my articles in about seven issues, putting ridiculous names of his invention on all but one of each issue. I sent the thirty articles to Alfred A. Knopf as a book, and he was very kind about them and said let him hear from me again but did not publish the book.

"I was released and returned to Germany. But my life after that never was the same. I wanted to get free and dreamed of earning my living by writing. When I did break with the Party I worked at all sorts of menial jobs—as porter for a banquet hall in the Bronx, as a house painter under a Negro boss and so on—about twenty jobs. Then I wrote two articles for *Ken* and they paid me just before going out of business. With that money I bought a tent and stove, settled on a place in the Ramapo Mountains between Bear Mountain and Suffern, set up my tent deep in the woods and went to work.

"It is true as the Communists say that Isaac Don Levine had a hand in my book. He did the cutting. It was much too long and he cut thousands of words from the first half. The second half is just about as I wrote it first draft. Many parts of the first half were condensed on Levine's advice. Also, he staked me to ten dollars a week while I worked.

"All this that has happened is hard to believe—it is impossibly implausible. Here am I, who, in 1938, was hunted, friendless, a slave working twenty hours a day for thirty dollars a month and living on scraps. I write a book. A book club takes it; thousands of copies are sold. I have just married a beautiful young American girl; I live in a comfortable country place. And I have so many plans! You would say, wouldn't you, that this could never have come true?"

AN INTERVIEW WITH THEODORE DREISER

The author of "An American Tragedy" looks back at the struggles of his youth

March 16, 1941

THEODORE DREISER has changed little during his years in California, save that he now twists paper handkerchiefs rather than linen ones while he talks. He came to the interview with a fresh, thick bundle and rolled this bundle about in his hands, gently tugging at its ends and running his thumbnail over the paper surface while he described the "impossible" factors in America's economic life. "Imagine!" he'd exclaim. "Imagine trying to live on four or five dollars a week! But that's all the part-time girls who work in the big Los Angeles store where I buy my booze and coffee get on a Saturday night. What do you think of that? They work three or four hours a day—the busy hours—all week. For four or five dollars. And the full-time girls only get twelve dollars a week. I'll tell you, if we don't have a revolution here with America modeling itself on Russia, then Americans aren't Americans any more. I won't know what to think of them."

Mr. Dreiser visited Russia in 1927-28 as a guest of the Soviet Government and was feted there, extensively entertained. "When I stopped in England on my way back Winston Churchill asked me, 'Well, what did you think of it?' I told him. I thought it was a wonderful country, a wonderful system. 'Nonsense,' he said. 'It won't last seven years.' That was in 1928. Imagine! Churchill as mistaken as that. After those seven years were up he changed his tune. A statement was issued over his name praising the Russian system as it works in Russia. Oh, you can't beat that system, you know. A whole country, belonging to the people and run by and for the people."

"Don't you feel that Stalin's pact with Hit–?"

"Why shouldn't he have that pact? Don't you know your current history, darling? Hasn't any one ever bothered to tell you the facts of life? Don't you realize that France and England were all set to attack Russia? Oh, you don't. Well, you'll see what happens. Russia may not be the greatest military power in the world now. But it will be. Then you'll see."

He had come East to speak under the auspices of a number of organizations many of the members of which hold similar views. He mentioned the difficulties that beset an outspoken man with beliefs such as his at this time. "Rows everywhere," said Mr. Dreiser. "Once in a while you'll find some one who agrees with you. More often the person you talk to won't agree at all. A conversation will start on a train and soon a row will start, some arguing on your side, some against. And intolerance. Some of them want to put you off the train."

"Any one try to have you put off a train, Mr. Dreiser?"

"They've talked about it," said Mr. Dreiser with a grim moodiness.

He at first refused to talk of writing. "At a time like this, when a man can't afford even to sit down in peace, when the whole world is at a crisis—no, darling, that's not the time to discuss literature. That is a hell of a subject for you to be plugging at now. Why don't you try to catch up with the world? Do you think this system is so good it can't be better? Have you ever seen Russia? No. And you want to talk about books—"

"What in Russian literature written under the Soviets do you feel is outstanding?" He mentioned "Quiet Flows the Don" as a book that he had greatly enjoyed. "Are we doing anything worthy of comparison with that?" he asked. "That colored fellow," continued Mr. Dreiser, referring to Richard Wright. "His was a good book, 'Native Son.' " "And Steinbeck?" I asked. "Wonderful. Yes, yes. Of course, Steinbeck. You know; they hate him out in California. They blame all their troubles on him. They curse him instead of the devil. They get a heavy rain out there, it is Steinbeck's fault. They think he is a traitor to his State. The smug people. They are so sure that they are right."

"When you were starting you were up against smugness. Was it in your opinion much the same?"

"Boy, were they smug! But they all came around. After Mrs. Doubleday had 'Sister Carrie' scrapped, kept out of circulation. Why, you'd have thought I was the devil. Nobody would have anything to do with me—none of the people in power. I took a copy around to the old Century Company to ask if they would take over the plates and republish my book. When I called to hear what they had decided the girl at the reception desk handed me the book. That was all. No one in the company would talk to me about it. The girl gave me the message that they didn't care to talk about it. That was all.

"Later I finished the first chapters of 'Jennie Gerhardt' and took it to John Phillips at what was then a big publishing house, McClures. He told me—he came out into the anteroom and told me—that if I wished to write such stories he supposed that there was no way in which I could be stopped, but he asked me not to come to him to discuss my writing.

"Years later the man at the Century Company told me—when he was giving me an advance for some travel articles—that he regretted what he had done, that he no longer felt that way. Years later also I met Phillips in down-town Fifth Avenue—and he told me that he was sorry, that he didn't feel that way any more."

He pulled at his paper handkerchiefs and laughed. "Don't look so anxious. What are you worrying about? I got through it. I took a room over in Williamsburg—a cheap room, $1.50 a week. It was out of the way, made a long walk to Manhattan. The Williamsburg Bridge wasn't finished and I had to walk down to the Brooklyn Bridge and then across to get here, to this island. I was sick, you see. Why? Because I could not feel that I had a place in the world.

"One day I went to a public charity organization in Twenty-second Street, near Fourth Avenue. They couldn't help me. You see, I had relatives who could have given me something and they wanted the names and addresses of these relatives so that they could go to them and beg for money to buy me food. I'd rather have dropped dead.

"Soon after that I told my landlady that I couldn't pay my rent any longer and gave up my room. I had 5 cents—no, 15 cents. But as I was putting on my clothes the morning that I was surrendering my room, I remembered my watch. I don't know why, but I hadn't thought of it before. I had paid $8 for that watch in St. Louis. I could pawn it.

"There was one of those State-controlled pawnshops next door, or almost next door, to the charity where they had told me that they could not help. I went to that pawnshop. Well, I hadn't eaten for a long time and I was sick. The cold-eyed clerk in the pawnshop must have seen the shape I was in, though he seemed hardly to look at me. He put the glass in his eye and examined my watch. I was thinking perhaps he would give a dollar. But I warned myself: 'Fifty cents; don't count on more than fifty cents.' After looking at the watch he asked for my name and an address at which I could be reached, not looking at me, looking at the paper, the chit, on which he was writing my name. Then he pushed the chit over to me. It was marked $25. It was hard for me to speak. 'This,' I said, 'this is for $25.' 'I know it,' he said; 'come in and get your watch back when you can.'

"Imagine! I bought a pair of shoes for $2. The shoes I'd had were very far gone. And my hat had blown off in a subway. I bought a hat. A room at the Mills Hotel—25 cents a night. I felt a slight return of confidence. Still, I couldn't find a job—wasn't ready for one in my own line. I had heard of a fellow who had had a chance to quit newspaper work and take a job as a conductor on the New Haven Railroad and I had heard that this fellow Chauncey Depew at the New York Central would help newspaper men if they went to him. I sent Mr. Depew a letter telling him what straits I was in and then went to see him. His secretary asked me what I wanted and I explained that I needed an out-door job, a job as a laborer, anything that would give me a chance to work and be self-supporting. He told me that Depew couldn't see me but he gave me one of Depew's cards with a message scribbled on the back and that card got me a laborer's job at $15 a week—all I needed.

"I worked for that railroad for nine months. Working with those men, sharing their strength, learning their lives, seeing the wonderful goodness in the gang boss who could hearten a dozen men, healed me. At the end of nine months, with a few pennies saved, I went hunting a job at my own trade and found one with Street & Smith, the pulp-paper magazine outfit. I was editor of a magazine of theirs at $15 a week, and, boy, is there a story in that outfit? Men writing 40,000 to 60,000 words every week, year in and year out, for $50 or $60 a week. Imagine! I'm not kidding you.

"It was while I was at Street & Smith's, Sixteenth Street and Seventh Avenue, that I started writing 'Jennie Gerhardt.' I had the turn-down from Phillips, but it wasn't so bad, as at least I had a job. Then suddenly everything changed for the better. I moved up to a better editorial job on another magazine that paid me"—he kissed his finger-tips—"$60 a week Baby! and from there to the Butterick group where I was general editorial director at $10,000 and up a year.

"Of course I went back to writing and then 'An American Tragedy' when I was 54 years old. . . . Now? I'll write a book of philosophy and then probably another novel. My autobiography? Listen, there's plenty of time for that. But now for matters of only personal importance. Son, don't you see the world is burning? In Russia—"

"The watch, did you redeem it?"

"The watch. Oh, yes. I redeemed it after I got the job with Street & Smith."

"Was the same man there? Did he say—"

"No, no. It was another man. I never saw that first man again. . . . But what's the matter with Americans? They're not the people I think they are if they keep on being suckers to this system when in Russia—"

AN INTERVIEW WITH MR. ARTHUR TRAIN

The creator of Mr. Tutt discusses his methods of work

April 13, 1941

"NOT TOO MUCH TUTT," said Arthur Train, almost fretfully. Since the Summer of 1904 Mr. Train has had more than 400 stories and articles published in magazines and only about eighty of these have had to do with Mr. Tutt. "But you'd think he was my only character. Thousands of letters have come in suggesting plots for Tutt. And when I step off a railroad train anywhere in the United States it is Mr. Tutt this and Mr. Tutt that. My best novel is 'Ambition,' which you seldom hear about—perhaps never did hear of. Tutt isn't in it, though it concerns a lawyer. Tutt is my best character—I'm grateful to him, I am delighted that he is popular, of course—but, remember, Tutt isn't me."

Nevertheless, Mr. Train is at present engaged in writing the autobiography of Mr. Ephraim Tutt. "How far along am I with it? Well, how much do you count done when you have the idea for a book and have its course of development worked out pretty definitely in your mind? I count it about half done, though I've only started the writing."

On his desk in the library of the University Club was the rather extraordinary manuscript of what will be the first chapter. The pages are jigsaws of typing and handwriting.

"You see, I make many drafts, often write a story eight or more times before it satisfies me. I try to keep all the heat in, the full excitement of composition, with the result that I'm verbose, make the same point three or four times, fill up pages with quotes that aren't necessary, use more dialogue than is necessary, and so on. I do a draft in handwriting and every evening mail the day's work to my former office boy, Frank George, who now has a government job in Washington and is the only person in the world who can read my handwriting. He receives the copy first thing in the morning, types it and mails it back to me. When I've completed a good-sized chunk of rough draft I go over Frank's typescript with a pair of scissors and clip out the paragraphs, even the sentences that I mean to use. I rearrange. Large amounts of the material that I set down when blocking in this first chapter will fit much later in the book.

"I connect the passages that I am salvaging with more handwriting, mail it to Frank again, go at the new draft with shears and pastepot and so on. It is a continual process of cutting and rearrangement. More cutting now than formerly. I've had a story printed, a short story so-called that ran to 12,000 words, a serial installment that was 19,000 words long. Think of the opportunity to personalize characters, to use colorful detail, that such lengths gave. Now, as you probably know, the short story length counted most desirable is 4,000 words, and all of it believable. It is—well—not easy to do."

The Tutt stories, he continued, follow a formula: "They are like three-act plays. The first act is given to the statement of the problem, the second act reveals the seeming impossibility of the triumph of justice over the technicalities of law, and in the third act Mr. Tutt pulls a rabbit out of his hat and justice triumphs."

The great difficulty in the writing of these stories has been the need to discover points of law that are sufficiently simple so that persons without legal training can find them interesting, that are "near enough the commonplace so that the reader may possibly exclaim, 'Why, that might happen to Jim or even to me,'" and that are dramatic in their possibilities. For many years Mr. Train advertised his willingness to pay for suggestions embodying quirks in the law that he could use for Mr. Tutt. He paid $100 for those suggestions that he used, has now dropped this honorarium to $50, but the letters continue to come in by the dozen. Of the eighty stories, however, only twelve are based upon ideas submitted to him. He keeps a file of all the letters he receives, usually lets five or six years pass before tackling an idea that has come to him through the mail. A short time ago he had quite a search on his hands trying to discover the addresses of a pair of young men who had jointly signed a suggestion while they were students in a Midwestern law school. Many years had passed between the receipt of this letter and the sale of the story. However, he finally reached both of them, with checks.

Mr. Train is inclined to talk rather pessimistically about the future of writing for entertainment. "I see no rising sun in that field—it is more a sunset. The times are such," he continued, "and perhaps it is because of the times, that I have thought that a life is perhaps better spent nearer the centers of action, in closer touch with the realities of the day as a moving force rather than as an observer.

"Of course, popular writing has changed. In my younger days there was a great deal of talk about art for art's sake—and that baloney. It is an encouraging sign at present that there is less talk of that kind and more accomplishment. So many of the young writers have come to understand that they can satisfy themselves, can touch a real personal success, only if they write with seriousness of matters that are of primary meaning to themselves."

It seemed probable that one reason he is just a little tired of being so commonly associated with Mr. Tutt is that, while it is true that the lanky lawyer is a wily foe of the law's injustices, the Tutt tricks remain tricks, machinations to spring a plot, while many of Mr. Train's novels that preceded the creation of Ephraim and some of those published since, have dealt with the problems and people of Mr. Train's times in less fleeting fashion.

Mr. Train became a lawyer at the turn of the century because the law was a family tradition and because among the conservative New Englanders who peopled his environment "no writer of less stature than the established masters was thought to be engaged in a respectable trade." He insists that he knows little law, never really worked at his profession. "Had I worked at it in any other way than I did—that is, the dramatization of cases in court—I could not have been a successful writer. The drudgery of the law would inevitably have ruined me for fiction."

His training was extremely useful, however, to his fellow-writers. The Authors League of America grew in large part out of the circumstance that Train happened to discover that a serial he had written for *McClure's*, "C.Q., or In the Wireless House," in 1911, had English rights worth $600. The magazine editor had sold these rights. Train telephoned him and asked for the money. By threatening suit he received it—though the threat "was rot—the magazine owned all the rights. I think they gave in because they didn't want to hire counsel." Train then examined the general copyright situation, found that every author was giving all kinds of rights away and that much of the work published in magazines was simply unprotected. The result of this was the League, the first meeting of which was held at Mr. Train's house on December 27th, 1911. Now most of the writers in the country are members of the League.

AN INTERVIEW WITH MR. ROBERT NATHAN

The author of "One More Spring" discusses critics and his theories of writing

April 20, 1941

"I AM AWARE that many reviewers consider me a milk-toasty writer," said Robert Nathan. He folded his hands on top of his head and leaned back in his chair. The remark had been made with some effort. He continued, carefully: "Perhaps one reason for their attitude is that they do not find in my books the strong meat of purely personal emotion to which they have been made accustomed by other contemporary writers. I do not believe that my irritations, my momentary joys, are stuff to fill a book. A book is something apart; it is itself; it exists apart from the writer.

"In a way a book resembles a relationship with a friend. That is, you put into a friendship what you want to put in it, and the other person does the same and neither of you throws himself around, permits himself to be influenced by passing irritations, wails at what he doesn't like. And so with a book. It is made for itself, made as well as you can make it. It is cool and clear, a little removed. Why not? Why should each of my books reflect merely a momentary me? What meaning is there for Mrs. Jinglebottom in Sioux City in my little personal antagonisms and dislikes? A book should be a clear statement, a—I won't say work of art—a piece of work that can exist alone.

"A Tom Wolfe puts all his life into his books as into a garbage pail and is hailed as a great artist. That is not art, to simply report emotion growing out of one's own prejudices and daily states of mind and temper."

"Not that you've asked me," he said later, "but my quarrel with the critics—and what I have to say holds less in literary criticism than in music and painting—is that they all too often prefer the obscure, the complicated and sometimes meaningless, to what is simple, melodic. I recently bought the album for Rachmaninoff's Third symphony and the notes—the guide or whatever you call it that comes with the album—talked of how great an advance this Third symphony was over the cornstarchy—or some word like that—Second symphony. Damn it, that is objectionable. Why should it be necessary to seek to destroy appreciation of the Second symphony, which, after all, a great many people like, in order to make a slightly better impression for the Third? Probably the Third is a better piece of work as the critic judges. But how snobbish to insist, how superficial to insist on the necessary superiority of that judgment at the expense of what is, there is no question, a piece of work that thousands have enjoyed.

"And again, to take an example from music, consider the vogue of Virgil Thomson, who lived a certain kind of life in Paris and cultivated a certain emotional approach to life, and whose work has colored music criticism for some years. Of course, it is understandable. The critics work very hard, they hear so much music that it is only natural that they tend to value what is new—to overvalue what is new. And particularly so if this newness also is associated with a kind and manner of life that in one way or another impresses them.

"And in writing—well, there is a brighter side there. The obscurantism in poetry is being gradually lifted by a group that has broken with the school fostered by Eliot and Joyce—yes, and Yeats. The poetry fashionable for so long might have been thoroughly satisfactory for people who had all day in which to read and then all night in which to sit about with friends and wonder now what did the poet mean by this phrase and why did he employ this form in this place and so on and on. But poetry that requires such analysis surely is worthless for the average reader.

Why is poetry so little known today? Because the average reader couldn't make any sense out of the stuff that the critics told him was the kind of thing that he should enjoy. So he says: 'I don't like poetry.' We now have at least a half-dozen poets who would be distinguished in any age. The public of none of them is large."

Mr. Nathan lives in East Eightieth Street near Central Park. Despite the sparing skill of his prose, he said that he never has been able to work when he has tried to shut himself away, "make a cocoon for myself." "I am always a part of the life of this house. When I try to make myself a vacuum center I can't write at all. The country where there is so little to do, I find most difficult as a place to write. Here in New York, where so much is going on all the time, it is possible to work at high pressure, to give, on occasion, all one's time to work and not feel that one is missing anything. In the country I grasp at every activity that offers."

He told of the amusement of a friend of his who had been under the impression that Nathan's work came from "some kind of ivory tower." He had been to see Dreiser, the great realist who supposedly lived in the thick of the life of which he wrote, and found him living in a house surrounded by a guarded park, the servants wearing slippers and whispering. "I have no ivory tower, never have had. I can answer the telephone, write a line, tell my stepdaughter to stop screaming, write a line, have dinner and return to polishing.

"When I'm really working I keep at it eight to twelve hours a day, usually writing by hand. I cross out a lot, insert a lot, revise constantly. In impatience I turn to the typewriter and write rapidly, then cross it all out and try again by hand. The work never gets any easier. How could it? When you wrote a description of Central Park at evening in 1921 and put all your heart in it and wrote the same scene in 1926 and put all your heart in it and again in 1933 and 1937, well, by 1941 you are a little at a loss. You sit down to describe Central Park in the evening and inescapably the thought comes to you, 'I have said this before.'"

"Gentle" is the word most often used by people writing about Robert Nathan or about his books. This gentleness seems to have developed primarily from a most extreme sensitivity. He has never, he said, "known what it is to be particularly happy, in my life, in my books, in anything. I have not been content or at ease. But when I let my irritations, my unhappiness show in my manuscripts, these personal things stick out like a sore thumb. So I strike them out. What I have to offer Mrs. Jinglebottom of Sioux City is, I hope, a piece of work with meaning in itself, clear and complete. And if it isn't running with blood and digestive juices and so seems to be milk toast, I'm sorry but it is the best I have to offer."

A TALK WITH CLARENCE BUDINGTON KELLAND

One of the most popular of all magazine fictioneers, he discusses some pitfalls and errors of the writing trade

April 27, 1941

"HOKUM! WHAT DO they mean by hokum?" Clarence Budington Kelland demanded, strenuously. He stepped up and whanged his golf ball into a trap at the left of the green. He commented briefly on the flight of the ball and walked on, maintaining for a few moments a stern silence. Then he resumed. "When *The New Yorker* reviewed my novel 'Arizona' it said some pleasant things about the book. The review on the whole was not unfavorable. But the reviewer wound up by saying that it was 'adroit hokum.' That remark doesn't make sense. Everything in that novel—the movies ruined it—but everything in the novel as it was written, every turn of the plot, the characterizations, was taken directly from historical records. So what was hokum about that? The word hokum is far too loosely used. After all, isn't it simply a synonym for the eternal verities? And what should stories be made of if not affirmations of the eternal verities?

"Young writers don't realize this. They turn out a lot of introspective tripe that has no meaning for any one and the magazine editors are forced to print it, to pay good money for it because they can't find anything better. The old-timers who knew how to tell a story have dropped away. Some are dead, others have quit writing. Where's Peter B. Kyne? Why doesn't Ben Ames Williams write more? Why no stories from Irv Cobb? Of all that old *Saturday Evening Post* gang, do you realize that only Tark and myself and, now and then—too seldom—Mary Roberts Rinehart, are left? The editors are eager to buy anything we write. And for good reason. We've learned to tell stories in a way that makes readers want to read them."

Mr. Kelland stepped into the sand trap, swung and topped his ball. The ball skittered a few feet and stopped, still in the sand. When the hole was finished an opponent who was keeping score asked with a touch of whimsey: "What did you make on that, Bud —a four?" Mr. Kelland responded with a hard look. "Seven!" He recently had returned from his Arizona ranch where he lives each year from mid-October until late March, returned here for the Dutch Treat Club dinner. Through the Spring and Summer his home is in Port Washington, L. I., though he often is away trailing major sports events across the country.

Many of his closest friends—John Kieran and Grantland Rice are among them—are sports writers. "I go less for the sports shows than to be with the crowd of people I like. You've seen my golf game. It isn't anything much. But Doc here," he nodded toward his score-keeping opponent, "and myself have played golf together about twice a week for more than twenty years. Seems to me that one mistake young writers make is that they don't stick close enough to people they really like. They go to Hollywood and hang around with heels and the first thing they know the only people they want to write about are heels. The atmosphere in which they live affects them; it is bound to.

"I see quite a lot of young writers. I lecture at universities every now and then. It seems to me that they tend to admire the wrong things. Realism. Lewis and this fellow who wrote about the Okies—they're realists—maybe. But any reporter can do realism. The good men go out on a story and get all the facts. The best man gets the facts—and something more. Seeming to report nothing but straight facts, he reveals a personality—something extra. The kids don't realize this. They are about evenly divided in their desires. Some want to get to Hollywood and make a hell of a lot of money. The others want to write what they call 'literature' whether any one wants to read it or not. I never have rated as a 'literary' man and as I have not vanity of that kind I don't care. But I am a storyteller. No one can take that away from me. If more kids aimed at that, they'd be better off.

"People talk about my versatility because I've turned my hand at most kinds of magazine fiction. There is nothing versatile about it. If you know how to tell a story, the form, the period, the location are not important. The story is what counts.

"Yes, my Scattergood stories follow a formula. That's right. But what happens in those yarns isn't of much consequence because they are read for Scattergood and little things he says more than for what he does. When you have a character people like, your main job is simply to keep him in character.

"There are three things that make a good story. Take characters people like—young lovers, yes; salty old philosophers, yes—and put them in an interesting situation. Let 'em work out of it. You don't need a novel solution. Hell, who cares about novelty? The eternal verities aren't novel. But what's better?

"And the third thing—first characters, then situation—the third thing is what I suppose you might call charm—an easy, pleasant, humorous way of expressing yourself. You don't get that by working for it; that is, by blueprinting how this writer or that writer achieves it. But if you have any of it naturally, you can develop it by writing.

"Too many people let six months pass while they wait for an idea. If they'd sit down at a typewriter and simply start to write about a fellow named Joe Jones, for example, in the lumber business, ideas on Joe and his job would come fast. It is work and, of course, that is harder than just waiting; but it is effective."

Mr. Kelland starts work at about eight each morning, types with great concentration until about noon. "Four hours of real work is about all a man of my age—pushing sixty—has in him. When I was young? I worked twenty-four hours a day then." He said that when he started writing, his hours on a Detroit newspaper were from three in the afternoon until three in the morning. "I wrote Sundays and early afternoons for seven years before I sold a line. When I was twenty-seven years old my first story was accepted. *Young's Magazine,* now deceased, paid me three dollars. What kind of story? Oh, tragic. Kid stuff. Kids have to write a certain amount of tragedy to clear their minds."

At present he tries to write one chapter (not one installment) of a serial—about 2,500 words—each day. "I don't manage it every day, of course. Writing wells up—and when it won't well up, you're stuck. I try for 2,500 words a day but settle for 10,000 words a week."

A TALK WITH THE SURPRISED SALLY BENSON

Who finds her new book's advance sales pleasant but amazing

May 18, 1941

"MY SISTER TOLD ME: 'I know you and I know just how smart you are. You don't write your stories. You get them through a ouija board.'" Sally Benson added that her latest series of stories were, in actual fact, coming from her older sister. "I have the diaries that she kept in St. Louis in 1902 and 1903 when she was sixteen or seventeen. I'm going to read you a paragraph and don't start squirming." She read from an old copybook a still-throbbing passage that was funny and very pleasant, a defense of a certain Major Schecklehauser who walked most erectly and spoke to his dog in a "divine military voice" and who was seen under the most casual circumstances yet was the object of much thought. The phrasing had the clean-freshness, the newness that is found more often in journals and diaries than in writing meant for print.

Like Dorothy Parker, Mrs. Benson shows a discontent with people as they are in her writing; again, like Dorothy Parker, she is as good company as you're likely to find and makes interview questions or work of any sort seem a bit drab. She comes from St. Louis, where she was born in 1900 and given the name of Sara Mahala Redway Smith, she says. In 1911 she was brought to New York, attended Horace Mann School and later continued her associations with Columbia by marrying Reynolds Benson, director of athletics at that university.

Mrs. Benson said that she hadn't cared any too much for Judy Graves, the main character in her most recent series of stories, "Junior Miss," and that after writing one or two had wanted to drop Judy. "But Ross (Harold Ross, editor of *The New Yorker,* in which the stories were published) told me not to be a fool, that I couldn't do better than keep on. And the response was good, and now that the stories are in book form, why, good God, the response is perfect." The story is that when Mrs. Benson heard that "Junior Miss" had been selected by the Book of the Month Club for June distribution and that the publisher had sold 40,000 copies in advance, she took a look at the check, left the office and within forty-five minutes an automobile salesman was in the publisher's waiting room wanting the bill for a new automobile okayed.

"They are even talking of movies and plays," Mrs. Benson continued, "but I don't see why, because the poor things have no plot, no continuity as movie and play producers understand continuity. What could be done with them I haven't the slightest idea. Of course, I like stories that don't have rounded ends and don't rise to climaxes; that aren't all wrapped up in a package with plot. I like them, that's why I write them. But all this that is happening to 'Junior Miss' is a really wonderful surprise."

Mrs. Benson has been writing short stories for ten years. Her working method does make you think that there might be something in her sister's ouija theory at that. Though her stories are very tightly written, close-packed, crowded with detail, smooth-surfaced, the words selected with great precision, they see print just as they come from her typewriter, first draft, and are written rapidly in two—or two and one-half—hours.

"I started writing as an interviewer on the old *Morning Telegraph*—did a piece each week. Saw authors, actors, actresses, all kinds. I remember a mass interview when a whole flock of girl reporters went to work on Sinclair Lewis. The questions were unbelievable. He was just back from England and they asked him how he thought English women compared with American women. I happened to have the seat on the sofa next to Lewis. He held my hand. I liked him. I didn't ask any questions, and after a while he looked down and said: 'What do you want to know?' I said that I hadn't any questions at all. That was the interview. But I guess I got some space out of it.

"After the *Telegraph* a pulp-paper house gave me a job reviewing movies. The pay was $75 a month and I had to do about thirty-two reviews a month. But I spaced that out a little by doing more interviews.

"In 1930 I got an idea for a short story and wrote it out. Some one told me to send it to *The New Yorker*. Mrs. White, who edited the fiction, sent me a check and said please come to see her. She told me that it was the best story of whatever its kind was that they'd had and asked me to write more.

"I didn't write any more for a year. For three months there was all the satisfaction I needed in just thinking to myself that I'd written a story and sold it. Then for nine months more—well, I didn't get to work. But I kept getting broker and broker so I started to write again and found that they'd keep taking the pieces, so I've just kept on turning them in. Yes, it's true that I haven't had a rejection, probably because I haven't tried other markets. My style fits here and it wouldn't most places. Every once in a while editors of some of the national magazines have asked for stuff, but what they really want are healthy, clean-limbed, hearty young people on a raft and that isn't for me."

Mrs. Benson makes a spare-time job of reviewing mystery novels for *The New Yorker* and goes through an average of one mystery a night. "There are weeks when seventeen mysteries are published." She is at present engaged in a campaign to draw attention to the work of "Joseph Shearing"—the name, she believes, is the pseudonym of an Englishwoman—whose books are usually classed among the mystery novels, "where they don't belong at all; they are really swell novels." The books of Joseph Shearing have had a puzzling history. Well-written studies in violence, novels based upon historic crimes, they have had practically no sale, yet other novelists, following Shearing to the same subjects and handling them, as it would seem to a reviewer, less competently, have rolled up large sales and built up huge popular followings.

Mrs. Benson said that one reason she spends so much time on mysteries is that she prefers straight history to historical novels "and then, too, I keep taking personal dislikes to authors. Why must all the men novelists get so damned virile, so chest-out, shoulders back, 'here we come' girls, as soon as they hit a success? Why must they go trucking all over the world and slaver with delight at wars? Faulkner—now, I'll always read Faulkner. He stays home. And Maugham. You know, consider all the stories Maugham has written and you find an awfully high average of really good work. But the big boys with all that virility—I don't know. However short their books are, they always seem too long."

AN INTERVIEW WITH GELETT BURGESS

Who found fame through a quatrain about a purple cow some forty years ago

June 8, 1941

"HUMOR?" GELETT BURGESS repeated, wandering the big room in search of a cigar. "All right, if you can stand it. But I've talked a great deal about humor. . . ." His voice trailed and the concluding phrase of his sentence seemed merely a private thought, "a lot of damn nonsense." He turned his back and walked away to poke around in his bedroom. There he found his cigar, but when he returned he continued moody. "Laughter originated in the yammering of monkeys in a tree. One monkey fell and the others 'Yaaa-yaaa-yaaed' at him because they were safe and so superior. You've heard all this somewhere, haven't you? Then what's the use of going on? There's another line I can take, though, if you really want it," he continued courteously. "That is the humor in the sudden break of ideas—the dreamlike substitution of the amazing for the unexpected. Accept the ordinary train of association as a-b-c. Humor is a-b-y or a-b-x. The unexpected but logical.

"I don't entirely approve of talking about humor. Most of what you say is just as well unsaid. I've written humor, books full of it, and some of them were very popular. But the funniest book, much the most delightful book that I have written, has, so far as I know, precisely one reader other than myself—Mrs. Ida B. Judd of the Mark Twain Association. Mrs. Judd enjoys it; so do I; no one else. Here. Read a page or so. Don't hesitate to say that you don't care for it. You'll simply be agreeing with every one except Mrs. Judd and me."

The book is entitled "Ain't Angie Awful?" "Nineteen is a terrible age," to quote from one paragraph, "and the longer you're nineteen the worse it is; neither girlitude nor yet womanability. Angie hated to think about it. To think about anything at all, in fact, was apt to produce vertigo. She had but one idea—it lived in her head like a cow in a tree. Its name was Get Married. For to Angie all men were holy. Some had money and some had mastoiditis, but she felt sure that she could fit right into any man's arms and take root. The only trouble was she never had a chance."

The copyright page showed that the material had first appeared in *Judge* in 1918 and had not been published in book form until 1923. "That's right. For five years all publishers turned it down, even though, among other things, it is a study of a nymphomaniac. But what I like is its ease, its high spirits, its freedom."

Mr. Burgess is a generous man, with no slightest suggestion of pose. The mild cantankerousness of his surface manner seems more scratched than scratching, and even brief association develops the complete ease that is possible only in reaction to honesty of mind. Born seventy-five years ago in Boston, he took, at the Massachusetts Institute of Technology, a degree as a civil engineer. He joined the faculty of the University of California, but late one night in San Francisco an ugly little statue that had been erected by a temperance crusader seemed to him at once a challenge and a reproach and he smashed it. Released from the faculty, he founded a magazine, *The Lark*, and for its first number wrote, among other things, the quatrain beginning: "I never saw a purple cow . . ." For reasons now less clear than in all probability they once were, this quatrain amused enormous numbers of people and swept Mr. Burgess from California to New York. His subsequent writings added a number of words to the language—sharp, inescapable words—among them "bromide" in its social sense, "blurb" and "goop." Other invented words such as "smagg" and "vram," that once were hailed with delight because they had the Burgess mark on them, have disappeared.

His rhymed manuals of manners for children, the "Goop" books, were classics for the nursery. His "Are You a Bromide?" combined with Theodore Roosevelt's doctrine of the strenuous life to decrease the smug self-satisfaction of the stodgy. But although one of the most popular of all writers for children, he was frequently at war with his editors when he wrote for adults.

"Once I wrote that my heroine had a 'laughing devil in her eyes,'" he recalled. "They changed that into 'laughing light.' A man came to call on her and I had him leaving at 11 o'clock. They changed it to 10 o'clock. I mentioned that she wore silk stockings. The stockings came out. She had no legs, of course; just head and hands. Hemingway . . ." he mused. "Now, with Hemingway . . .

"I suppose it was the war. When I started writing I thought that Robert Louis Stevenson was the great man in the world. But, do you know, Stevenson was the ultimate dude. Ornament, figures of speech, decoration—the period of dudism in art reached its climax in Stevenson's style.

"I don't like the photographic realism that has been popular. I have no use for it at all. But I do like the directness, the honesty, the clean efficiency of much of the writing today—of the main stream of today's writing. No decoration, no lazy figures of speech.

"There is much to be learned about tactics from the movies. Have you noticed that the movie people are remarkably expert in handling the episode. They are weak in the strategy of storytelling—that is, the grand plan of the story as a whole—but in the parts, the tactics, they are superb. They know exactly what to show and what to let the onlooker fill in. And to know this is to know a great deal about fiction writing. They understand pace and rhythm."

The difficulty of a satirist who is no longer young, he agreed, is that satire is not quite practical; the quick, self-confident bite tends to fail before experience. The successful satirist is in part a fashion, and fashions change. There is, then, the problem of sincerity. A mind habituated to find the false in a popular idea is essentially a rejecting mind.

"When I find an idea that I can accept, the heat goes on automatically and I enjoy writing; really enjoy it. But, of course, such ideas aren't common. And there's not much use working on things you don't believe.

"The mental activity here—that in general is helpful. I spent eleven years or so in Paris and I miss the beauty, the trees, the cafés where you could meet people as you liked and talk to them or pass them by as you liked; not take them home or go to their homes; see just as much of them as suited you with no responsibility created on either side. But Paris was asleep. Our minds were rotting and we didn't know it. To come back was to find new life, new energy and new ideas good enough so that I could enjoy writing again."

AN INTERVIEW WITH HERVEY ALLEN

At his place in Maryland, the author of "Anthony Adverse" drives ahead to finish a two-volume novel on a vast canvas

July 6, 1941

HERVEY ALLEN poked with a long forefinger at a mound of manuscript that is his next book in the making. "Let's not be absurd about it," he said, "but it is a sort of—well, Peace and War."

The novel will appear in two volumes. (Note: Two volumes have been published and the book seems hardly started.) It will be very long. The time: 1763 to the late 1920's. The characters: a multitude of Americans engaged in creating the America of our time. Mr. Allen said that he now is working fairly steadily, that for the first years of his effort on this novel he frequently allowed himself to be distracted "by a dozen and one interruptions that had nothing to do with my main job. After all, the job of a writer is to write. People don't seem to realize. Speeches, appearances in bookstores, committees—that stuff is all right for a young poet striving for recognition. But when you've had one really widely distributed book it is damn nonsense. You try to do the best you can at these other jobs and they throw you off your main job for weeks at a time. I feel in stride now, as though the work would go fairly rapidly.

"No, the war doesn't confuse me much. I know what side I'm on; there never could have been any doubt. The threat is strengthening. It helps cut clear—cut away doubts and wonderings and lets us feel with cool certainty what our ancestors felt. It's great, this country; greatness built on what were always great beliefs. Why be confused by the war? There's only one side. And I can tell you this much: Americans are damn good fighters when the muddling stage is over and the fight begins. I was kicked out of Annapolis just as the last war was starting for us and joined the Army. There weren't any better fighters in Europe and there aren't better fighters there now."

Bonfield is the name of the Allen estate. It was bought with the movie money paid for "Anthony Adverse" in 1933, "when all the land in the country, pretty near, was for sale." Even with the whole country to pick over, Bonfield seems very nearly ideal.

To reach Bonfield you leave the narrow coastal road a mile or so north of Oxford, which is a small fishing town on Maryland's Eastern Shore. Brick gateposts mark the entrance to a pocked cinder lane that bisects flat acres of corn and wheat. Another gate opens to an avenue of trees. The blue-shuttered white house is on a mound that was built by eighteenth-century slaves who carried earth for the mound from a sector that is now a marsh. The estate has a river at each end, and the waters of an inlet of Chesapeake Bay come within fifty yards or so of the house. Huge ancient trees and smooth lawns make a frame for the water of the inlet.

Across a formal garden a large white guest house; near the inlet's edge a capacious boathouse. Mr. Allen's study is a house, a very old building, a story and a half high, with small, infrequent windows. Well beyond the study, out of earshot, is a fully equipped playground for young children—swings, rings, horizontal bars, a slide and a shallow pool in which small children can learn to swim.

The flour used on the place is made from wheat grown there and ground in a room adjoining the garage. A workshop contains a power lathe and dozens of tools. "I formerly hired a mechanic, kept him on full time, but I had to let him go. When you try to do so much the costs become fantastic." Bonfield, he went on, is now nearly self-sustaining. A couple of cows supply the milk, hens provide eggs and white meat, the inlet is "full of crabs and fish and oysters. Fishermen come very early in the morning and raid the fishing grounds, but the one way I could stop them would be to sit on the lawn all night with a shotgun. I don't care to do that." The gardens provide all the vegetables that a far larger family could eat.

But because the many houses of Bonfield are difficult to heat in winter, the Allens commonly winter in Florida—"We live in the woods down there; no telephone"—where the children go to school.

No, said Mr. Allen, the leisurely pace of life at Bonfield and in Florida does not, he believes, slow his production. "The mind makes its own time, keeps to its own schedule. I doubt that nervous bustle can help a novelist in the least, whatever it may do for a journalist. The great necessity when working on a novel —once the fundamental of having something to say is taken care of—is to have a wife who knows that when you are not actually writing it is not because for some selfish reason you don't want to or are being lazy, and who knows that if you get up and walk away or are moody at meals that you are not mad or hurt, that nothing is wrong with you except that your mind is on its job and that that job is important."

When he has found an idea for a novel Mr. Allen draws up a plan and divides the plan into panels of action. He works out these panels one at a time, treating them as units. He puts down his first draft in longhand, completely and carefully. Then, with his longhand sheets to guide him, he dictates the second draft to a secretary. "I dictate so that the sound will be right. I have had enough experience in poetry to realize the importance of the sound of words." Also, he finds that when you are writing speeches for characters of another day there is a tendency to let forsooths and egads creep in. Dictation knocks them out, is a great aid in making dialogue natural. Allen then edits the dictated draft, rewriting extensively and filling in sections when he fears that he has not made himself sufficiently clear. When he has finished marking up his copy Mrs. Allen types the final draft.

Many letters about "Anthony Adverse" still come in despite years have passed since the novel's publication. The novel has been published all over the world; the war has pretty well dried up the stream of royalties that flowed from a dozen countries, but the letters come anyway. "Bankers and other businessmen write to me to discuss the theories on credit that are worked out in the novel and that have considerable relevance today. There still are a lot of people who want commas changed." He answers as many of the letters as he can, but those that ask for minor typographical changes usually go into the wastebasket. One such was sent by a clergyman who protested that at one place in the long book "Heaven" was spelled with a lower case h.

"After the first hundred thousand copies had been printed we assembled a board of savants and they took the book apart for errors. There were no great changes to be made but naturally in a book of that size some corrections were needed and we made them—we had to make new plates anyway. After that I gave up. I'd just as soon have 'Heaven' spelled with a capital, but I can't say that I'm greatly interested one way or another. The first volume of the new book is giving me enough to do just now."

AN INTERVIEW WITH KAY BOYLE, EXPATRIATE

She has returned from France with material for a novel set in a concentration camp

August 3, 1941

THE CLIPPER FROM Lisbon settled on the water and was towed to the shore of LaGuardia Field. Five children raced down the gangplank and with great energy started playing games. The last passenger off was Kay Boyle, mother of three of these children, stepmother of the others and holding her youngest child in her arms. "She looks as though she were answering a challenge," a woman said, with considerable enthusiasm. Miss Boyle is tall, thin to the bone, shy at the first moments of meeting, remote and withdrawn until her interest is caught—generally by her own intense curiosity. Laurence Vail, her husband, came from the plane carrying a stick of wood. (Note: Miss Boyle has divorced Mr. Vail and remarried.)

"Test it." He pressed at the wood with his thumbnail. "Wouldn't you think this fine wood to carve? To carve little figures? I'm sure it must be. Test it." He lowered his voice and said confidentially: "I have a fine lot of it packed with my luggage. They didn't want me to bring it but I persuaded them." Mr. Vail is an artist as well as a writer. The children created a chase game, using customs men as obstacles. In the restaurant they were amazed by the plenty all about them, scooping up handfuls of sugar and cramming their mouths with it and sticking slices of bread into their pockets. Newly come from a hungry land, the restaurant seemed a Paradise.

Later, in the offices of her literary agent, Anne Watkins, Miss Boyle accepted one cigarette and smoked it down to its last half inch. "We'd stand in line a half-hour or more for a packet of matches. And cigarettes were even harder to get, of course." She said that she is writing a novel on concentration camps. "I have one version finished but I'm going to do it over. And short stories —I have the material for dozens of them. I want to find a place in the country and do nothing for a long time but write. Under the conditions writing has been so difficult. We were held up for two months arranging passage. Rich refugees literally pushed us aside—big rolls of money in their pockets."

I asked: "If the Germans are so efficient, and these stories of rich refugees are true, how is it explained? How do they get out with money?"

"There are many legends that every one tells and that, of course, no one in France believes, because the wonderful thing about France is that no Frenchman believes anything, really. But one of the legends is that people who knew they'd have to leave Germany bought quantities of platinum and had the platinum made into automobile tools. Then, with the tools of platinum simply lying on the floor of the car they'd cross the border. That's one of the many legends. Every one tells these tales."

Kay Boyle married a Frenchman when she was eighteen. "It was necessary for me to accept French citizenship." She now has a dual citizenship, American and French. She has lived in Europe —mainly in France—for nineteen years.

"In what section of this country was your home?"

"It is difficult to say. I was born in St. Paul and lived there for six months. I suppose that's the nearest thing to a home that I've had over here. I've lived in New York, many cities. But I've never lived in the country here in America. I want to. Somewhere in the West, I think. Perhaps Arizona.

"While I was growing up I spent much of my time in Europe. Switzerland for the skiing, France in Summer. I love France. We had to leave it because we couldn't get enough food, especially milk. We stayed near Marseille and for a time had a share of the milk sent on American ships. When the milk ship stopped coming there was nothing for us to do. You cannot imagine, in this rich country, the misery, the poverty, the complete lack. . . . Is it really necessary, do you suppose, to starve France? What is hoped for?

"About 40 per cent of the people, I think, are for De Gaulle. Another 40 per cent do not know; they literally do not know. Not more than 10 or 20 per cent favor Germany—10 per cent. But these last are the noisy people, the shouters and talkers. It is so disheartening to hear them. And the Germans are so efficiently taking what they want, always under their own rules. The phrase most often used about the Germans is that they are *très correct,* that they are very proper. It is horrible to hear that phrase. And one hears it continually. It is almost as bad as the other phrase: 'I am ashamed to be a Frenchman.' To hear a Frenchman say that!

"Every one is so puzzled, lost, without leadership. The German officers stride the streets; they are everywhere, in the unoccupied zone as well as in Paris. No, they do not push; they are not feared. If they were feared—but they are not even noticed. The people seem not to see them or think about them. They are already—it is hard to believe—they are already an accepted part of the new life that isn't life, the waiting without hope. One hears of no revolts. How can there be? What can men without arms do against that military machine? If there were incidents—a German killed on a dark street. But there are no incidents."

The most memorable study of the emotions out of which Naziism grew was in Kay Boyle's own novel "The Death of a Man."

"I was called a Nazi for writing that. Perhaps I was at fault. The emotions were there and I put them down and the picture was not thoroughly rounded—it couldn't be in a novel of that kind. But I am not a Nazi."

She talked of the plight of men who had fled Germany and found refuge in France. "But when war came and on September 3—no, that was a Sunday—on September 4, when they went to enlist in the French Army to fight for the country that had given them refuge, they were marched from the enlistment places to concentration camps." She feels that this measure revealed a weakness in France, a weakness that may help explain the defeat.

"When will you have concentration camps here? Soon, do you suppose? Oh, but finally you must come to it."

With so much material she expects to write a great deal during the next year. "Does my style seem involved? It doesn't to me. I write very rapidly and thoroughly enjoy everything to do with writing. I even like the smell of carbons. I shall write many short stories. While waiting in Lisbon I read all the American magazines, but I suppose I'll have my old trouble when I try to write for the very popular magazines. I'd like very much to write for those with large circulation, but when I put down a sentence that seems to me the sort of beginning that an editor of such a magazine might like, I find something in that sentence that I must change so that my meaning will be exact—and then it is all over. The chance is gone."

AN INTERVIEW WITH BUDD SCHULBERG

The author of "What Makes Sammy Run?" discusses Hollywood, writing and glickism

August 10, 1941

Budd Schulberg said that after the publication of his "What Makes Sammy Run?" he had to leave Hollywood for a couple of months. "It was too embarrassing." "Sammy" is the novel in which Schulberg traced and analyzed the rise of a newspaper office boy to a mogul position in the movie studios.

"Almost every one I met asked who I was taking for a ride. Was Sammy Glick So-and-so or So-and-so? Every one thought it must be the wonderboy whom he personally hated most. I didn't know how to answer. I hadn't written a Paul Pry, a gossip column, to stick a knife into some individual's back. I was trying to show a type, of course, and maybe behind the type a kind of cause of evil, not impale a person. Here in the East I find more people who seem to give me credit for being something else than just a gossip and when they talk about the book they consider it as a novel, not a scandal sheet."

Hollywood is Schulberg's home town. Son of the producer, B. P. Schulberg, who quit a reporting job on the *World* to become Adolf Zukor's press agent in the days when movies were new, Budd Schulberg has met a number of Sammy Glicks.

He is big-shouldered, heavy-handed, looks as though he possessed a great deal of physical endurance. His mannerisms are those of one who is quite shy but who has his shyness under control so that it is no block in the way of whatever he proposes to do. He is in Class 3A on his draft-board list, is twenty-seven years old, married and the father of one child.

For a first novel, "What Makes Sammy Run?" is a very hard-headed job in which many of the techniques employed to keep a motion picture rolling at a good pace are used. Every incident and bit of dialogue propels the story onward and makes a relevant point, and the main character takes his pounding on every page.

"I didn't want to write an autobiographical first novel so I took a subject that I knew but that was outside myself and tried to be as interesting, honest and at the same time inventive as possible. I kept it all on one man because I don't feel that I know enough to do counterpoint stuff with a big canvas and a lot of characters developed. It was difficult enough to write a novel. By keeping the story as simple as possible I gave myself a break that I needed. Early in the Fall I'm going to Vermont and expect to write another novel. Of course, I'll keep it simple, too. I need what breaks I can take.

"Yes, it is a temptation to make a first novel autobiographical, and plenty of them have had a lot of swell writing. But who wants to read them? I don't know, it seems to me that you shouldn't write autobiography until you are far enough along so that you have some perspective. You can tell pretty well whether something outside you is important. But to handle material in which you yourself are mixed. . . . I'm not ready for that, not smart enough."

As though to bolster this he expressed the conviction that "the war shouldn't be allowed to turn a writer from the work that he has outlined for himself; that is, culture must survive." He told of a telegram that he had received from John O'Hara. The telegram read: "It is all fixed. We are going to drive ambulances. We leave this week."

"The first day I was sure that I would go and I spent about twenty-four hours wandering around and mentally saying good-bye to my wife and the life I'd known and so on. The second day I was just as certain that I wouldn't go, that it was up to me to keep to the jobs I'd planned. No, O'Hara didn't go either. I don't know what happened; haven't seen him."

Schulberg said that he started writing when in his early teens, edited school papers and the Dartmouth paper. After graduation from Dartmouth he went home to Hollywood and found a job as a reader. He said that to hold the job it was necessary to read on the average of one novel a day and write a twenty-page synopsis of plot, sketching in characters and the main situations. The pay was $25 a week.

"Then I was given an undercover chance to work on the script of 'A Star Is Born.' A writer and a director had turned in an original story and the producer sent for me and asked me to read their story and make suggestions for improvement. I worked all night, got some ideas that I thought might do and kept a seven-o'clock appointment—the next evening—in the producer's office. But in some way word of what I was doing must have gotten out, because the director who was co-author of the story pushed open the door, saw me and was sore as the devil. He said he didn't want a punk like me fooling with stuff he'd written."

After a stormy session with the director, Schulberg was fired and sent home. On arriving there he found a message containing instructions to keep right on with the job but to be very secret about it. Dorothy Parker and her husband, Alan Campbell, were called in on the script and some of Schulberg's suggestions were used, one of them making perhaps the most effective scene in the picture. "It was like laying linoleum, different people working on different little squares."

This job brought him a contract as a junior writer. "The pay started at fifty a week and rose in slow degrees through five years—on the contract. But the trouble is that when they hire you as a junior writer they rate you as kind of excess baggage—you are supposed to sit around and mature and nobody much fancies the idea of letting you work with them. After months of sitting around I asked that my contract be allowed to lapse. I couldn't see that I was doing them any good and certainly it didn't seem to be doing me much good. But I guess that asking to be fired was a mistake, because then, of course, they didn't want to fire me. Finally I quit coming to the office. Other studios offered me temporary jobs and I took them. The people who held the contract telephoned me that I couldn't take other jobs, that I had to go on working for them and I said that I was sorry but that I'd quit. So after a while they let the contract lapse.

"Meantime I had started knocking out short stories just to fill in the time. . . . They sold—the first batch was taken by *Liberty* and then *Collier's* took a few. When I'd sold a dozen short stories I decided that I could support myself on the story checks while writing a novel.

"I got started on the novel and then when I needed cash I knocked out a story. It came back. I think that I was pressing too hard, trying too hard for sales, and whatever natural touch I'd had in the beginning had been strained away. Also, I'd been reading the magazines—that's bad, I guess, because it sort of influences you to try to write what they seem to want rather than what you want to write.

"So I gave up short stories temporarily and plugged at the novel. One thing about studio work is that it teaches you to keep busy. You're expected to put in a full day and to produce. They figure out just about how long it should take you to do a job and they expect the job to be finished when the deadline comes around.

"Writing 'Sammy' I kept pretty close to the schedule that movie work had accustomed me to. The actual writing took five months, then I spent about three months fooling with it, trying to tighten it up. Then my publisher, Bennett Cerf, told me that I had fooled with it long enough, to get it up, and I did.

"I think one hopeful thing about Hollywood is that they are getting away from the Sammy Glicks because it is more and more realized that the story is the most important part of a movie and that stars, production, nothing, can take the place of a good yarn. As the story comes in more and more the Glicks are bound to fade."

AN INTERVIEW WITH REX BEACH

Who has some trenchant things to say about eating and writing

August 17, 1941

"FOR MANY YEARS the only way I could earn a living was by carrying something heavy," Rex Beach said. "My hands were calloused and my muscles and thews a sight to behold. My brothers were lawyers and I'd intended to be a lawyer. To this end I attended a decidedly churchy school in Florida—it amazes me when I go back there in these later years to hear an undergraduate say casually: 'Guess I'll have a highball—sort of tired. Can I make one for you?' When I was there lollipops were all right and no one kept count of the amount of pop you bought if you could pay for it, but a likker drink—I guess if you'd taken one you'd have been ridden out of school on a rail. The suavity you find in colleges now, the ease, the sophistication. What a jump they have—to that extent—on the old boys!

"I went to Chicago to learn law in the office kept by my brothers. They were young, just starting. They gave me all that they could afford for food. It wasn't enough. I'd been hungry most of the time all my life, never gotten used to it and it seemed I was getting hungrier. Big Bill Thompson let me play football for the Chicago Athletic Club and that gave me the right to lay waste the training table. I was so bruised after the games that sometimes I couldn't reach the whole length of the table and some one would beat me to the last four or five lamb chops. However, I did fairly well.

"The Alaska gold rush started and I joined in. I've beaten you into the market with descriptions of that period. Back in Chicago I was selling firebrick, lime and cement—made a heavy sample case to lug around on a warm Summer day—when I met a Yukon acquaintance who told me that he had sold one of his mining experiences to a house organ for ten dollars. There was an empty desk in the law office. I snagged a chair and wrote.

"I'd never planned a writing career, hadn't even thought of one, but in a way I was prepared. While doing the work of a mule on a windlass on Little Minook Creek I'd had the pleasure of listening to an old fellow named Bill Joyce who had as fine a knack for telling a story as any man I've listened to. One of Bill's stories came to my mind. I wrote it and sold it to *McClure's* for $50.

"No, I wasn't the first man to capitalize on Alaska in fiction. So far as I know Jack London broke that trail—I'd read his first book of Alaska stories while I was on the scene and before I'd had any notion of writing. But when S. S. McClure came on to Chicago after buying a batch of my short stories and suggested that I try a novel I discovered—once the shock of surprise had worn off—that I did have the material—at least, the fact material—on which to base a novel. That was 'The Spoilers,' an account of how some prospectors had been knocked out of rich claims by slippery higher-ups. It was muckraking but true. The novel bogged down when I was part way through it, McClure showed more interest in a factual account and I turned to John O'Hara Cosgrave of *Everybody's.* He thought the novel was pretty good as far as it went but wanted to know where it was going. He almost had me there. I didn't know. But under that pressure I evolved the rest of the plot on the spot. It must have been pretty good because he said he'd buy it. Later I couldn't remember what I'd told him, but I slaved through, doing the best I could."

Mr. Beach was one of the first major figures in the Authors League. He said that he didn't remember all the abuses that the authors then faced, that his clearest recollection was of the weak business judgment that his colleagues showed. "It seemed to me impossible to get it through their heads that movie rights really had value—big value. Finally I gave up." He himself early adopted the policy of renting his stories to the films rather than selling them outright. This, he said, has proved itself smart. " 'The Spoilers' is now a picture for the fourth time, and one of my other books has been made over three times. Had I followed the usual practice, some movie company would have owned my rights and collected on the additional filmings.

"The only real gauge of success that we have is profit—honest profit. I don't slap down my stories. They come hard, always have. I've traveled widely to get the material because I felt safer if I had fresh fact to bolster my fiction. I figure I've earned whatever they've brought in."

In recent years he has done comparatively little writing. He mentioned the "commissar method" of choosing stories for the big-circulation magazines. "When one man of normal tastes chooses a story because he likes it, then it seems to me perfectly reasonable to suppose that a great many other people will like it. But this present custom of asking Miss So-and-so, who is just out of Smith, for her opinion and Mr. Jones from Yale for his and then testing their opinions against those of Dick and Eloise, and if they all say, well, they guess it won't poison any one, buying it and printing it—I can't keep up with that. I don't have to."

Mr. Beach maintains a penthouse home in New York, though he doesn't spend a great deal of his time there. "We come up for the Summer." His real home, as he counts homes, is in Florida, where, in recent years, he has been "writing stories with tractors." Out of vastly rich but never-tilled stretches of the Everglades he is making new farms—among them flower farms—and experimenting with large-scale cattle ranching.

"There's much the same kind of fascination in running down a new feed for cattle that is cheaper than the old feed, but makes the cattle just as fat or fatter, as there is in finding a new setting and fresh situations for a fictional hero. You start with nothing, work like the devil and if you play it right, probably come through."

His recently published autobiography, "Personal Exposures," he expects will be the base for a radio program. "I've been around more than most people—that's been my job, cutting new trails, finding stories in Panama, Alaska, the Southwest oil fields. And it's been an active way of getting around; I have plenty of anecdotes that seem good to me. The idea was that some one else could write the sketches. Can't seem to connect with the right person so I'm doing them myself.

"In fact, I may go into this new thing even deeper. It turns out that my voice has what they call microphone appeal. Same as in the movies. Cameras like some of the actors and do wonders for them; microphones like some voices, and mine is one they like. I'm glad to be mixing in radio. Radio is in much the same phase that the movies were in when I had a crack at them. Radio still goes all-out for personalities, for example, and never mind the material. That's sure to change, because finally it is the material that counts, not the stars. And something should be done about those commercial announcements. They can't all be gagged up, of course, but there must be some way to knock the boredom out of them. You see, the fresh field. So long as you can keep on finding new places to go, new fields to look into, you don't get old very fast."

AN INTERVIEW WITH H. ALLEN SMITH

Who wrote his humorous "Low Man on a Totem Pole" at the rate of a chapter a day and is happily amazed by the fact that his book is selling a thousand copies each week

August 24, 1941

H. ALLEN SMITH, author of the best-selling "Low Man on a Totem Pole," said that a number of people had come down hard on his book, complaining that it was worse than ribald, that "it wasn't anywhere near pure enough, clean enough. I put those things in that they object to because there was the dough. I don't think I'm wrong in saying that Hemingway's 'For Whom the Bell Tolls' got about 85 per cent of its hundreds of thousands of readers not because of the beauty of Hemingway's prose—and it's beautiful—or the greatness of his theme—and it's great—but because they knew that every thirty or forty pages that sleeping bag would be in the middle of the plot again or the earth would turn. So my book ain't pure. No. If it was, would it sell?"

He said that no matter how he might make out as a humorist—and he was laying no odds that he would make out at all—it was his most sincere hope that he never would be foolish enough to forget that he was "just a little guy who can watch people and not feel that they are watching him."

"I don't have any message to offer or reforms to further or any desire to be respected or loved. I hope that I don't change. I know people who changed. About all that I have to contribute is detachment. I have no fealty to any one or any institution. I love some people, of course, but I don't love humanity."

But, if that were true, where did the emotions originate that provided him with copy, that supplied the drive for the expression of his.

Mr. Smith is thin, of medium height, has a rather long nose with a double tip on it, is nervous, quick of mind. He is only now approaching his middle thirties, but has been in newspaper work for eighteen years, quitting his job as a rewrite man only after "Low Man on a Totem Pole" had become successful. He was sweeper-out and bootblack in a Midwestern barber shop when a man whose shoes he was shining made it known to him that there was a job available on the local newspaper. Smith got that job, worked on newspapers in many parts of the country.

"I have peasant tastes. I like to bear Bing Crosby sing, but I can't listen to Flagstad. I rarely go to the theatre—too much trouble. I go to the movies a lot and like double features. I find movies that are very bad quite funny; sit in the front row of the balcony with my feet on the rail, smoke cigarettes and enjoy them. I doubt that I ever read a whole book until after I was twenty-one and the father of two children. I didn't know from nothin'. I'd heard of Robin Hood and knew Washington crossed the Delaware, that's about all. Maybe it was a break at that, because when I discovered books they seemed wonderful and I was old enough to know what I was reading for. By then I knew that I wanted to be a writer, and while I was reading I'd make notes—put down this bit of information and that. History more than anything else. I still fill notebooks as I read, and I'm a great clipper-out. Sure, I look at the notes again. I've got two big cardboard boxes full of them and what I'm going to do now is buy a steel filing cabinet. Mencken has all kinds of stuff filed. His family saved all the bills they ever got—he has a complete record of the life his father and mother lived and of his own life. He even has the bill for his own delivery—$10."

Mr. Smith said that he discovered the writings of H. L. Mencken at about the time that he first discovered books and he never has wavered in his loyalty; that for him Mencken is the great humorist—"practically all bright journalistic writing now stems from him; his style and his satirical or humorous point of view.

"That question mixes me up. The hell of our interview system is that no one who has done a lot of writing can be half or a quarter as competent when talking as when writing. I'm crippled in talk. Even H. L. Mencken doesn't talk anywhere near as well as he writes. . . . If I were at a typewriter now I wouldn't need to x-out that stuff about having no fealty; I could fix it up and make it fit, though admitting contradictions. There are contradictions. For instance, I see myself as a guy who doesn't even worry about the future of his family. I think I don't even worry about my two kids; that is, about the world they'll live in, slave or free, about anything. Yet, though I would sort of like to move out of the city into a country place—in fact, I would damn well like to do it—I can't because the kids have all their friends where they've lived and I remember how much I hated having to make new friends when they moved me from one school to another.

"I like to think I am absolutely without sentiment—I run over with sentimentality. And as for emotions, I am full of them. I am bound to be since I had a Catholic childhood and then broke away from the church. You can't eradicate the fear and the mystery, and I don't look forward to ever being in anything but a kind of stew.

"But perhaps because I did break away from what was meant to be my strongest loyalty my emotions work on me in a kind of off-side way. For instance, to me most of the ceremonies that men have worked out for themselves are plain funny. Funerals. It is wonderful to watch the pompous dignity that politicians have at the funerals of other politicians. Ever go to them? And much as I respect the President, which I do—a lot of people don't like Mencken because he's a Roosevelt hater, but I practically worship Mencken and at the same time practically worship the President—anyway, I can't help but think that when the President is piped aboard his yacht—these little whistles, tweetle-tweetle-tweet—it is funny."

AN INTERVIEW WITH MR. AND MRS. PINKERTON

Who found their material and learned to write while pioneering in the wilderness

September 7, 1941

THE PINKERTONS have been writing for thirty years, have turned out enormous quantities of fiction for the pulp-paper magazines but always until just recently "we wrote to live: our pleasure was in building houses, varnishing boats, exploring country that was new to us. Writing was simply the job that made it possible for us to live as we wanted to." Their efforts, however, were strenuous. "We kept a record of output for ten years. The total came to 4,500,000 words written and sold." Robert Pinkerton completed a book-length serial every twenty-eight days for a long period. "Now we're getting along and writing seems more interesting." Mrs. Pinkerton has written three books covering phases of their life, and Mr. Pinkerton writes one serial a year for the slick magazines.

They have now a rather turtlelike scheme for existence. That is, all that they require to make a home they carry in a specially constructed oversize luggage compartment in their automobile.

"We carry twenty-two pieces of luggage; everything that we own fits into the back of that car. The astonishment of bellboys when we pull up to a hotel where we are strangers always amuses us. After the first ten or twelve suitcases their eyes pop."

They range the country, summering in Maine or Oregon or New York, spending the Winter in California or Florida, in no set places.

"For example, we left Los Angeles one Sunday morning to go to breakfast at Santa Barbara, and a friend, met at breakfast—a friend who is an aviator—said that she wanted to go away for a couple of months on flights. We rented her house, worked there for two months, then moved on. Within thirty minutes after arriving anywhere we have all our belongings unpacked, our typewriters set up and we're at work."

Mrs. Pinkerton said that she was first uprooted only by necessity. Mr. Pinkerton was a roaming newspaperman when they met in Milwaukee. His proposal to her was that she accept one end of the figurative shoestring on which he proposed to live. Soon after they were married ill health made it necessary for him to give up newspaper work and he was advised to stop living in cities. They decided to pioneer in the Canadian wilderness, "though I," said Mrs. Pinkerton, "never had been off the sidewalks, didn't know how to boil water, had never done any work with my hands." Funds to take them into Canada were raised by the writing of their first story—a 30,000-word novelette that they turned out in five days and that Bob Davis bought for *Munsey's*, paying $150 for it.

"It seemed very easy. There were six five-day units in each month and seventy-two in a year. Seventy-two times $150—we thought we'd be mighty rich pioneers." But for the next two years, while they were establishing themselves in a cabin in the woods and while Mrs. Pinkerton was learning to run a trap line, drive sledge dogs and do the housekeeping, they wrote stories endlessly. None sold. Now and then one of the outdoor or nature magazines sent them a small check for nonfiction material. Robert Pinkerton guided some hunters, they farmed and trapped and so survived.

"The trouble with our fiction was that we didn't understand the necessity for plot and conflict. We'd been lucky on the first yarn—it had been a natural with natural structure. Finally Kathrene sat down and analyzed the stories of Jack London and some of the other popular fellows of that period and made graphs of them to find out just how they got their effects. She skeletonized their stories and in that way we found out what was wrong with ours. We immediately started to click, and for the next four years every story that we wrote was sold."

On three other occasions in their thirty years of writing they have been similarly stuck, Robert Pinkerton said. "We lived aboard a boat for several years and met a lot of people in out-of-the-way places whom I found very interesting. I started writing stories that were all character, that presented a hero but never provided any circumstance to kick him in the teeth. We studied that out and I learned that to write the kind of stuff I aimed for I had to keep kicking my hero in the teeth from the beginning right up to the last page.

"But later I was stopped again by becoming too interested in vocations. For example, we went to the Mother Lode to live and I did a lot of mining. My stories in that period contained everything you'd want to know about the work that the characters were doing—more than you'd want to know—but the characters were simply stuffed figures.

"The fourth break came when editorial requirements changed sharply. I had become accustomed to using a great many words to tell a story, introducing two or three situations to show one character trait. But an extreme tightening up was required by the editors. What had been a 30,000-word story had to be told in 12,000 words. Each situation had to make clear about three character traits.

"At about the same time the pulp magazines became a poor market. Fellows who had been making $30,000 a year—or even double that—had their incomes cut down to almost nothing by dropping wordage rates and the change in what the editors wanted. Now the maximum that one man can make out of the pulps is about $600 a month; the stuff is mostly written by young fellows who burn themselves out in about a year and a half. I switched to the slicks."

The Pinkertons indulge in a perennial argument on whether it still is possible for young people to pioneer as they did. Mrs. Pinkerton thinks that it is easily possible and has a list of places where, in her opinion, one can move in with very little money and find security living off the country. Mr. Pinkerton believes that very few people could get away with such an attempt, though he admits that it might be done on the Alaskan coast where the Winters are not too severe, the seas are full of fish and you can pot a deer in half an hour.

AN INTERVIEW WITH MARGARET LEECH

The author of "Reveille in Washington" discusses some echoes of the past

September 14, 1941

MARGARET LEECH spent five years writing "Reveille in Washington," the story of the capital during the Civil War. She said that one cheerful aspect of all this work was that she always could break up those conversations that start: "To fight Hitlerism we'll have to give up the very freedom that we're fighting for, we'll have to form a totalitarian State as tough as his, so what's the use of fighting? We'll lose, whatever we do."

"If there's one thing I found out, it is that democracy is tough enough to take anything. It needn't change much to make a fight. It need only wake up. The Fifth Column—Washington in the Civil War was just about filled with Fifth Columnists. Lincoln was bitterly and noisily hated. And it was a slow change. But when the North woke there was no possible stopping it."

Miss Leech is a tall, attractive woman, very pleasant in talk. She is the widow of Ralph Pulitzer, son of the founder of that fine newspaper, the *World.* The Susan Pulitzer to whom her book is dedicated is her daughter.

She hired an office and there did most of her work. "I kept at it pretty steadily. For bedtime reading I'd take up biographies of Lincoln, histories of the Civil War, and so on. At first I did my best to keep Lincoln out of the book because, after all, it was the story of Washington. But that was like doing a book about the disciples and not mentioning whose disciples they were. Late in the writing I realized this and sort of inserted Lincoln. Some reviewers have said that the book is all Lincoln and some that he isn't in it enough. So I guess the amount is about right."

Excerpts from the book were published in the *Atlantic Monthly.* Miss Leech has received about thirty letters as a result of this. One woman wrote from Essex, England, that she had noticed many parallels between actual events in England during this war and Miss Leech's account of events in Washington during the Civil War. A man wrote that his father had served in the Union Army and that he had his father's sword in storage, but that not until reading "Reveille in Washington" had he become thoroughly converted to the Northern side. He said that he always had tried not to read too much about the war, that most of his friends were Southerners and he hadn't wanted to be prejudiced.

She said that before the book was published some readers wanted her to cut out much of the material in the early chapters. "But that would have made a static picture. I wanted to show development. And isn't it lucky that I insisted on leaving all that in? Because it is the early stuff that is so quickly realized as applying now."

An unneeded bathtub* just off the study of her large East End Avenue apartment is the filing place for Miss Leech's penciled notes. Thousands of notes, most of them made from newspaper stories, represent writer's cramp and that special illumination that brightens this history.

"Most of the details I used came from news accounts. Historians look down their noses," she said, modestly disregarding the fact that some of the most respected of all contemporary historians have given her work high praise. "Depending so much on newspapers isn't considered at all the thing to do. It is held to be irrelevant and incompetent. But they were the best sources I could find."

She said that she always has liked to read old newspapers, and

* Miss Leech reported that after this was printed many people questioned her as to why she didn't need a bathtub.

that with all the resources of the Library of Congress at her disposal it was the newspaper files that she asked for. The Washington *Star,* which was a particularly lively paper through the Civil War years, filled with sprightly comment on what people were doing and saying and thinking, was perhaps most useful. The *Chronicle* was helpful, and she took a great deal, particularly for her chapter on Mrs. Lincoln, from the New York *Herald.* Mr. Bennett of the *Herald* employed as a kind of off-the-record correspondent a somewhat villainous character who had rather too much influence on Mrs. Lincoln.

Miss Leech remarked on the curious contrast between the coarse tone in which so many of the news accounts were written in the Civil War period and the extreme emphasis on respectability that society in general was so anxious about.

"They'd write of prostitutes so intimately, give the pet names of the girls and sort of laughingly chide them for getting in trouble with the police. And the publishers behaved in such a—well, high-spirited way. One time the publisher of one of the New York papers met Mr. Bennett of the *Herald* on the street and was so infuriated at the sight of him that he seized Mr. Bennett's head, pulled Mr. Bennett's mouth open and spat down Mr. Bennett's throat. Bennett went hurrying back to his office and made the story of this encounter the big story of the day in the *Herald.* He told the story in full on the front page. And of course it was good news judgment, probably delighted the readers. Try to imagine anything like that happening now.

"Of course, while I was making notes, I was continually pulled aside from my subject by things I couldn't use. And I made hundreds of notes that were no use to me. Also, I'd often find that I hadn't bothered to note things I really needed. You see, I didn't do all the research and then write the book. I couldn't possibly have kept at it if I'd done that. I started writing very early. There's nothing like having concocted an ironic description of some one to send you on to find out all about that person so that you can enlarge and better the description.

"By writing as you go along you can keep yourself amused and interested, keyed up. Just doing research and no writing would be so dull as to be impossible."

Miss Leech wrote three novels in the 1920's. One of these, "Tin Wedding," was well received. With Heywood Broun she wrote a biography of Anthony Comstock that was popular.

She said that she was not very proud of being unable to say that she had slaved at "Reveille in Washington" through an inner compulsion. "The fact is that the publishers asked me to write the book and suggested the subject. . . . Later I asked Cass Canfield how he happened to make the suggestion and he said that he had a theory that there was plenty of room in the field of American history for other than professional historians and that he had asked me to make a try because he was pretty sure that I would turn out something that was, anyway, adequate, of which he needn't be ashamed."

Miss Leech said that she preferred to work "on a smaller canvas." "I'd like to do short stories, but I'm afraid they call for a talent that I don't have. I'm through with fiction because I haven't enough invention.

"To do this kind of writing" she continued of historical writing, "requires much that is necessary in fiction. That is, you must have your own light, your own point of view for each scene. If you don't have that, you're simply copying, of course. But, as I'm not inventive enough, fact writing is much the best kind for me because the material is there and so half the work is done by drudging, by learning the material.

"But next time I'd like a smaller subject. I enjoy writing and intensely admire brief, perfect things. This book is too sprawling."

AN INTERVIEW WITH REX STOUT

The author of the Nero Wolfe detective stories discusses his work and the war

September 21, 1941

WITH REX STOUT you have one certainty: that, whatever you are, you won't be misunderstood. The author of the Nero Wolfe detective stories is more articulate than are most writers and has more free energy. One has the impression that he has lived more and worked less than the majority of his peers. His beard is not a particularly good beard. It has rather the sparse look of barberry bushes that have been trampled by the house painters. The beard's purpose, probably, is to ambush one's attention from the eyes above it, which are not cataloguing eyes and seem to reflect open judgments but are intent and observing to a rare degree.

Mr. Stout said that he writes detective stories because they pay well. Before turning to Nero Wolfe he wrote four novels. Two had very good notices here and were even better received in England and in France.

"But I know of only three reasons why a man should write serious fiction. One, if you love words and want to put them together in a way that pleases you—that was my reason for writing the four novels. The second reason: if you're burning to tell other people what you think is wrong; that is, if you're the preacher type. Some of the best writers now are fundamentally preachers. Johnny Steinbeck, I think, is one. The third reason to write serious fiction is if you are a great writer. There are damn few great writers and I'm not one of them. While I could afford to, I played with words. When I could no longer afford that I wrote for money."

Born in Kansas, the son of a superintendent of schools, Mr. Stout left the University of Kansas while in his freshman year and enlisted in the Navy. "I wanted to see the ocean." That was in 1906 and the term of his enlistment was four years. He was made yeoman paymaster on President Theodore Roosevelt's yacht. "As it happened there were only seven men in the wardroom and that left them one short for two tables of whist. So they fixed it up to make me a warrant officer, which would give me the freedom of the wardroom and would fill out the second table. After a time I got tired of whist, and as a warrant officer can resign, I resigned."

Then a succession of jobs, including clerking in a cigar store. Mr. Stout heard that an uptown New York hotel needed a manager. He bought some striped pants and a cutaway and applied. The costume clinched the job, and the elevator man and the telephone girl—old hands in the hotel business—tutored him so that he could keep it. He left this post to write for a living.

"But if I was paid eighteen dollars for a short story and it was Summer, I went to baseball games until I was broke again. If I got $3,000 for a 90,000-word story that Bob Davis had bought and it was Winter, I went to the opera until I was broke again. Never even got my laundry out. I decided, hell, that life wasn't getting me anywhere. And the stories weren't any good. I made up my mind to go into business until I had $150,000 or was forty years old. I was three months short of forty when I had the $150,000. I wrote my novels but in the depression I lost my money."

"What was the business?"

"I invented a system of accounting that I sold to banks."

"Had you ever worked in a bank?"

"No."

"Were you an accountant?"

"No." A pause. "You see I have a—a sort of a trick mind for figures. When I was a kid, nine, ten, eleven, along in there, I toured Kansas as a sort of exhibit. I'd stand in a schoolroom with my back to the blackboard, or blindfolded, and rows of figures—eleven or twelve across and eleven deep—were written on the board. I'd look at this block of figures for, well, six seconds, then turn my back again and give the total, the total that they added up to.

"My father didn't like it. You see, it made me a freak. I realized that, too, and I didn't like it. No, I've lost the trick. I think I consciously lost it. But even now I find it impossible to make a mistake in addition.

"I turned to words instead of figures. I'd always loved words—had read the Bible through when I was three and a half, read Macaulay when I was three. But with words I wasn't a freak."

He said that until the war started he had thoroughly enjoyed writing stories about Nero Wolfe.

"I never worked more than three months a year. Not quite three months. Thirty-nine or forty days on each novel, and I'd do two a year.

"No, there's nothing much to planning them. Of course, I was lucky in having hit on the name—Nero Wolfe. Simple but odd; people remember it. And Wolfe was born; he wasn't synthetic. I didn't have to sit down and decide: What color will his eyes be? Well, they'll be blue. How much will he weigh? How will he walk? What expressions will he use? He was born.

"I tried another detective later, Tecumseh Fox—because *The Saturday Evening Post* editors wanted a fresh detective—and he never was born. He was put together piece by piece and wasn't worth a damn.

"As for the story, you take a setting that interests you, think of what might happen in that setting, choose the most entertaining happenings and then ask yourself: 'Well, why would a man want to buy that champion bull? Why would some one murder a man because of a bull?' The answers come right along. You have your plot. You write it.

"It was pure pleasure—a game.

"Then Munich gave me my first belly-ache. I'd always been healthy; I became dyspeptic. That's true. I had pains most of the time after Munich, a nervous stomach.

"I started making speeches, debating these America First fellows, going on the radio to answer them, doing all I could to wake people up to the danger.

"Listen, if we get in now, right now, 200,000 American lives and fifty billion dollars probably will be the cost of beating Hitler. If we listen to the isolationists and wait until Hitler is ready for us, until we are next on his timetable, we'll spend five million American lives and two or three hundred billion dollars. What in God's name is the sense of that?

"I'm not dyspeptic any more. The nervousness is all going out, you see, in these speeches. But Nero Wolfe gets smaller. Can't keep my mind on him."

Mr. Stout led the way onto the sunny roof of his house. The Stout place is called High Meadows. It is near the crest of one of the long slopes to the south of the Berkshires. Straight ahead a ten-mile view of meadows, trees and hills. Mr. Stout gestured toward Pawling.

"Quite a colony of the subversive element over there." He named a number of prominent isolationists. "With a 75-millimeter gun placed right here, I'll bet I could pot them," he said, with great cheerfulness, a cheerfulness that had in it no indication that he did not mean exactly what he said.

AN INTERVIEW WITH CHARLES MORGAN

The author of "The Fountain" discusses his work and the war

October 5, 1941

Charles Morgan has the casual charm of honesty that probably is inevitable in a poet who has survived the toughening training, starting at the age of twelve, that is a prelude for a career as a British naval officer. The author of those mystic but popular bouts with love and death, "The Fountain" and "Sparkenbroke," can—it soon becomes comfortingly clear—take poetic introspection or leave it alone. His manner is assured to that farthest point—the unself-conscious writer. This is nearly as rare a being as the unself-conscious actor.

"I was ten years old when, one day, I went to my father and told him that, please, I should like to become a writer and, please, might I be educated with that aim in view. My father was an engineer, a very good one, an eminent engineer—he built the Victoria terminal in London, was president of the engineering society—a solid Victorian father. Looking back, I wonder a little at the way in which he received my request. It seems that it would have been natural for him to say: 'Pooh, pooh, nonsense. There never has been a writer in our family.' I believe that he did say that there never had been a writer in our family, yet he was very open-minded about it. He told me that I might find that I wanted to write but that a first necessity would be to find a job that would bring me a steady income, some leisure and perhaps allow me to travel. With that we left it.

"Two years later I went to him again and said, please, I'd like to go into the Navy. No one in our family had been in the Navy. He found it hard to understand why I wanted it and I did not tell him. I had settled on the Navy because that seemed to offer a career that fitted his specifications—steady pay, travel, some leisure. But I didn't recall to him our earlier talk. He questioned me, found that I was sincere and arranged for me to start the training course.

"Though I had taken this step with a double purpose I became very keen on the course, wanted very much to make good at it, took the proper firsts, did well at games and so forth. When I had time I wrote.

"Later, as a midshipman, I was on ship soon to leave for Singapore and from there to China. We were still in harbor and one day in the gunnery—the wardroom, I suppose it might be described, for midshipmen—I took out my books and papers and began going over them. Time came for me to go on watch; I left my papers and went on deck.

"About half an hour later one of my contemporaries, another midshipman, found me and said: 'Morgan, you're in for it. The sub came in and saw your papers scattered around. He took that marble-covered book that has your poems in it, put it under his arm and went away.' 'Lord!' I thought. A midshipman writing poetry and the sub-lieutenant finding it out—the man with power of life and death over midshipmen, who can beat you, do anything to you, finding it out.

"Nothing was said at the next meal. The next day I was told to report at the sub's cabin. He said: 'Will you have Scotch or Irish?' and I knew it was all right. In fact, it was very much all right. The sub was a descendant of Matthew Arnold, and a great many of the best writers in England were family friends or relatives. He said that he had read my poetry and thought it rather good and that if I liked he'd send it to friends for an opinion. I knew no writers. I was delighted. He sent the poems home and word came back that they were quite all right and that if I wanted to make a career of writing I seemed to have a fair chance of doing well at it."

Morgan persuaded his father to buy him out of the Navy and

returned across Asia to England. This was in 1913. He was preparing for Oxford—studying Latin and Greek—when the war broke out and he returned to service. In one of the early battles of the war—that at Antwerp—he was captured and interned in Holland. He said that there is nothing like a moderately comfortable captivity to help along a writer. Only the imagination offers freedom. While in Gelderland he wrote a novel, but lost the manuscript when the ship on which he was returning to England struck a mine and sank.

Continuing to follow his father's advice, he found a job on the staff of the *Times* and before long became dramatic critic on that newspaper. Until the start of this war he held that post, doing his own writing on evenings that he did not go to the theatre—"that is, I could work at my own stuff two or three evenings a week and on long vacations when we'd go to some small town on the Continent and really get down to work."

He said that until the last two years he never has permitted himself to become dependent financially on his imaginative writing. "I wanted—more than that, I felt that I required—absolute freedom to write in my own way, admitting no urges from outside, no publisher hurrying me or asking me to repeat a novel that had proved fairly successful, no need other than my own need to do the work."

He said that his way of work is, in a sense, wasteful. He has tried plotting a novel in advance but found that this caused him to become bored with his characters and with the task. It is better for him to start with characters that are real and alive to him and, in writing about them to let them take their own way. Often this means that he will get on a wrong track and write thousands of words, even tens of thousands of words, that lead to a dead end and must be thrown away. "I throw them away and start again." Because he is independent of the money, this is less difficult for him than it would be for most writers.

He left the *Times* when the war broke to do a prearranged job for Naval Intelligence. When that was finished he was told to return to writing. He is not now working for the *Times* because there "is no longer space for articles on the theatre." Lack of paper is profoundly affecting publishing of all sorts in England. "New writers are in the soup. No one can afford to chance their paper on men who are not established." He is in this country on a nonprofit lecture tour.

I gathered from his talk that one purpose he had in coming here—though this never was stated—was to give such assurance as one individual can that the English are not as interested in hanging on to property as they formerly were.

"One thing we know is that there is to be no reward for us of ease or gain or comfort. Perhaps for our grandsons. But we do not seek in victory vengeance, profit or even the preservation of what we possess. All victory can mean is an opportunity to replant, to safeguard the early growth, to leave the maturity to others. We're dedicated to the future—only sensible thing to do. What possible use is care for your possessions with bombs smashing them and flaming bombers dropping into your street?"

He recalled a night when the sky was so filled with flame that the birds in his garden thought it was sunrise and woke and sang.

He said that the leaves of the calendar no longer represent measurable dates to people in England. "They are not 'next Spring' or 'next Summer.' They are just pieces of paper until you come to them—but then they are very much alive. The root fact is that it no longer is of any use—if it ever was of any use—to play for safety or for gain in one's own life." It is simply ineffectual to think of life in terms of air raids and shelters. "Man is not a mole—his life has to be lived, his work has to be done. There is everything to be said, when the bombs are whistling and the windows of your house are falling in, for staying in the room where you happen to be and continuing the work you happen to be doing."

THE AUTHOR OF "A THOUSAND SHALL FALL"

Hans Habe, a youthful journalist and novelist who fought for France

October 12, 1941

HANS HABE, the young, tall, brilliant author of "A Thousand Shall Fall"—which is perhaps the most effective book that has been written about the fall of France—is living on the reservation at West Point and taking lessons in English from a teacher in the local school. Beyond his writing table one of the fine views of the East—the long, wooded slope to the Hudson far down below. At the table Habe works, producing in tight-fisted Hungarian script the slow, difficult opening pages of a novel—"A novel I have hope for. I try very hard."

He rejects thoughts of the difficulties added by his circumstances to the normal difficulties of composition. Of writing, he says: "Most important is system, to write twenty lines a day as Thomas Mann does, or twenty pages a day as Zola did. The quantity does not matter. The consistency does. As for inspiration, one is born with inspiration or not. If one is born so gifted, what more does one require? One is inspired at eight o'clock each morning."

He spends about six months brooding over a novel then writes rapidly. "I become crazy in a pleasant way." The planning period is dark with doubts. "I doubt that I am a writer, that I have a subject, that I have anything to say."

Of his new novel:

"My theme is the constant struggle, the unending war between the generations. It is, perhaps, unusual because I am on the side of the older generation; I think they are right."

"Do you mean that you believe that Hitlerism and Stalinism represent the point of view of youth?"

"How could any one dare to answer that in the affirmative? But it seems to me that there is no doubt that the young in Europe are in the position of confused children who have only gangsters for teachers, the codes of gangsters to live by. They know they were born—I mean borned—into a crazy world. They themselves are not criminals. The mass never is criminal. But the criminals tell them that there is no hope, that they must destroy. And they incline to believe that the criminals may know. Yes, I am afraid so.

"I myself had my first taste of Nazism when I was a student at the Franz Joseph College in Vienna. You, an American, could not conceive of the cruel bitterness, the vicious, violent acts that grew out of politics in that school. The students hating one another. True hate, very strong. Out of the hate and confusion, so much that it would be impossible for you to comprehend, I saw boys who had been my friends turn to Nazism as the answer. And many times since, the same thing. I could not be on that side. So in my book the ideals of the older men and women are the ideals that are good."

Habe was the first man to say in print that Hitler's real name was Schicklgruber. The year was 1931. Habe was twenty years old and employed as a reporter on a Vienna newspaper.

"Every day for a week a man who did not give his name called my editor"—he held an imaginary telephone to his ear, then banged his hand to the desk—"and he would tell him something like this: 'You must send a reporter to Braunau Inn. He will find out Hitler's real name.' Then, bang, the call would end. Every day for a week and each day he would tell a little more of what we might discover at Braunau Inn. So I told my editor: 'It is not very expensive. Let me take the bus to Braunau.' He did.

"For ten days I was there. I talked to old friends of Hitler's father. I obtained photographs of Hitler's earliest records—of the old church book, all the official papers. I talked to every one who would talk to me and learned of Hitler as a boy and as a young man and of his father and mother—everything.

"It was a very, very small town. Each evening I drank in the little bar. There was a girl there who worked in the bar and drank with me.

"This girl was the special friend of an architect who lived in a town some miles away. He came regularly to visit her. On the tenth night we were having our drinks and the girl said: 'You must leave here. It is necessary that you leave here now. Do not go back to your lodging. Go to Vienna.' She told me that the architect's car and his chauffeur were waiting for me around in back of the bar. The chauffeur would take me to Vienna. She would send my belongings after me.

"I had nothing but human feeling to believe in. I had spent all these nights sitting with this girl and I thought she was good. I had talked many hours with her friend, the architect and I believed in him. It might have been a trap but I believed in them. So I got in the car, and surely it was wise, for as we passed my lodging there were three or four men in the brown shirts waiting. Well, we drove along ten miles—more than that—and I was thinking to myself that, however right my friends had been, my own part was none too courageous, when we heard German motorcycles behind us. And then shots. They were shooting at our tires. I suppose it was not more than five minutes before we lost them, for it was a fast car with a good driver. There were bullet holes in the back of the car, four or five. I felt as though I had been on the road two years."

Hundreds of thousands of copies of his story of Hitler's origin and boyhood were distributed in Germany. Mr. Habe likes to think that they were helpful in depriving Hitler of victory in Germany's last free election which was coming up just at that time.

Habe became a correspondent for one of the last newspapers printed in German and with large circulation to campaign against Hitler. His headquarters were at Geneva, but he ranged all Europe covering the biggest stories of the time.

When the war started he enlisted in the French Army and his regiment, made up of foreigners, held a sector of line for a considerable period after neighboring troops had been driven back. On this he bases his theory that men who understand what they are fighting against, who fully realize what is in store for the world if Hitler wins, can hold their own against the Germans even when their weapons are inferior; that there is more to war than panzer divisions and superiority in the air.

The collapse came and Habe was one of the war prisoners. He said that in his book "A Thousand Shall Fall" he pulled his punches when he described the life in the prison camp. "I did not want people to say, 'Ah, here is another liar come out of the night,' and I knew that if I told the truth in its entirety that is what they would say. What you must understand is that I was not in a concentration camp—I suppose that they are worse. I was a prisoner of war, soldier just as the Germans were soldiers. We were honorable enemies who had fought courageously and well. Had they known my identity—well, then, of course— But I was not known to the Germans. I was simply a prisoner who could be employed to translate commands because they could know that I spoke German well and thought that I spoke French well, though in fact I spoke it moderately.

"All of us were men who had fought honorably. We were made to feel that we were less than men, so far as the Germans could make us feel that. And do not believe that this was impromptu on their part. No, it was not. All their moves had been planned. They were under orders to impress upon us that we were slaves and they had had instruction in how best to prove to us that we were less than men, less than cattle, slaves cheaply held."

Because he was a translator of commands and so had had some contact with the German authorities at the camp, he was shown a list of names of men wanted by the Gestapo. His own name was on the list.

Out in Hollywood now this situation is being used as the basis for a movie that will use much of the detail taken from his book but will center on this dramatic circumstance—a man employed by the Gestapo to hunt himself.

Mr. Habe escaped from the camp, sent a message to his wife in Switzerland and crossed Spain to Portugal.

"At the Portuguese border the sentry knew about me—he knew that I was entering with a forged passport. He said to me: 'Come in. Eat well in this country. Drink well here. This is a free country.' "

A special visa granted by President Roosevelt permitted him, as a man whose life was in danger, to avoid the long Lisbon wait and come to America.

"It is not only that I owe to your President my life; it is not only that he is the best English teacher in the world—I know his speeches so well; they have meant so much to me.

"As you ask what I think of him, I can tell you, though perhaps as a foreigner I have no right to say. I think him the greatest man in the world today and one of the very greatest men that ever lived. I have thought that for many years—yes. Most people in Europe—well, I did not hear one word of criticism of Roosevelt, ever, until the day our ship entered New York Harbor. Believe me, we in Europe who hate Nazism see in your President the great hope of the world."

JOHN GUNTHER, WHO WROTE "INSIDE EUROPE"

He has gone to London for a vacation before starting on the U. S. A.

October 26, 1941

JOHN GUNTHER said that sometimes he wakes in the night and thinks: "My God, suppose I hadn't written it!" He was talking about "Inside Europe." Since writing that book he has been well paid, with no boss, can make his own assignments. He has assigned himself to Asia and Latin America and during the next two years will write an "Inside the United States." Today he is in London on a vacation that will leave time for some broadcasting and perhaps some articles. He thought that he might attempt to wangle passage to Russia. He said that a number of his friends talk about taking a little house in Vermont and living in quiet comfort. "I can't understand that."

Gunther looks bigger than his 218 pounds, a tall man with shoulders like those of the men in "Lorna Doone"—big enough to block a wide doorway. His features are Byronic, set in too heavy a frame. He respects structure in talk, persists in answering each question fully before going on to the rest. This sense of structure is a great aid in writing. His method is to "type very fast—like a madman—getting the stuff down. After that it's just copyreading, revising for finish and clarity. The structure usually stands up." He produced a manuscript sample, a typescript pasted up in places and interlined with handwriting, the words written in probably totaling more than the words first set down. He revises the revised scripts and makes a lot of changes in proof.

What is most important to him is that he has succeeded in putting together objective guides to the politics of three continents, that in two more years he will have completed "profiles" of all major States on earth.

"Not to sound too stuffy—Gunther-explains-success, that kind of thing—but I believe that one reason the first book went well, and the second, is that though every one knows where I stand there are not more than six paragraphs of overt editoralizing in all the half million words. The books are craftsman jobs and what I've tried to do is be interesting but a mirror, interesting because the facts are worth knowing and so presented that no one stands between the facts and the reader. By good luck I have no messianic impulse. But, of course, there's no doubt about how I think. The Axis governments ban my books automatically."

Mr. Gunther said that he took a great deal of knowledge as his province in 1910 or so, when he was ten years old and wrote 200 pages of an encyclopedia. "It sounds childish—of course, it is childish," he said, like a man making a discovery. "There were five sections: Great Dates of History, Battleships, Animals, Greek Mythology—I don't remember the other. I spent a lot of my time reading and working at stuff like that. Never took much interest in games. As I grew older I developed a split personality—if you don't take that too technically I was schizophrenic. I was interested in the world around me, in who ran it and how, but the main thing I wanted to do was write literature, stories, novels. And I was hungry for travel."

He made a trip to Europe aboard a cattle boat, returned to his home in Chicago and found a job with the Chicago *Daily News*, where he did very well. "I had that curious mixture of brashness and shyness." When the Teapot Dome scandal came along he went to see his managing editor. " 'Look,' I said, 'we're running thousands of words about the Teapot Dome, but has any one ever seen it?' 'What of it?' 'Well, could I go to Montana and look at it?' He thought it was a good idea, so I went out there and wrote the obvious story that it didn't look like a teapot or like a dome. . . . Then I asked to be sent to Europe.

I was twenty-three years old and he said that they liked me all right and I was doing a good job but was trying to rush things too much. So I quit. I went direct to London and called at the *Daily News* office for my mail. Hal O'Flaherty sort of drew my story out and made the most wonderful gesture any one has made to me. He told me to come to work on Monday.

"Well, that didn't work so well because in a couple of weeks my by-line began cropping up on the cable stuff and it was pretty clear that if I was allowed to get away with that the whole local staff might quit and come to Europe for correspondent jobs. I went over to the United Press, saved three of the ten pounds I was paid each week and when I had enough went to Southern France and lived in a police station on a little island. There I wrote a lousy novel. More than anything else I'd like to write a novel and I keep trying but they are never any good.

"The *News* relented and hired me back and I had fine experience covering during vacations at the various bureaus all over Europe. I was the emergency man sent out to where the stuff was breaking.

"Along in 1925 I started to keep my private morgue—magazine and news articles that interested me—and I've kept it faithfully ever since. There are about 75,000 clippings in it now.

"But always I looked on the news as the day's work. My real work, I thought, was that which occupied me after I left the office, the novels and stories. It wasn't until the early 1930's that I suddenly broke out with a rash of magazine stories on what was going on in Europe and the men who were running the countries. I had nearly a clear field. Publishers thought there might be a book in these articles and they'd write me, but I didn't want to take on so big a job. Finally I came back home on leave and my agent asked what figure I'd set to do the book. I named a tremendous sum—$5,000. She raised it and still I wouldn't sign. The morning I was to sail Cass Canfield—as he will tell you with relish—came to my hotel room before I was out of bed and said that he was going to stay there until I signed. So I signed.

"Soon after going back to Europe I was transferred from my spot in Vienna which was not really a loaf but was sort of a loaf—after all, I'd been there five years and knew the ropes—to London. They had a general election that year, the old King died, big news stories all over the place. I worked hard all day and some nights at the job but just about every hour that I wasn't working for the *News* I pounded on that book. All my friends, the other correspondents, helped tremendously, gave me plenty of the material. My eyes were in the back of my head when I finished it after six months. I still didn't have the title. One night in Wales I got on a train—it was raw, I was tired—I went into the dining car and ate cold mutton and drank a Scotch and thought: 'It's an inside view of Europe—Europe from the inside—inside Europe.' That title made a big difference. No one thought the book would do much, but it came out at exactly the right moment. Curiosity about Hitler had just gone into high. The book sold even better in England across the counter than it did here. I quit my job and headed for Asia to do another one."

"Isn't it difficult to work without the daily deadline?"

"Not very, because I make my own deadlines. I toured South America for my new book—spent five and one-half months down there—and every night I wrote a long report on everything that I had heard and seen. It's the only way—the edges are blunted if you let that kind of thing wait too long. I rarely had a meal alone; in all I interviewed 338 people. But a lot of my life is wasted getting ready to work when I have writing to do. I don't know—I hate to get up and I hate to start. Along about the middle of the afternoon I get at it and work until sometime in the evening. Same way with a book; the first chapter may take me thirty days. The next, twenty days. But then I really get into it and knock them off. Sometimes as much as 5,000 words a day."

IRVIN S. COBB DISCUSSES HIS WRITING

In an interview he talks of humor, homesickness and publicity

November 2, 1941

"WHEN I WANTED SOMETHING—a trip to Europe, a couple of new cars—I'd say to my friends, 'Excuse me for two weeks,' and I'd write two li'l sheafs of typescript," said Irvin S. Cobb, "that were already bespoken. Suppose they were tricky with professional humor, suppose they were nothing that would be remembered long! There was too much involved in those words as they stood; I couldn't afford to scrap them. And back there in the 1920's—the time I'm talking about—I worked. Sure I did. But I played, too. I'd been robbed of childhood and youth because all my waking hours went into work. So when I could I played and I wrote what was wanted. And, make no mistake, the magazine editors wanted my stuff bad. I was a good salesman and they'd been sold. But the novel that might have come out of it never was written.

"There's nothing so perishable as humor," he said.

"How about Dickens and Mark Twain?"

"Now you're talking of great novelists who sometimes wrote humorously. I'm not talking about that. I mean professional humor. That self-deprecatory trick of 'you know you're an ass, you make a fool of yourself all the time, but if you want to meet the champeen, that's me.' That kind of line. Laughing at yourself and it's not hard to do, but no man can do it very long. It spoils.

"And don't think Mark Twain didn't slip. He did. I'm not comparing myself to him any more than I'd compare a tumble-bug to a fast horse. But when he started running with that Hartford crowd he did some mighty poor work. Now you're asking me how it is that I've done pretty well when I've written about Paducah and my early days in New York and slipped when I've written of my later years. The later years just don't mean so much when you get along. When Twain wrote 'Huckleberry Finn' he was homesick—he was hungry for fried catfish and he dipped his pen into the innards of a li'l tough-footed boy. And don't think Dickens didn't use all the homesickness there was, because he did. So when I did better when I wrote out of homesickness for things that were gone from me, there's nothing strange about that. I'm in the best company—way back yonder on the list, but the best company.

"And in the '20's you know it, there didn't seem to be time. The novel, the things that might have lasted—seemed they'd take too much."

He talked on the uses of publicity for a writer. A few minutes before, with more misery in his face than befits the mask of even a professional humorist, he had slowly approached the Algonquin Hotel, in front of which a large crowd, shepherded by twenty amiable policemen, waited because the Duke and Duchess of Windsor were scheduled to visit the Union Jack Club, next door. A woman acquaintance had greeted Mr. Cobb as he came to the outskirts of the crowd and he had swept off his oversized Western hat and remarked in round, clear tones, drawling, that of course he had expected some notice, and was not in the least surprised by the size of the crowd, but how had they known what time he was coming in? At this there were many nudgings, some pleased laughter, and whispers: "Yeah, that's Irvin S. Cobb." The hundred who were nearest turned to look at him.

They saw a man who is not exactly flattered by his pictures but neither is he maligned by them. He must once have been considerably heavier than he now is, for he has been forced, he said, to just about give up eating, "because I liked to eat too well and did too much of it. I never was an inebriate but I enjoyed drinking when I was a younger man. I've had to just about give that up, too. Now and then a smidgen, no more." He spoke of illness and said that he wrote his autobiography, "Exit Laughing," at a fast pace, "because I thought I was about to die, and there were facts in there I wanted to set down." He stated that the book was "without professional trickery—you won't find any stunts to force laughs, because there aren't any such stunts in it. I wrote those 130,000 words in sixty-five days. You've got to write honest at that pace."

In the hotel lobby and on the sidewalk he had a way of disregarding what was said to him, implying that when a lot of people were listening he'd do the talking. But in private talk the flush of long public attention disappears and a strong, thoroughly conscious temperament makes itself felt.

He said that when he started to write fiction it was with the full knowledge that "I didn't have one-tenth the talent or ability that some of the other men then writing had.

"I figured out that it was up to me to keep moving and to keep my name in the papers. I'm a pretty good publicity man and I took my own account. Every opportunity offered me to get my name in print was accepted by me, with thanks—and a photograph. If the editor of a Pittsburgh paper wired me that he'd like an interview when I was passing through the town, why, I'd leave a call for 3 A.M., if that was the hour we hit Pittsburgh and I'd be up and dressed and waiting when the reporter came on board. If a lady interviewer said she'd like to see me in Atlanta, I'd wire back an invitation to dinner and I'd say to my manager, 'Buy me six, seven dollars' worth of flowers.' Yes, sir, those six, seven dollars' worth of flowers meant six, seven hundred dollars' worth of publicity.

"I could go on a picnic with writers who could write rings around me. But when the reporters came it was always old Irv Cobb who was happiest to see them, who had a special angle to talk about and who made the headlines.

"Same way I broke up my assignments. I did nonfiction pieces, lectured, took up acting. I've done every damn thing there was any call for me to do, and when a big news story broke and no one asked me to cover it for them, why, I'd borrow a police card and cover it for myself. It all helped. The scenes you see as a reporter, they change around, they're fiction some day."

He said that finally he caught on to the fact that editors considered his stories old-fashioned. "It was a matter of quit or be thrown out and I quit. I couldn't do these things they publish now, with no beginning and no end and a little incest in the middle. Of course, the ex always hates the new champ. Maybe that's where I'm wrong. It's all bein' made over, anyway. My generation gave the world the two greatest massacres of all time, the most people starved, the worst mess. Time for us to say, 'Good luck. Here's the reins.'"

AN INTERVIEW WITH JOHN DOS PASSOS

On American writers and middle age, autobiography in fiction and other matters

November 23, 1941

JOHN DOS PASSOS said that he had been particularly interested lately in what happens to American writers when they reach middle age, what it is that confuses them, what checks their careers. He shook a last drop of gin and bitters out of the ounce-and-a-half measure onto the ice in his drinking glass. "No, I don't know the answers. I just wonder about it." Did he think that a possible cause might be a tendency to form such close attachments, to become so closely entwined in the lives of others, that detachment was lost, that the imagination was too much caught up in complicated relationships? The more formalized relationships of the Europeans probably helped European writers to avoid this.

"Yes, there is a possibility that that is so. The cool detachment of a young writer—well, that's hard to keep into middle age. And then I wonder if that curious anarchism that is possible here once a man gets on top doesn't cut a man off from life, from his material.

"The Sunday-supplement heroes—no, that's dated—the gossip-column heroes—they seem to have a hard time avoiding a tendency to become a little like movie stars going in ermine to premieres, living up to press notices. And that cuts them off.

"Of course, in Scott's case," he continued, referring to F. Scott

Fitzgerald, "the notices weren't important. Neither was the alcohol. He could do without alcohol and did. It was something else that held him up for so long. What? I don't know. More than any one else I know he lived to write. Nothing meant much to him except in how it might be translated into words. A taste, a meal, a view was nothing in itself; it became important only in what he might make of it in words. He had so much talent that even when he announced that he was writing a potboiler and tried to write a potboiler the talent came through unmistakably. Yet there was something blocking him that he couldn't get around."

He mentioned possible blocks that were in the way of other writers who now are well known. Stage center, he suggested, has been rather too much for several of them. What about his own case?

"Well, I'm working on a novel, making fairly good progress. But all this talk about puberty being so hard on kids. Puberty isn't in it with middle age, not by a damned sight. I took a long time out from fiction to dig into history for my last book. Now I've come back to fiction and it seems to be going along all right. Of course, just lately, the last few weeks, I've been traveling more than writing. I made a fast trip to London for the P. E. N. Congress and then there were a lot of details here."

With no taste for the spotlight he makes quick trips to localities that seem to promise material for fiction. His writings have proved that he has a singularly unerring instinct for the important men and developments of a time. Where did he find the best hunting these days?

"In Washington when you go out for an evening you have a better chance of running into a good story, a man who is doing something that is new and interesting and really important, than you have in New York just now."

Spending most of the year at Provincetown, he said that when well into a story he usually writes five or six hours a day. This is at one sitting, from about nine in the morning until two or later in the afternoon. The amount of work accomplished varies with each day—"there is no average that I've ever estimated." In Summer he spends the afternoons sailing or gardening. He finds that he is fairly successful at putting the work out of his mind when he leaves his desk. His eyes have been in bad shape for years but he finds that they give him less trouble if he reads without glasses, even though this necessitates holding print very close to his eyes. "I was pretty worried about them for a time, but now I guess that my eyes will last about as long as I last." He tries to limit the use of glasses to occasions when he is driving or walking.

His books have been given the greatest praise, but rarely have had large sales. How has he escaped the temptation of trying to write for money?

"I haven't escaped it. I once tried to write a murder mystery but it was no go. I couldn't handle it at all. But I haven't tried to do much writing for money because the way I do write is the only way I can write.

"You see, though, of course, I am a professional writer, the realization that I'm a professional has come very slowly to me. In the beginning I meant to be an architect. I wrote my first novels in the belief that as soon as I found the time I'd go into architectural work. The illusion that I was about to become an architect stayed with me a long time. And even now—even now I'm sort of looking forward to becoming a farmer. But, of course, before doing much about farming I have this novel to finish and then I suppose there'll be another."

He denied that his novels have contained any considerable amount of direct autobiography, "though, on the other hand, autobiography certainly is all mixed in. There is a part of me in every character, naturally. That's why novelists rarely write good autobiographies. You start one and it becomes another novel—bound to. No, I make very little use of other people, directly. It is like those museum skeletons that are built up from a knuckle bone, something like that, reconstructed from a part. Walking around London, for example, during the blackout you hear a few words, a part of a conversation, and in them you may find a situation or a character. But it is all building up, reconstruction.

"Naturally, when I write of a childhood, that is autobiography to a large extent. There's no getting away from it. You can be a part of many other adults, but you've only yourself to remember when you write of a child."

A TALK WITH MARJORIE KINNAN RAWLINGS

The author of "The Yearling" discusses her way of life and methods of work

November 30, 1941

"WRITING," SAID Marjorie Kinnan Rawlings, "is agony. I stay at my typewriter for eight hours every day when I'm working and keep as free as possible from all distractions for the rest of the day. I aim to do six pages a day but I'm satisfied with three. Often there are only a few lines to show."

"Is it worth such complete dedication?"

"I'm sure it is. Without the work I'd be a tangle of frustrations. An ivory tower," she continued, "is impossible now. The news is always with you wherever you go. But physical isolation has its uses." She lives in a cottage on a sand dune about ten miles south of St. Augustine, breaks the routine of work by occasional drives into St. Augustine to see a motion picture. "Della and I drive in, with the dog in the back seat. Della, my maid, is a graduate of Bethune College at Daytona. She doesn't mind the loneliness as long as there is enough around the house for her to read. I'm holding out a set of Proust for the long Summer afternoons."

Mrs. Rawlings does most of her work during the Summer because there are fewer interruptions during that season. "Writing as I do, out of emotion rather than through a mental process, I find that I can make progress only if I keep living with my characters and let nothing come between." She lets the new issues of two magazines, *Nature*, published by the Museum of Natural

History, and the *Atlantic,* break into her working hours. But even in the evenings, during her months of writing, she reads no fiction. "I am avid for biography, history and essays." When not actively writing on something she reads new novels and returns to the backlog of her library only to reread Hemingway, "John Brown's Body" by Stephen Vincent Benét, and Proust.

In most of her writing Mrs. Rawlings "makes with the heart," but she discovered a year or so ago that she possessed a hitherto unsuspected talent for high comedy. Her rather searing short story, "The Pelican's Shadow," was published by *The New Yorker* and has already been reprinted in anthologies. There is no more sweetness in this tale than there is in the bulk of the work of Sally Benson or Dawn Powell. She said that she was delighted to discover that she could do that kind of thing and intended to do more.

She spoke of the helpfulness of her Florida neighbors. "When I was planning 'The Yearling' I needed some good bear-hunting scenes because I knew that they were to be part of the book. I told the old guide why I wanted to go on bear hunts and he took me out on a number of hunts and told me all the facts he could think of. All the people down there are very good in that way. They realize that they are helping to preserve a way of life that is passing, helping to make records of what they have learned and what their ancestors knew."

It was suggested that one fortunate aspect of this was that she was dealing with people who had no intention of writing books themselves and so had no reason to hold back.

"No, you're wrong. Many of them do intend to write books. They come to me and ask me to collaborate with them. I'm to do the writing but it will be their story."

Born in Washington, Mrs. Rawlings worked on newspapers in many cities as a reporter and feature writer. She mentioned employment on a Hearst newspaper as a sob-sister and commented that it was "a rough school, but I wouldn't have missed it. So long as you can avoid the stereotyped pattern you learn a lot when you must put down what people said and how they acted in great crises in their lives. And it teaches you objectivity." Continually while she supported herself through newspaper work she attempted to write fiction for the magazines.

"I tried to write what I thought they would be most likely to buy and all that brought me was rejection slips. Then in 1928 I had an opportunity to buy an orange grove in Florida and I bought it, left the newspaper and settled down to give all my time to fiction. Still the stories didn't sell so I gave up. I thought the best thing might be to write poetry—that would satisfy the urge to create and would bother no one. I wouldn't have to worry much about getting it published as there'd be very little chance of that and I could rule writing out as a means of income.

"But then I thought—just one more. And I wrote a story that seemed very far from 'commercial,' that—it seemed to me—no editor would want to buy, but that had meaning for me. It sold like a shot and I've had no trouble about selling since, though I never have tried to write 'commercially.'"

Perhaps because of her long efforts to give editors what they presumably wanted, every line continues to come hard. "I have no free swing in what I write, no little miracles. I let my novels mature for several years, know almost exactly what I want to do in them and slowly do it. I make the first draft as perfect as I can and do comparatively little rewriting because what I toilsomely put on paper is the best that I can do. For me there is no improving it. The phrase, the line, the paragraph—they never are quite right, as it seems to me, but I keep plugging, getting them as near right as is possible for me. Every thought, every description, every bit of dialogue, is as compressed, as tight, as I can fashion it. It is all self-conscious and perhaps that is wrong, but it is the only method that I can use."

AN INTERVIEW WITH GEORGE R. STEWART

Few novels have been more minutely planned than was "Storm"

December 14, 1941

FEW NOVELS HAVE been so minutely planned as was "Storm" by George R. Stewart. The notes are most efficiently compressed but they make a sizable bundle.

Mr. Stewart said that the idea for "Storm" came to him in 1938 when he was at Cuernavaca, Mexico, on sabbatical leave from the English Department of the University of California. "I was just completing a novel and naturally I was very open to a fresh subject. A storm hit California and the local papers considered it of so much importance that they ran quite extensive accounts. Reading these accounts, in a foreign country, a foreign language, the storm took on a special interest for me. I thought of using a storm such as that one as the main character in a novel.

"You said in your review that 'Storm' would hardly set a new style in fiction but that it might provide a new pattern for nonfiction. All I have to say is, I'd like to see some one use that pattern in nonfiction. It could be done with a storm because there you have a natural plot—the biographical plot which is about as sound as a plot can be. First the static situation, then disturbance, then disturbance passes. I had the birth of a storm, its growth to maturity, it even reproduces—another storm develops, you may remember—its strength in maturity and its death. How many subjects for nonfiction would be suitable for a soundly plotted book in 'Storm's' pattern?"

A grasshopper plague, he later agreed, might be a suitable subject, but if the procedure used for "Storm" is followed, the book is still some years off. Before starting to write, Mr. Stewart figured out what his scenes would be and what works of man and nature in those scenes would be most vulnerable to attack by a storm. Then he walked the scenes with a camera and made photographs of switches and transformers, switch poles, outdoor telephones, waterworks and so on. A sheet of his notes contains, as an example, three photographs of electrical equipment and pasted up with these are two larger photographs of reports of power trouble written by the repair men who went out on the job and took care of it.

A sample report that later was used in the novel:

"At 1:20 P.M. the Southern Pacific Co. reported that the electricity was off at Emigrant Gap. Upon investigating it was found that 2 fuses on the 2 KV and 2 fuses on the 11 KV were broken. The fuses were caused to be broken from snow and ice thrown against them from the S. P. Co.'s snowplow. This accident happened on the transformer pole at Emigrant Gap where the 11 KV is cut to 2 KV for S. P. Co. use. The fuses were replaced and service restored at 3:30 P.M. Jan. 15."

One series of episodes for the book was taken complete from a page in *The California Highway Patrolman,* a periodical. A man and wife had driven from Nevada to San Francisco to the East-West football game on New Year's Day, had started home after the game but had not reached there. Searchers found their automobile almost hidden in deep snow in one of the deep ravines below Donner Summit. According to the story in the magazine the bodies were at some distance from the car and were found because coyote tracks were noticeable in the snow above them.

"I learned that coyote tracks had had nothing to do with finding them. But I used it anyway because it seemed a good touch."

This story of death below the pass is woven through the book and like the other threads of interest, was timed to fit into a tight time schedule. Mr. Stewart fashioned a chart with a column for each day of the storm and noted down each part of a series of episodes that he would use on each day and the information that he would offer the reader.

To gather his material he went out into a flood and made photographs showing the water markers, the construction of the weirs, workers piling sandbags, uprooted trees, a flooded by-pass, a swollen river, a flooded farm. He made up complete schedules for two airports, with times for arrival and departure for planes from and for Los Angeles and Seattle. He talked with a ship captain on a river line. A sample note from this interview:

"Fog. Heavy fog is bad but the boats run anyway. From S. F. to Sacto [Sacramento] a captain must steer about 150 courses. In a fog he does this by time and sound. He steers a compass course for so many minutes; then gets an echo by sounding his horn. Then he knows it is time to turn to a new compass course. Allowance has to be made for current, tide and wind conditions. Worse coming downstream because boat cannot be stopped easily.

"But in general weather makes very little difference. Except that it makes it harder to load and unload in the rain."

He made several visits to the Weather Bureau and set down his impressions of the place and how the work was done. "The worker putting marks on map with deft strokes. Seldom an error in spite of rapid work. Ink eradicator used. He now and then senses an error in the radio report."

"I knew ridiculously little about meteorology when I started." Before his preparations were finished he had drawn complete meteorological maps for every day of the storm and they were checked "and not found wanting."

"Were there any slips, any mistakes in the factual matter in 'Storm'?"

"One scientist told me that I was wrong in associating thunder with the advance of the cold front from Canada. But another weatherman said that he himself had heard thunder under the conditions I described. Otherwise I haven't been accused of a slip."

He asked the power company, the airplane company, the telephone company and representatives of other outfits from which he had received information to have his manuscript read for inaccuracies. A few suggestions were made such as: "Reference to money may be misleading; 'service' is of paramount importance to all employes at all times." And when, in the manuscript, a telephone repairman drives along a road thinking about a girl the committee wanted that changed. "Manner of driving implies careless habits. Suggest revision to reflect careful driving as a matter of habit, still thinking about girl." The committee was perhaps most troubled by the tragic death of an imaginary telephone repairman in the performance of his duties, it being felt that death was rather out of place.

Nevertheless, the checking was helpful. Comments such as: "Statement, 'ready to keep them working at risk of his life' is not typical of company policy. Employes' welfare and safety come first; employes have been known to risk life to save life" were followed by the more concrete remarks: "The pole was probably pine or fir, not spruce," and in relation to the speed of telephone communication, "Change to 'sound travels in about one-tenth of a second the 3,000 miles.'"

Mr. Stewart's next book will be a history of place names in the United States. At present he is touring the South digging into local history.

AN INTERVIEW WITH IRVING BACHELLER

The dean of our practicing novelists looks back over his long career

December 21, 1941

IRVING BACHELLER is the author of "Eben Holden," which sold more than a million copies a long generation ago. His also was one of the most popular books about Lincoln, "A Man for the Ages." This and his "The Light in the Clearing" are, in his opinion, his best books. But in any accounting of his work his newest novel, "The Winds of God," recently published, is not to be neglected. Of the main character in this novel—a frustrated backwoodsman—Mr. Bacheller says with wonder and amazement that have endured for sixty years, "that man, but for God's grace, is myself."

Wide-shouldered, his big head well covered with white hair, he sat reading his mail, without glasses, before a savorily odorous open fire in the library of the Century Association. Now eighty-two years old, Mr. Bacheller must be just about the dean of producing American novelists. He talks of his age, probably because he believes that this topic is expected of him. "Perhaps you don't care to mention my new novel."

"Why in the world not?"

"I believe that when a man as old as I am writes a book literary editors must advise their reviewers to treat the old fellow gently but not commit themselves. I presume that they can hardly expect a vital contribution. But if you are interested in a story, perhaps I can tell you one connected with 'Winds of God' that you may like. First, though please join me in a cocktail."

His scotch and soda was followed by a lunch of flapjacks and honey. "I like scotch at lunch. At dinnertime I prefer gin."

He was leaving, he said, the next day for Florida where he and Mrs. Bacheller spend their winters at their home in Winter Park. When the weather is right he plays golf with a friend who is slightly his senior. "We do the first nine holes in about forty strokes on some days, not every day. On the second nine we don't do as well, but that doesn't lessen our cheer at the nineteenth hole." He occasionally visited the late John D. Rockefeller during the Florida winters, he said. "Mr. Rockefeller was about ninety-four. I found him a merry-hearted old boy. He loved a good joke and would double up with laughter. I once saw him throw his legs playfully over the head of a young great-grandchild. 'I suppose you leave the business to others?' I asked. 'No,' he answered, 'but I drive with a long rein.'"

"Did you know him because he liked your books?"

"I don't know. He wasn't the kind of man who volunteered things of that sort. He was a brilliant man. If he had read the books, I presume he would have found much to criticize."

During lunch Mr. Bacheller sketched his writing career. "I was the son of a pioneer born in a log house in St. Lawrence County, N. Y., at the edge of the great Adirondack wilderness. Darwin's 'Origin of Species' and myself appeared at about the same time. I knew the taste of liquor and of tobacco before I was twenty and I knew the woods—I was an expert shot, an excellent canoeman. I might have been a guide and timber cutter, the two occupations that paid best in that neighborhood. Three dollars cash a day was the wage of a guide.

"But I seemed to have a tubercular tendency—and it was my mother's strong wish that I go to college. I went to a man and asked him what I must do about my lungs. He told me that my great requirement was oxygen in large quantities, that I must learn to breathe very deeply for five minutes each day and very deeply and rapidly for three minutes each day. I took that treatment as prescribed until my chest expansion equaled that of John L. Sullivan. Now I breathe deeply when I think of it.

"After college there in the Adirondack country I came to New

York and won a newspaper job by writing a piece of light verse about the country people who blew out the gas in their hotel rooms and died in their beds. This accident had occurred twice during my first week in New York. The editor asked me what salary I wanted. I answered nervously that I would work for $10 a week. "I wouldn't hire a man worth less $25," said the editor but he hired me. Two years later, when I was dramatic editor of the Brooklyn *Daily Times,* Sir Henry Irving introduced me to an English novelist. The novelist suggested that I might be able to arrange for American newspaper publication of a manuscript he had, and out of that grew the first American newspaper syndicate, for I did place his book. He shared with me generously and soon I was selling each week enough material to fill the old *Century Magazine.*"

When he had acquired $40,000—as he promptly did—he sold his syndicate and gave the money to a millionaire who guaranteed certain investments. The millionaire dropped dead soon after that and Mr. Bacheller never saw his $40,000 again, but meanwhile he had started work on a novel, a tale of the Adirondack country. When this novel was about one-third finished the late Joseph Pulitzer offered him a place as Sunday editor of the New York *World* after being impressed by an honest answer Mr. Bacheller had given him one day at lunch.

"What do you think of our editorials?" Mr. Pulitzer had asked.

"I never read them," said Mr. Bacheller. Mr. Pulitzer banged the table.

"By God, gentlemen," he said to his other guests, "I like that kind of talk!"

But Mrs. Bacheller was determined that her husband should finish the novel. She sent the part that he had completed to a publisher. "It was not great art but it had humor and people." The publisher proposed a healthy advance, Mr. Bacheller retired from the *World* and completed "Eben Holden." That book was extremely popular as were many of those that came after it.

Mr. Bacheller devoured the third flapjack, lighted a cigar and led the way back to the library. He talked for a time of the changes that have come over New York since he came here as a young man. He named the ministers who had filled the main pulpits during his first years here and the great actors.

"It seemed to me that both the pulpits and the stage went into decline as enormous fortunes were piled up.

"Certainly I have no prejudice against wealth. But when I hear talk of social ills I remember some customs in the Adirondacks when I was a boy. If a man was sick, Tom Peters came to sit with him until midnight and gave him his medicine, and from midnight on Joe Smith took over. It was expected. The family needed rest. That kind of thing became too rare when wealth and fashion came—sometimes I think wealth crowded out more values than it gave.

"But I was intending to tell you of the new book. The main character is an Adirondack guide with a rough tongue and all the bad habits. In off seasons he is a scholar. He is rowdy when the hunters come because they like to hire colorful characters and because he had married at sixteen and had a family to support.

"The point of that is that I was so nearly that guide. When I was sixteen I wanted to marry; the girl wanted to marry me. If I had married we'd have had six or eight children and the hard life of the woods would have been all that I'd have known. I'd be dead."

"You've thought of that a lot during the sixty-six years?"

"Of course I have," said Mr. Bacheller, emphatically. "The longer I live the better I realize how closely we misstep how many perils. Married at sixteen! I'd be dead!"

AN INTERVIEW WITH GEORGE JEAN NATHAN

He tells of old days on the "Smart Set" with Mencken

February 1, 1942

A BEAUTIFUL WOMAN turned to nod good-bye. "There's a fine girl," said George Jean Nathan. "Do you know her? She was the great love of So-and-so's later life. Made all his funeral arrangements. . . ." He seemed to find it difficult to talk about himself. Conversation idled pleasantly through the romantic attachments of prominent novelists; the physical disrepair that is apt to result from too much sitting on cushions—"The rowing coach at Cornell was my diagnostician. 'Throw away that cushion you have on your chair; sit on the hard wood,' he told me"; the quality of Scotch whisky—"What do you mean, have I tried Scotch lately? I was up until four o'clock this morning, and then I couldn't sleep. Yes, I've tried Scotch, and if you think it's been weakened you're wrong"; the possible marital intentions of a playwright; the financial expectancies of a luncheon neighbor; the salary that So-and-so made on his last job and what he is getting now.

"Ring Lardner told me that one of his great desires was to be a football coach. You know, he could drink a lot without its having much effect, and when he'd finish a highball he wouldn't let the waiter take the glass away. He'd string the glasses in front of him and then push them around in formations. I once asked him why he kept the glasses, and he told me that he had always wanted to be a football coach and used the empty glasses to work out power plays.

"But you want something about me, don't you? . . . A funny thing about Dreiser. One time when Menck and I were running the old *Smart Set* we said—as a joke, you know—'Dreiser, all you do is write about brakemen's daughters and laundry girls. Why don't you do us a society piece, a story with fashionable people in it?' He agreed. A few weeks later he came in with his version of a real society yarn. A novelette. It was about a Midwest traction magnate named Diamondberger—and there was one scene that I'll never forget: Diamondberger's daughter, the heroine of the piece, slowly descending a staircase. She was dressed in 'shimmering green satin.' We printed it. No, I don't believe that he was turning the tables on us. It was his idea of upper-crust . . .

"But you want something about me. . . . Do you know the geography of this place?" The place was the bar of the Twenty-one Club. "In this corner the magazine crowd gathers—it saves a lot of letter writing to meet editors here in the afternoon and talk ideas over a drink. In the corner over there some of the playwrights get together—Bob Sherwood, some of the others. Down there is a kind of doghouse for the *PM* crowd. . . . Now, about me . . . I was born in Fort Wayne, Ind.—my father was French—he owned coffee plantations near Bahia in Brazil and vineyards in France. My name—my father's name—was Naret. I went to Cornell because all the boys from our neighborhood were going to Cornell that year—Ithaca's a beautiful place, one of the most beautiful campuses in the world, probably the most beautiful. I stayed with Red Lewis for a week-end last year in that house he took for a short time in the Berkshires. He was too lonely, he had to give it up, but when I was there he took me around in the big new car he had bought to go with the house and he showed me what he said was the most beautiful town in the world—Litchfield, Conn. Do you know it? Yes, I think Red was right. It is the most beautiful town in the world. . . .

"About me . . . after Cornell I went to the University of Bologna for a year. Then came to New York, where my uncle, Charles Frederic Nirdlinger, had pull with William C. Reick, who was then boss of the *Herald*. Reick gave me a job but he treated me like a rat; that is, no matter how many stories I covered or how well the work went he wouldn't raise me above fifteen dollars a week.

"I've always been a snob about food and wine—will you have wine? No, I don't want any, either. I don't know how things happen, things like last night. Ordinarily I like to be in bed at a reasonable hour. Once in a while my friends of the Drama Critics Circle drop in—You haven't seen my place lately, have you? It is more crowded than ever. The books on the chairs reach almost to the ceiling and there are cases of liquor stacked all over the place. Anyway, that gang drops in—the entire gang—and they not only drink my brandy, they complain about its quality. With every glass a complaint.

"Anyway, there I was on fifteen a week and wanting the best. It was hard to manage. After two years as a reporter the *Herald* offered to send me to London—they had a good-sized bureau over there. But the salary was still to be fifteen a week. Just at this time I met a friend on the street. He offered me a job—that was all there was to it. You walk down a certain street at a certain time and meet a man, and there's your start. *Smart Set* brought Menck and myself together—the day we were hired we went to the Beaux Arts Bar and drank and told one another how lousy the magazine was. We were very critical then—and in agreement on the great changes we'd make, Menck in books and myself in the theatre. That was in 1908, when I was two years out of Bologna."

A project that pleases him at present is that of digging through the old files of *Smart Set* and other magazines of the period of his editorship of *Smart Set*, and discovering the love stories that he liked when they were new and still likes but that have been forgotten. He mentioned "Little Girl," by Lee Pape, a story of a soldier who asks a flower girl for a kiss. "She kisses him, the boat with the soldier on it pulls away from the wharf, and one of the soldier's friends says, 'Aw, she kisses every one.' Does it sound good? Another I want to use is one called 'Without End,' by

Edwin LeFévre, and a story of some French sailors and their effect on lovers in the next room. That was written by Lilith Benda. I can't recall the title."

Mr. Nathan has written almost as many books on the theatre as there are theatres in New York—the books are, in the main, collections or reworkings of material that he has contributed to magazines as a critic. He said that he likes "the editorial jobs."

"I can't write in the morning, so I spend most of my mornings reading. I write from one to about four—usually have an engagement in the late afternoon, and after that the theatre."

Richard Watts, a fellow member of the Drama Critics Circle, crossed the room and stopped for a moment at Mr. Nathan's table.

"What do you hear of the play for tomorrow night?" Mr. Nathan asked him, referring to Samson Raphaelson's "Jason." "Is it about me?"

"Why should it be about you?" asked Mr. Watts. "A young playwright steals the wife of a critic—is that you?"

"Then what happens?"

"The wife goes back to the critic."

"I guess it couldn't be about me," said Mr. Nathan, a modest bachelor. "I'm afraid I'd never get her back."

AN INTERVIEW WITH EDGAR LEE MASTERS

The author of "Spoon River Anthology" evaluates other modern poets

February 15, 1942

"REMEMBER THIS," said Edgar Lee Masters, prodding busily at his teeth with the butt end of a match. "I don't want to be tied up with any one, with any group. As a writer I have no relationships."

In other words, he was not to be included in a "Chicago school," or a "revolt-from-the-village" group. His judgments are severe. Chicago was a desert so far as literary life was concerned when he lived there and when he left there, he said. He pictures "the amateurs" eating the virtue out of the magazine *Poetry,* like a grasshopper plague. The old Press Club was a hangout for "drunks, gamblers and amateurs who wrote sentimental ballads." As for his contemporaries and near-contemporaries, "Dreiser has depth and in 'Sister Carrie' he knew his people. He knew what he was writing about. I like 'Jennie Gerhardt' almost as well. I am sorry to say that I have not been able to share the general enthusiasm for 'An American Tragedy.'" Sinclair Lewis is "a wonderful mimic," but to Mr. Masters it seems very doubtful that his novels will long endure.

Mr. Masters walks very slowly and erectly. He wore a blue suit that, it is reasonable to believe, some tailor considers a masterpiece. The suit shows off good shoulders and a trim waist. His face is ruddy, with a combative expression, but it is as though the combativeness were an old habit that has been broken, for his tone is mild and his manner, though impersonal, essentially friendly. He is now in his early seventies, and when he comments that he "has always been vigorous" the statement is easy to believe. Looking about Cavanaugh's, the old West Twenty-third Street restaurant, before ordering lunch, he remarked that the food was good but that the attitude of the management did not suit him. "It is a Tammany kind of place. On New Year's Eve I had reserved a table and I brought my lady here. She is temperamental, spirited. Our table had not been held for us and the management gave us very little satisfaction. Everything seemed to go wrong, so we moved on to have our bottle in another place." He ordered rye with his lunch, explaining that Bourbon, which formerly had pleased him, no longer "seemed to have much in it."

"Are there any modern poets who interest you, Mr. Masters?"

"No."

"You spoke of Stephen Vincent Benét—"

"Mr. Benét writes folk tales very well. I am sorry that I do not find his 'John Brown's Body' worth reading. I do not consider that Brown was the sort of man who should be celebrated."

As for other modern poets, Mr. Masters continued, they are worthless and he cannot make anything out of them at all.

"They have no principles, no individuality, no moral code and no roots." They are air plants, he went on, using the technical name for air plants.

"What are your roots?"

"The American of Jefferson—of Jeffersonian democracy. I date back a long time. I believe in an America that is not imitative, that stands alone, that is strong, that leans on nothing outside itself and permits nothing to lean on it. I date back. I have a number of Revolutionary ancestors. Israel Putnam was a collateral ancestor of mine—in my mother's family. And a soldier of the Revolution who was born in Virginia and died in Tennessee was my grandfather. Hilary Masters—I once saw his grave."

"Your grandfather?"

"No, certainly not. My grandfather's grandfather. But that was his name—Hilary."

Bitterly opposed to the "Lincoln myth," and arguing that Lincoln was hypocritical, slow-witted, vindictive and cold, Mr. Masters is convinced, at the same time that he believes in America standing alone, that "Americans are provincial." On the other hand, "I am a Hellenist." Every two or three years until recently he read all of the great Greek plays. "The great marvel of the world is Greek civilization. They thought in universals, as did the Elizabethans. We are provincial in our thoughts.

"Some one should write an article on America's Cinderella complex and the many men it has destroyed. The man in the country dreaming of being the guest of honor at a city banquet. The Cinderella complex—the destroyer of virility, of sound workmanship and honest thought. William Dean Howells—do many people think of him now?"

"Probably not very often."

"He had that Cinderella complex. So did Hamlin Garland. They wanted to associate with bankers, the rich and influential."

"And Mark Twain?"

"Badly. He had it badly. Spoiled him for me."

"Weren't you flattered when, after 'Spoon River,' so many people came from New York, and even England, to see you?"

"No, I think not."

"Spoon River Anthology" was not, in Mr. Masters' opinion, his best book. He prefers his "Domesday Book," which appeared in 1920. "But I am aware that the majority of readers do not agree with me."

He said at first that there had been nothing unusual about the conditions of his life when he wrote "Spoon River Anthology," but after a number of questions he told the story of that year, 1914, when, a lawyer in Chicago, he wrote "Spoon River," and published it anonymously in *Reedy's Mirror*.

"In April, 1914, I went into court on perhaps the toughest law case I ever had. I was on the side of a union of underpaid waitresses there in Chicago."

"Did you take the case because of interest in its sociological side?"

"I was very much interested in that side of it. I no longer would be."

"You feel that economics . . . ?"

"Don't mean anything. These strikes today don't mean anything. . . . Almost every day during that year I was in court, and doing a full job. For a time it was as though I was living two lives. The life in the courts and the life in the poems, for at that same time I was writing from seven to ten poems each week—the "Spoon River" poems—and sending them to Bill Reedy. I published them anonymously because I knew that if it got out that I was the author my law business would be destroyed.

"I wrote the poems on menu cards, on the backs of letters, at home, in my law office—anywhere and everywhere. Later I was offered $5,000 for the manuscript of 'Spoon River,' but a man doesn't keep menu cards. The manuscript was thrown away.

"All through that Summer and Fall I carried on the two lives and felt, after a time, that I was outside the world. Oh, I had vigor; I never was better in court; never felt better. But sometimes I'd look about the court and everything was there in plain sight, yet I'd feel that I wasn't part of it. One day in January that feeling was very strong. The next day I was at home reading Goethe's 'Faust,' sitting in front of a blazing fire, but I felt cold. I took my temperature. It was 102. I had pneumonia and if my nurse, my wonderful nurse, Bertha Baum, who fought for my life like a rat fighting a cat, hadn't pulled me through I'd have died then. But the poems were finished."

"And the case?"

"It was a dog fall. Can't say we won and can't say we lost."

Meanwhile Reedy had made a trip to Chicago to ask him to acknowledge authorship of the poems. Mr. Masters agreed and "Bill came out with a great blast for them and for me, and your New York *Times* with another great blast. People from everywhere came to see me."

"Did it ruin your law business?"

"I had my most profitable case after that, but the business was ruined. Utterly."

He gave up the law and left Chicago. He has spent most of his time here for many years and has written a great many books. He continues to write poems every day. He has, he said, hundreds of unpublished poems.

AN INTERVIEW WITH ELLIOT PAUL

Novelist and co-founder of "Transition" discusses movie scripts vs. writing

March 1, 1942

Elliot Paul, author of a number of novels but perhaps best known for his "The Life and Death of a Spanish Town" and for his detective stories that some people like very much and that other people dislike in a thorough and wholehearted way, said that when writing he was ready to sacrifice anything for spontaneity.

"When you write rapidly you write in your own style. There is no good in trying for style by rewriting, by torturing sentences. You knock the life out of it and probably out of your ideas."

He said in effect that persons who have not overcome the effects of education are pretty sure to be handicapped as stylists. The years of daily themes, of "correct" papers, hardly lead to originality or to any natural expression.

"And another thing—this note-taking. Your memory retains what is useful to you. When you make notes you remember only the notes. And when you start writing, the notes aren't enough; most of what you have seen and heard has disappeared.

"Making mental notes—this business of looking around when you are in the midst of what seems to be 'material' and thinking of phrases, doesn't work out. You can't get full value out of material by 'observing.' If you try that, you shut a lot out that is part of the story."

Mr. Paul is one of the easiest men to talk to. Most exceptionally responsive people are likely to keep their companions on edge. One is conscious of a strong tendency to try to provide them with something worth responding to. Mr. Paul shows no alert eagerness to be amusing or amused. His manner is deeply polite, entirely tranquil, and at the same time seems to reflect curiosity and interest.

He remarked that he could think of no first-rate writer who had not done most of his writing rapidly and spontaneously. The manuscripts of Tolstoy and Dickens were clean, swiftly written. He agreed with Mark Van Doren's observation that if Shakespeare's lines had been solved problems, Shakespeare would have had time for hardly one play in his entire life, that the great plays could not have been written in any other way than naturally, easily.

"How about Balzac and Flaubert?"

He was inclined to believe, he said, that in neither case had the struggles for the right word been so pressing as the authors liked to make out.

"In France a man who becomes in any degree public—and even those who do not—decides what part of himself he will open to the public, what picture of himself he will provide for those who may be interested in him but in whom he is not interested. He may exaggerate tendencies so that his public picture will be clear, easy to understand and easy to remember.

"Here we try to give out, to be natural with acquaintances as well as friends, and are affronted by formality, with the consequence that—well, leaving a cocktail party, as an example, we usually are dissatisfied because we've tried to go all out with every one and every one has gone all out with us but the conditions were such that the naturalness was affected. We don't like or understand the public face; the French do. They grade the view of themselves that they offer, one view for their intimates, another for good friends, and so on."

Here on a brief vacation from the movies and staying at the Hotel Lafayette, "I feel that I need a passport to go above Fourteenth Street."

He answered the inevitable question of how he liked Hollywood by saying that he lived almost precisely the same life there that he had lived in Spain.

"I know a great many people who live and work in my neighborhood—extras, grocery-store keepers, fishermen. I see very little of the big-shots."

He said that he had attained what he hopes is a valuable reputation for eccentricity by refusing to argue about the scripts that he turns out, or worry about them, or use high-pressure methods to sell them.

"I write the best script that I can manage—it is a fascinating medium with a devil of a lot about it that you can't possibly learn except by experience—and if the producer tells me that it is no good, I say that I'm ready to change it in any way that he likes. That's eccentric. But it's the only way I could do it. I can't use that trick that is so popular there—the author thinks out the scene about two weeks ahead of the conference but when he is asked what he will do with the scene he says that he doesn't know. No one else knows, of course, but they all have a shot at it, and talk, and get nowhere. Then when he thinks that the time is right the author suddenly leaps up, clenches his fist, pounds the producer's desk and shouts that he's got it. Every one listens. If he'd said in the first place that he had the answer, they wouldn't have heard him. But when he pounds the desk and shouts—then it's drama. Every one listens, every one is relieved to hear a solution, and the author is considered a good and valuable man. The producer is happy because he has had a part in creation. I can't put on such shows so that makes me a little different, which probably is an advantage, too."

Born in Malden, Mass., fifty-one years ago, Mr. Paul left home after graduating from high school, worked in the West for a time with his brother Charles, a hydraulic engineer, took a newspaper job, and went to France as a private when we entered the First World War. He had become a sergeant when the war ended. Re-entering newspaper work, he spent much of his time in Paris, where he and Eugene Jolas started *Transition* in the Spring of 1927.

"Would you start *Transition* again?"

"You're thinking of the publicity—Stein and Joyce. You must admit that they were influential. We published first works by about two dozen Americans, who have since done very well, introduced all the Russians who have come up since the revolution over there and most of the French writers who have turned out well. Of course, with the world as it is now, there's no possible place for such a magazine. But individuality had its little time to sprout."

Leaving Paris, he spent five years in the little town of Santa Eulalia, on the Island of Ibiza. This is a part of the Balearic group, bordered by Spain and near Africa and Sardinia. A central location in ancient times, these islands are on trade routes.

"A large part of the world was accessible. We weren't isolated. We only felt that we were."

The life was idyllic. Mr. Paul organized an orchestra and played at weddings and pig killings. He plays the accordion and piano. He retained his habit of working in the early morning.

"Most of my life I've had a job that started at nine in the morning. The greater part of my writing has been done before nine. For two or three hours before I've spoken to any one I type rapidly.

"The whole thing is to have something that you want to say, and if it is based on a life that you've lived some time before, so that your memory has had a chance to go through it and slough off what is not important, what doesn't fit—then much of the work is done. All that remains is to put it down as naturally as you can."

AN INTERVIEW WITH LOUIS BROMFIELD

The novelist and short story writer talks of his life and his work

March 29, 1942

IN RESPONSE TO a question of whether he didn't feel hurt or perhaps doubtful when people discussing him as a writer more often mentioned his old books than his new ones, Louis Bromfield said:

"The reason for that may be that my old books continue to sell so well in reprints. They sell thousands of copies a year. . . . Oh, you mean that the reviewers speak more highly of the old novels. My critical standing. No, I don't care about that. It is now about eleven years since Willy Maugham (W. Somerset Maugham) told me—he's a good friend, an old friend, a wonderful guy—that if a writer wanted to imitate another writer, that might be all right, that it might be possible to get away with it. But that when a writer imitates himself he is through.

"That's true. There's no quicker way to become simply slick. Hugh Walpole did that and it was fatal. When you imitate yourself, you go over and over the old emotions, the old scenes, that meant something to you once, but must be artificially resurrected, to be polished, refinished, and it is all mechanical; the life isn't there any more. There's a tendency to do that so that you won't let any one down, so that your readers will continue to get from you—as nearly as you can give them—what they got before, what they expect and look for.

"But, you see, the quality that a writer needs beyond any other is independence. Your readers know what they like and want you to keep on giving it to them, your publishers know what the readers want and what you should do about it, and your agent and maybe your wife and your friends. That's the way to go to hell in a handcar. If you pay attention to other people, you are licked, because the stories are part of you, not of them. If you are not independent, you'll be spoiled because you'll try things that you haven't it in you to succeed with.

"Now, for example, my last book is a pretty rough-and-tumble tale, a melodrama, a kind of book that I've always wanted to write. It has done me good, as a writer, to do it, even if it doesn't go, even if a lot of people say that it is a failure. They don't know what I need to do. I'm the only one who knows that."

He mentioned all the hailing of genius that was performed in the press of the early 1920's.

"You probably never heard of or wouldn't remember dozens of the great names of that time—fellows who wrote one book and heard it called the great American novel and then couldn't write any more. I lived through that. I didn't fall for the publicity then and won't now. I'm too old for it, but at that, speaking of age, do you realize that Hemingway and myself are still just about the youngest steadily producing American novelists?

"And as for reviewers, look at the going-over they gave Ernest for so long. There are fashions. A couple of the big boys say that this guy is no good any more and all the little ones take up the chorus that the guy is no good. You've seen that work.

"But about me being a young novelist—at forty-five. Steinbeck? He's forty-two or so, isn't he? The same generation. The new ones don't come along for one very good reason—Hollywood. What happens, some one writes a good novel, or two perhaps, and Hollywood says, 'Come on out.' They go out, they start at $500 a week, they learn the business. Then what? About the most they can hope for is $1,500 a week and they are reworking the stuff that some one else created, and they are working for a boss, and they are, at least to a degree, dependent on the boss. While if they'd stuck to their own job they'd be making twice as much money if that's what they want, and be dependent on no one."

Mr. Bromfield once wrote a novel about a man who could turn on charm "as from a tap," and some of the reviewers threw the phrase back at him, employing it as evidence that he was talking of himself at the time. There is no doubt that he has a most likable manner, but one has no sense that it is calculated, that it is a charm that turns on and off through effort. Rather, it seems the result of perfect health, an uncommon vitality, an entire adjustment to life. It was only ten in the morning and he said that he had been out until five, ending up in a place where an entertainer named Bricktop, whom he had known in Paris, was featured in the floor show. In spite of this the meal of corned beef hash and a triple order of coffee had a festive quality to it.

About twice a season for many years chroniclers of travels in Europe usually produced a couple of paragraphs that described a week-end or a week spent with the Bromfields at their house outside Paris. Mr. Bromfield said that he always collected people at whatever house he had, that it was a habit that he had developed in Ohio, where his grandfather and his father had had the same habit before him.

"We live in Ohio now and it's just the same. We have a 600-acre farm with thirty-three people living on it all the time and there is never any shortage of guests. Now our children are growing up and they invite their crowd. But we built the house with that in mind; it's big—plenty of room to work there, or play gin rummy, or milk cows, or fool around in the garden—anything any one wants to do."

He believes that with the farm he is as secure as any one is likely to be. He runs it on a co-operative basis. He put up the capital and draws 5 per cent on it. Any profits over that are divided *pro rata* among the men who work it.

"Of course, every one pretty much lives off the place. A gardener goes to each house each morning and asks what vegetables are wanted that day—you take what you need. And the same with meats. The farm is no plaything. We don't spend money that our neighbors can't afford to spend except on experiments that may help us all, the neighbors and ourselves.

"I know a lot of people who bought stocks and bonds and have nothing to show. We spent our money as we got it, went everywhere, traveled, met all sorts of people, had a wonderful time, and have the land to show—and stories to write. The land and an ability to tell stories—it looks all right to me. They never can get rid of the storyteller, never have been able to and never will. I got checks just last week from Switzerland and Sweden for book rights. Sure, they still are signing contracts and publishing in Prague, and in Paris there's a full publishing list and some good sellers. Not in Poland. There the Nazis have really had time to go to work."

He continually travels around the country making speeches about soil and water. He said that despite the governmental efforts of the last nine years Ohio has far less rainfall than it formerly had—partly a result of deforestation—and that unless remedial measures are taken by every one concerned one-third of the industries will be forced from the State in the next twenty-five years because of water shortage.

"My job is to try to talk bankers and industrialists into doing what must be done. I'm at home only about three days a week."

"When do you write?"

"The thing is that I don't fiddle around when I do write. When I have two hours for work I write every minute of the two hours, simply because I know what I want to say before I start trying. No, I don't do much at a session. My maximum is 3,000 words of first draft. And I like to rewrite.

"This time I brought three-quarters of a short novel with me—that is, 45,000 words. I've been on that since November. So though I don't do a great deal each week, it counts up. I'm practiced enough now so that I know what I should get out of a situation; but, of course, the real stuff is what goes on when you get hot. And you get hot in your work faster and easier when you live—you know, when you keep going, when there's so much to do and think about that you haven't the time to tie yourself up in knots."

"What they mind most is the blackout. They long for lights—especially the older people. Look, when we peeled off the convoy, and got in the harbor, the people ran out and called to each other: 'Lights! Look, lights!' And the mothers held their children up and explained about lights to them. But the children weren't excited at all.

"Then, by gum, you realized suddenly that there are children of three years or so toddling round in Britain who can't remember in their lives ever having seen a lighted street. We're raising a race who don't mind darkness—they have known nothing else.

"You know, the ham actor in me wants to make a parable of that. Talking with my mouth—I'm liable to. Writing it, I'd cross the parable out and just let every one draw his own conclusion. I'd probably edit out of existence every word I've said."

AN INTERVIEW WITH GRACE ZARING STONE

The author of "Escape" and "The Cold Journey" talks of her life and work

May 3, 1942

GRACE ZARING STONE, a very spirited writer, answered a comment that her novel "Escape"—the authorship of which was so long secret—had been rather "slickly" written, which was to say as though to meet the requirements of a magazine.

"If the word 'slick' means what I think it does, that is nonsense. I don't like to read loose, loosely constructed stories or books. Naturally, I try to write the kind of book that I like to read. That is, tight, with plenty of incident, all of it going somewhere. I know that my stories can't resemble in the least the books of Virginia Woolf. And you mentioned 'Wuthering Heights.' What kind of comparison is that? 'Wuthering Heights' was the work of a genius, filled to splitting with romanticism and running wild. If Emily Brontë had had one atom less genius the book would have been a mess. Must I be called slick because I can't write as Emily Brontë did?

"There are too many people imitating genius—its way, its methods of production. This stream of consciousness they pour out—a genius may be able to do something with writing of that kind, communicate something that can be communicated no other way as clearly, as well. But who in hell wants to read the gallons of that kind of thing that come from people who have no personality worth expressing in the first place, no particular talent to express it with, who simply like to write and write in the way that calls for the least effort, characters and plot running every which way, expressing themselves? Expressing what?

"I don't try to imitate genius—naturally. Why should I? I work terribly hard to tell a story effectively and do a good, tight construction job, because I can do that much, I can be a craftsman."

Mrs. Stone is the author of a number of excellent novels, including "The Cold Journey," one of the soundest historical novels of the last decade; "The Bitter Tea of General Yen," and "The Heaven and Earth of Dona Elena"—the last, she said, a title that she finds it very embarrassing to repeat. "It was one of those fancy titles that were modish in 1929 when the book appeared. You know how titles go: a Hemingway sets the style in them for a time, then a Steinbeck comes along and perhaps changes it. This was my first novel and the title was picked by the editor. I didn't understand at the time that I had something to say about it. It seemed to me that all that Winter I was going to cocktail parties in Washington, where we then lived, and old ladies who were hard of hearing were saying, 'My dear, I am told that you have written a book. What do you call it?' And as in a bad dream I'd take a deep breath and shout—the title. Of course, they rarely got it the first time and I'd have to keep on shouting it."

She said that she had had two reasons for keeping secret her authorship of "Escape." Her daughter was living in Czechoslovakia, and Hitler had invaded that country while the novel was being written. "And my husband and I were in Paris; he was naval attaché there. It seemed a mistake for me, in these circumstances, to publish what could hardly be construed as other than an attack on a country with which we were not at war, at least under my own name. I thought of not publishing the book for these reasons. But the secret was safely kept and my daughter is now in this country."

Mrs. Stone is the great-great-granddaughter of Robert Owen, the British idealist who founded the communistic colony of New Harmony in Indiana.

"I spent most of my childhood visiting around" (her mother had died when she was born) "and in all the houses of the

Owen descendants there were many books being very thoroughly read and almost everyone kept diaries. I spent some time with an aunt, Caroline Snedeker, who wrote books that children read in enormous quantities. Diary keeping, writing in general, was just something one did.

"Then I married into the Navy and, of course, that was very, very different, because the Navy—well, doesn't express itself in diaries. But when my husband was stationed at St. Thomas in the Virgin Islands the place seemed to get me started.

"It was the time between the wars when we wanted excitement—hard to remember now, isn't it?—and I'd look forward to the hurricane season, not above hoping for a hurricane. Everything was all ready to take care of things if the hurricane struck—and the seasons passed with no hurricane. Then finally one came along and I wrote down everything that happened. The account seemed interesting and, of course, in the Navy you always can do with a little money, so I shipped it off to the *Atlantic Monthly*. They bought it. I wrote a short story. The *Atlantic* bought that and Bobbs-Merrill wrote to ask me if I had a novel in mind, by any chance, and, of course, that was a most amazing question to me, because I'd had a novel in mind practically forever, but the idea that some one might publish it—

"Since then I've spent a great deal of time writing. Of course, there are difficulties. When I'm chasing up and down a coast following my husband from port to port I can't write, and when he is on shore duty I have very little time for writing. I'm aware that these difficulties are not insuperable. But I bring them up for myself because writing is very hard work for me. When I'm doing a book I slave at it until about five in the afternoon and then go out and have myself the best time that can be arranged. That's why I like to work in New York. Always something to do after five."

The "big hump" in writing is getting started.

"I ease myself into it by simply making notes, an outline of what I'm aiming to do. This outline always is terrible, but that doesn't matter; I can throw most of it away. Then I write a first draft and that is always frightful. Another draft, which is almost as bad and so on until finally, with all its faults, the manuscript seems to be the best I can do.

"I start writing a short story with less dread because I always think that they are easier to write. In this I probably am mistaken as I don't do them very well. But, of course, now it is practically impossible to write anything. How can any writer of fiction compete with the newspapers? 'Tokyo bombed!'—that's better reading than anything else possibly could be."

AN INTERVIEW WITH JAMES T. FARRELL

A realistic novelist talks of his views on writing, and of his aims

May 17, 1942

JAMES T. FARRELL works in the living room of the apartment near Columbia where he lives with his wife and their small son, Kevin.

"Isn't it difficult to concentrate—the telephone, doorbell, visitors, the kitchen, and the baby running around at your elbow?"

"If you let conditions stop you from working," said Farrell, "they'll always stop you."

He has an owlish seriousness that is enhanced by fogged spectacles.

The baby is about as good-looking as a baby can be—curly yellow hair, deep-blue eyes—and it is a mystery outside the realm of realism that at the same time the child manages to look like his father.

Down the street and around the corner, at a place called the Gold Rail, Farrell sat over beer and answered questions about his work. He said that he works very hard and consistently but takes a long time with each book—"As much as two years for a novel." He starts at eight each morning, keeps at it intensively well into the afternoon. Formerly he could work ten and twelve hours at a stretch but such bursts of energy are less frequent now.

"Do you rewrite much?"

"All the time. I finish a draft, however bad it may be. Sometimes the first draft hardly even suggests the scenes that I can use to make my point. The second draft may have a scene or two that I want. I never work steadily at a novel, though, except when I am finishing it off. I break it up with articles, notes and short stories."

"Do you consciously keep the dialogue rather stylized?"

"I doubt that it is stylized. The dialogue of Ed Lamson in 'Ellen Rogers' was consciously formalized because Lamson spoke differently than most characters I have used—he was a ready talker. I had to accentuate his readiness of speech a little.

"In general I try to build up characteristic speech through small differentiations. For example, I don't know if you've noticed, but Jim O'Neill's speech is always common, commonplace, dull, with no imagery. His wife, Liz, speaks flamboyantly, with color, and so does her mother. Uncle Al talks like a salesman and so on."

He talked of the real people on whom many of his characters are based, of how well some have turned out and of the deaths some have died—there have been many deaths among these people—but he wanted these comments kept "off the record."

He said that "Basically and in the main part my novels so far have been a remembrance and reconstruction of what I saw and heard when I was very young. But, of course, they are not wholly that; they couldn't be. It is what you know now that gives the shape and meaning to what you remember. New impressions go in along with the memories. For example, part of a barroom scene in 'A World I Never Made'—though it was dated as taking place years ago in Chicago—was based on a conversation that I heard in a bar in Sixty-sixth Street here in New York."

"You use so much autobiographical stuff—do you consciously gather material?"

"That doesn't work for me because when I've tried it I've gone too literal and the material gets out of hand and occupies a false place. I'm too inclined to use such material in full, and whatever actually was done goes into the story though it may not have a place in it, and all that was said goes in and throws the story out of focus. Of course, I remember and utilize a phrase that sticks in my mind, or a scene that I've noted without trying to make notes. But a writer—any writer—can't be so all-inclusive as to use all life. It is a mistaken notion that the realist tries to."

"Just what are you trying to do?"

"I am working on a projected series of twenty-five volumes of fiction, of which I have completed thirteen. What I want to do is to make these works an integrated re-creation of what I've seen happen, or what I think can or might happen in American life.

"I've been consciously working at this from around 1931. By then I had more or less developed the plan and had in mind many of the books and stories that I have written since. Danny O'Neill appears in 'Studs' and Jim O'Neill in 'Gashouse McGinty.'"

It can safely be assumed that Danny O'Neill is Farrell.

"Is it true that you are writing so much of your childhood and the Chicago of that time because you hate your memories and want to get rid of them in this way?"

"It is overstating to say 'hatred.' I suppose that I am recompensing myself, but I'm not doing it out of anger, because in literature anger is a luxury that you cannot afford. Anger throws your concept of a character out of line; it destroys an honest and true depiction."

So far as honesty and truth are concerned, it is improbable that any other writer of this time has so little falseness in his work as has Farrell.

"But how about dramatic values? They seem almost entirely lacking in your books."

"My books aren't concerned with what is called dramatic values. The term is a very relative term. As a whole in modern literature there is less emphasis on dramatic value than in the nineteenth-century novels—this is not completely true but it is to a considerable extent.

"My attempt as a twentieth-century realist writer is to give an intensive and detailed report of a certain way of life, of certain characters. We don't have the same outlook on life as did the great Victorians; we don't have a panoramic view of life. We live in a period in which many perspectives are being destroyed and it is necessary for us to forge new perspectives. For me there is the perspective—socialism. But socialism never has been realized in all this world; you can't build up a complete literature in terms of that perspective. A serious writer struggles for a way of seeing life, for a perspective, for making a greater conquest of experience, of human beings.

"By conquests I mean real attempts to penetrate the mysteries of life. We are surrounded on all sides by mysteries. There are many in our own consciousness—we do not know our own beings. All serious writers unravel mysteries, creating a sense of what these mysteries mean.

"Also, literature now is profoundly influenced by science, and one effect of science on literature is this concern with the more precise realization of details. Just as science breaks up problems, attacking them in their parts, so has literature attempted to break them up. That is one reason why there are fewer broad and panoramic works of literature.

"The great Victorians, Dickens and Thackeray, wonderful novelists, focused differently on problems. They had a settled, bourgeois point of view. The apparent security of middle-class England strongly affected the writers.

"In Russia there was not that security—there was a sense of change, and Russian literature from Pushkin to the young Gorki worked in change, among the new problems and new questions posed by the introduction of capitalism into feudal Russia. General sociological and economic developments were translated into individual psychological terms and individual problems. For all cultivated people were asking themselves a whole series of questions about matters that in England seemed settled, established and done with—questions about economics, about God, about class relationships, morality, etc. One reason for the all-sidedness in Russian literature is because the Russian writers more than any other group in Russian society dealt with these questions. And by doing this they raised to the level of world literature the history of nineteenth-century Russia. Tolstoy alone made the whole world conscious of the Russian muzhik.

"Similarly here in America we are asking ourselves many questions as a result of war and the world economic crisis; all kinds of Americans are finding that similar questions are occurring in their consciousness and in the consciousness of their neighbors. This is one prerequisite for the development of an all-sided literature in this country."

He spoke of a tendency, apparent since the days of Stephen Crane, of American writers to follow their interests through descending social classes. He mentioned Dreiser and Anderson and topics they chose. "A dozen years ago writers began writing more and more of workers, racial groups that were down the scale, delicatessen storekeepers, tenant farmers. There was a sociological line going down. It is no accident that the rise of the C. I. O. and this development in literature were parallel."

"But do you ever feel that you are writing almost in a vacuum, when you know that the mass of readers come from groups that don't care much to hear about the people you want to write about?"

"Of course, I know that women who belong to ladies' clubs don't want to be told that the life of the majority of people is banal, that it is gray, that it is dreary. But Gorki told a story of Chekhov, of a gray, sad, dreary people who couldn't react against oppression, who couldn't lift a finger in their own time, and who dreamt that in three hundred years everything would be better. There passed among them, said Gorki, a wise and observant man who said in a voice beautiful and anguished: 'You live badly, my friends. It is shameful to live like that.'

"In a sense that is what realistic writers have been saying. It is more important than entertaining the women who belong to ladies' clubs."

AN INTERVIEW WITH CARL SANDBURG

The poet and biographer of Lincoln discusses himself and his work

May 31, 1942

"THE POETS SUSPECT that I may be a good biographer and the biographers believe that I may be a good poet," said Carl Sandburg in a rare moment of relaxed talk, as he finished dinner at an Automat on Sixth Avenue. Earlier he had answered a question that had been prompted by his frequent comments of "There should be a good poem" behind this or that news item. The question was: "Do you think of yourself as primarily a poet or a biographer?"

"I think that there is little in my biographical work when it approaches my best," he said, "that I could not space into free verse. But here is a better answer—that I would rather have a good photograph that had not been monkeyed with, that had clear, definite lines, than an interpretive painting by any one. And I would rather make the good photograph in words in a biographical work."

He did not continue this, but from other things that he said it seemed clear that he considered that a poet had a far better chance of supplying an exact "photograph in words" of another human being than had a member of the "tribe of historiographers"—a phrase that he uses for the professors who said that Sandburg's "Lincoln" would have been improved had he supplied more exhaustive footnotes that gave the sources of all the material that he used. He believes that there are more readers who are grateful for the comparative absence of footnotes in his "Lincoln" than there are "historiographers" who feel superior because their books have a great many footnotes.

However, he is extremely alert to any criticism, has a very thin skin for it. Though he sometimes thinks of a good phrase with which to castigate his critics and laughs, when he talks on this subject his eyes reflect no laughter and the laugh stops abruptly.

He said that his monumental "Lincoln" was, as he first planned it to be titled, "The Life of Abraham Lincoln (For Young People)."

"But when I got into the material I found that that wouldn't do, that I must go on and do a complete work."

"Why had you planned it for children in the first place?"

"So that I could give free rein to my naïveté," he said, and laughed in the same way that he had laughed when he had talked of his critics.

"Then you actually felt that you were naïve and needed the protection of being able to say that you were writing only for the young?"

He did not answer this at the time but later he said that in all his writing "I have followed almost a formula—that is, to write the books that I most wanted when I was a boy and that did not exist. That is not altogether true, but it is true of much of my work. . . . There is another need in me that does not go back to my childhood—a want to make full use of the American speech. There is not enough of it in poetry. And, yes, there's another need that I did not feel in my childhood, the need to prick a bubble here and there, to point out now and again the men who don't know as much as they think they know. That is my horse laugh at the bar."

The interview took place under unusual circumstances. Mr. Sandburg writes a weekly newspaper column that is syndicated from Chicago. He said that he was behind with his column, that he couldn't seem to get started on it at his hotel and suggested that he come over and use my typewriter. An old reporter, he said: "I think the stink of a newspaper office may help me get going."

He is a straight-standing man, now in his middle sixties. He keeps at high tension but apparently not through effort.

"Though I can't keep going as I once did. When I was younger I worked so steadily that I had time for only four or five hours' sleep each night."

I asked: "Did you drive yourself to that, keeping up a schedule of some sort?"

"Oh, no. I was interested. To lose yourself in some character or intent. That is the way to work."

He said that when he was completing "The War Years"—the second section of his "Lincoln"—"it was as though I were living in a period as taut, as exciting as this year is. Of course, that war was tremendously exciting, too. A great emotional tension. At eleven o'clock at night, when I should have been settling to sleep, I'd take a cigarette and then a drink. Another drink and another cigarette until four in the morning. I had to break that. It was new to me, for I am not a hard-liquor drinker. I suppose I was 40 years old before I had my first cocktail—a glass or two of beer in a week, that had satisfied me. For those few months only, I wanted drinks. Then it passed. Now I've given up cigarettes. For me there is no such thing as smoking in moderation."

He surrounded himself with a scattering of newspaper clippings and began slowly pecking out his column. About every ten or fifteen words he would turn in his chair and talk. I had asked him to give me some practical tips on the preparation of a biography.

"When I was writing of Lincoln I determined that it would be a mistake to use any phrase that tended to draw the reader's mind back into the present. As an example, in one draft I described Cyrus McCormick of the McCormick reaper as the Henry Ford of his day.

"It was then that the thought came to me that I was asking the reader to return to the present, picture Henry Ford and then go back again to a period when Ford did not exist. When possible, avoid making references to situations, to circumstances, that came into being after the moment concerning which you are writing."

He sorts his own voluminous notes both by subject and in chronological order.

Speaking of timing, he said that he felt that he had been fortunate in the "spacing" of the writing of his "Lincoln."

"I am glad that I wrote 'The Prairie Years' (the section dealing with the years before Lincoln became President) while I was in my forties. I was closer then to the long, long dreams of youth—I remembered growing up more clearly then than I did when I was in my fifties. And it is better that I wrote 'The War Years' in my fifties and early sixties because my judgment of men was better. I completely rewrote the notes I had set down on two members of Lincoln's Cabinet—Chase and Seward. I understood them as I had not when I was a younger man . . ."

The column went slowly. Mr. Sandburg discarded his first page and started anew. That also was slow going. He suggested a walk and we went to the Museum of Modern Art, where his brother-in-law, Lieut. Comdr. Edward Steichen, was supervising the setting up of "Road to Victory," a show of photographs. Mr. Steichen had selected the photographs and Mr. Sandburg had written the captions. It was as fine an exhibition as I have ever seen, as effective as the best drama. Dinner at an Automat followed and it was on this dinner that we came in.

AN INTERVIEW WITH EUDORA WELTY

A short story writer of exceptional talent talks of her work

June 14, 1942

EUDORA WELTY, the short-story writer, said that when she was younger she was very much interested in herself and always projected herself into her stories.

"The stories were awful. I'm from Jackson, Miss., and never had been much of anywhere else, but the action in my stories took place in Paris. They were awful. I remember the first line in one of them: 'Monsieur Boule deposited a delicate dagger in Mademoiselle's left side and departed with a poised immediacy.' This, of course, makes no sense at all. I loved the 'poised immediacy' so much that I've remembered the whole sentence.

"When I wrote the stories about Paris I thought that I was very good. I think that you're likely to believe that something you write is good so long as it is about something of which you are totally ignorant. You project yourself into some situation of which you know nothing but that pleases you.

"Then I went home and started writing about what I knew. I was older and I guess had a little more sense, enough sense so that I could see the great rift between what I wrote and what was the real thing."

"Do you ever feel, in your stories, that you have closed the rift?"

"Sometimes in the middle of a story I have the illusion that I've closed it. But never for more than a minute. Your common sense tells you that you haven't done it. When you see yourself in proportion—as you're bound to do when you get some sense—then you see how much greater what is real is than anything you can put down."

She writes easily, perfectly naturally, enjoying the job and lost in it.

"I sort of hang stories in my mind and let them hang for a long time. As an example, I have just heard that a long short story or a short novel—I don't know which it is—that I have written is to be published. It's a wrong length and I guess no one will pay much attention to it, but I enjoyed doing it. It is about the Natchez Trace, and planters' beautiful daughters and Indians and bayonets and so on are in it—and a lifetime of fairy-tale reading. Everything in it is something I've liked as long as I can remember and have just now put down."

"You write for yourself entirely, don't you, without the reader in mind at all?"

"Oh, no, I certainly never think of who is going to read it. I don't see how any one could. I don't think of myself either—at least, I don't believe I do. I just think of what it is that I'm writing. That's enough to do.

"Anyway, so long a time elapsed between the original writing of most of my stories and their publication that I lost all sense of connection between writing and print. A lot of the stories that have been published lately were written five or six years ago.

"Yes, I changed them. I revised as I recopied. I think that as you learn more about writing you learn to be direct. When you start you don't say the thing that is behind the writing—maybe you're not sure enough of how it should be said, or maybe you yourself know it so well that you don't feel that the saying is necessary, or maybe you just don't realize what it is. So you write around it.

"In some of the stories, as I retyped, I simply put the kernel, the nut, in. Now that my stories are beginning to find a market—or rather, now that I have an agent who has drummed up a small market—I don't revise as much and the stories don't hang so long. It may be that in ten years I'll wish they had never seen the light of day."

Miss Welty has written some of the most memorable short stories to appear in print during the last few years. Each story is distinct, purely individual, born of its subject and a point of view that is so wide and deeply understanding that it is as though there were no brand of one mind upon the stories. Their outstanding similarity is formed of the intensity that went into their writing. They create moods as powerful as the moods developed by good poetry.

But Miss Welty obviously finds it difficult to talk about herself and not only difficult but not interesting. She is without a public attitude.

Born and brought up in Jackson, Miss., the daughter of the head of a Southern insurance company, she studied at the University of Wisconsin and then came to New York, where she attended Columbia's School of Business, specializing in advertising writing. "I quit advertising because it was too much like sticking pins into people to make them buy things that they didn't need or really much want. And then, too, advertising is so filled with taboos—you are scared to say this thing and that thing; scared to use this page and that kind of type, and so on. What's the use of learning fears?"

Returning to Jackson, she took a variety of jobs. "I used to write everything that was said over a small-town radio station—and to keep the job wrote myself a lot of fan letters each week. At the same time I was writing society for the *Commercial Appeal* at Memphis, and then I moved into a government publicity job that let me get about the State and gave me an honorable reason to talk to people in all sorts of jobs.

"One day I was on an assignment at a fair and talked to a man who was building a booth at the fair grounds. He told me the story that I used in 'Keels, the Outcast Indian Maiden'—about a little Negro man in a carnival who was made to eat live chickens. That's the only actual story I've used. I guess if you read it you must have known that it was true and not made up—it was too horrible to make up.

"When I decided just to go ahead and write stories I no longer could meet as many people, but that doesn't seem to matter much. Why, just to write about what might happen along some little road like the Natchez Trace—which reaches so far into the past and has been the trail for so many kinds of people—is enough to keep you busy for life."

AN INTERVIEW WITH ESTHER FORBES

Who discusses some of the reasons for the contentment of historical novelists

June 28, 1942

IT HAS SEEMED TO ME that historical novelists are in general just about the happiest writers. They tell of the notebooks they have filled with solid research; mention the helpfulness of their wives; their lives seem more enclosed than the lives of most writers. Esther Forbes said that there were a number of reasons why this should be so.

"The historical novelist is like God himself," she said, "so far as knowing his people is concerned. He knows the people in his book really better than he can actually know any one in life. He knows exactly why they fall in love or can't stand being snubbed. He works from the inside out.

"And his people stay in frame. I've tried to write modern novels and I am not sure that I understand what the trouble with them is, but I think it is something like this: As soon as one attempts to transfer actual life—whether by painting, say, or fiction—to some art form, one is conscious of needing some frame about it. This is natural and easy when you are dealing with the past.

"In my book 'Paradise,' for instance, I could build a house—a village, when it comes to that—put the Parres in the house, in the village, and there they pretty well stayed. In the books, as in their lives, they stayed put. Nobody turned on the radio to tell them what was happening in China. They did not even see a newspaper. If they got tired of each other, they couldn't get much farther than out into the woods. The light was on them, I knew them and the light wasn't diffused over a world.

"Today people of that same type would be sashaying about—New York, Florida, a dude ranch or what not. They would constantly be getting out of the frame—either mentally or physically—and it would be quite a job to follow them.

"You notice how many novelists dealing with our own times use frame devices. That is why there are so many artificially limited novels—I mean, a group of people held together by a department store, a liner or even a bridge. The writer has to limit himself in some way because his imagination can't roam the whole world nor can his knowledge—so he jumps at some chance that does group certain people for him.

"Think of the endless novels about one week-end, one day, one week. On the other hand, the historical novels go on and on with the greatest of ease, and then on and on some more (those are the grandchildren of the original characters who are beginning to appear over the horizon), but these novels are held together and framed by the very simplicity of the lives with which they deal.

"When I was working on 'The General's Lady' I went down to Dedham four times to the Bartolini trial (he was an Italian who killed a Mrs. Asquith). I'd read all the accounts that I could find of murder trials here and in England at the time of the Revolution and they have wonderful records. You're too apt to get generalities in a diary. For instance, you will read that Goody So-and-so was sent to the stocks for complaining about the Reverend's sermons. In the trial record of Goody you have the words that she has said, she'd 'liefer hear a cat mew than the Reverend preach.' With that you're getting somewhere. You know how Goody talked. There are many of those straight quotes in the trial records.

"Well, I went to Dedham because I thought that I might get something from seeing a trial in action—for neither human emotions, the courtroom reactions, the expressions of people's faces can change much. But I must admit that any good movie producer can put on a better murder trial than the Commonwealth of Massachusetts. And as I listened to one expert testify after another—not understanding anything they said, and practically no one else in the place understanding, either—I was glad that in the days of my Morganna Milroy there had been no experts on ballistics or fingerprints, and no psychiatrists. A kind old clergyman was all I needed for the fundamentally unchanging humanity of such a story.

"The real reason, I suppose, that I like to write stories about the past is that human nature—which interests me the most of anything—can be seen more clearly without all these trappings of experts on this and that.

"Of course, it is not hard to lose human nature in the past, lose it under trappings. I think many writers do when they describe costumes that are not important, when they spend a lot of time telling of how this or that character stopped at a tavern and ordered sillabub. If it is important to the story, you can go into considerable detail in a modern novel about a man stopping at a Howard Johnson for a soda. But the soda usually isn't important to the story—neither is the sillabub."

"The historical novelist has his frame and unchanging human nature. The biographer (Miss Forbes' new book, 'Paul Revere,' is a biography) "must be something of a detective—which may be the reason why so few novelists write biographies. He assembles his clues, follows this scent and then another, working always from the outside in—while the novelist starts at the very center. And yet no matter how hard the biographer works, those innermost secrets, with which the novelist starts, are forever unsolved. I've not the faintest idea, for instance, why Paul Revere married Sara Orne. I don't know why he was so fond of horses, what conditioned him. I felt greatly concerned about his dancing around in the streets in jubilation just a few evenings before his wife died. And what was he doing at a wedding party so soon after her death—having a good time, too? There is so much that doesn't fit. I had one break, though. You know, Revere had made many of the bells in the churches—the fine church bells all through New England. How my heart warmed when he died on a Sunday—to the tolling of his bells, you see. That was a fine touch."

Miss Forbes said that she turned to biography partly through accident, that for two years she had been working on a novel about a man who remained neutral during the Revolutionary War, "saw both sides, waited and judged, and so on. I thought that I had a fine character. Then the Nazis attacked Poland and I was suddenly the most unneutral woman in the world. That destroyed all that I'd been writing about. A person who could stay neutral in war! The character was absurd. But I had a great deal of research completed—that is, my mother had done an enormous amount of research for me, and I'd done a lot—so I wrote of Revere and his world."

There probably are few scholars who know as much about New England before 1800 as does Mrs. Forbes, the mother of Esther Forbes and the author-compiler of a number of source books on New England's past. The family lives in Worcester, Mass. All of Miss Forbes' American ancestors settled in New England before the Revolution, and as a child, she said, she was steeped in tales of the past. "I was mad about witches. My mother stitched little red devils on my handkerchiefs. But it wasn't until years afterward that it occurred to me to write of the things I knew. When I wrote my first novel—at the age of thirteen—my subject was the fall of Troy. And the next one had to do with Renaissance Italy. All through school—I went to a school that was not very strict—I wrote instead of learning to spell or do arithmetic."

Passing up Vassar for the University of Wisconsin, she failed to graduate, leaving school to work on a farm during the last war. After the war she went to work for Houghton Mifflin in their editorial department. "That was a busy time. I was writing my first published novel, doing a full-time job, and getting engaged to be married. I almost never got to bed before three in the morning but it didn't hurt me in the least—never felt better.

"Of course, I enjoy writing, always have. I like the pile of paper, the sharpened pencils, and use them rapidly—writing in my own shorthand. I let myself go in the first draft because you can cut and chop as much as you like later, but if the first draft doesn't have vitality, you might as well abandon the whole project. It is wasteful to write about four times as much as I ever can use, but that seems to be the only way in which I can find out what it is that I need. Then I cut and redo and fool with it until the publisher takes it away from me."

AN INTERVIEW WITH KATHARINE BRUSH

Who discusses her own experience with problems that confront many writers

July 5, 1942

"WHEN YOU GET THINKING that you are smarter than your subconscious," said Katharine Brush, "you are licked. The only good writing you do is almost automatic; you make a connection with a voice that seems to come from outside your head but doesn't, of course. It is the subconscious and it is useful only when you are really rolling. That is the only time it can come through. When you can make that connection you do all right, but if you try to contrive, do it all with your conscious mind, then you write crippled stuff. Of course, that is hard to believe. Naturally you don't trust the happy accidents, the writing that doesn't call for sweat, because that is too easy. But it is crazy not to.

"I had a long, very stale period when I tried to carve every page and then every paragraph and then every line. I don't know just why I went so stale—I guess there were a number of causes.

"One was the huge apartment that would have made Winter quarters for a circus. It was a big white elephant and it had to be served. And then travel. I'd always wanted to travel and had the chance. I was practically a commuter on the Atlantic during the years that were so bad for everyone else—the 1930's—and I lost touch with what was going on here—I'm still trying to catch up. Of course, the European scene didn't help. I didn't know enough about it to write about it, and anyway no one wanted me to write about it. I'd pop over here, a stranger. Pop over there, a stranger. I lost touch.

"And I always had thought that when I could afford it I'd write the kind of novel I wanted to write. I guess every one thinks that. Well, I did it. In a way, at least. I wrote the novel called 'Don't Ever Leave Me'—but it was not written; it was carved. When you carve you can spend all day on a sentence. And you lose perspective. Believe it or not, practically all of the sentences in 'Don't Ever Leave Me' scan. I would read the manuscript over to myself and enjoy the lilt of the lines. I understand that some other writers enjoyed it also, bless their hearts. But you could hardly call it a hit. I had lost the story; it was all spread out thin and hard to find among the gently swaying lines.

"Then there was insecurity. I used to think that insecurity about money was a pretty good spur for a writer. It put you to work and no nonsense. But the trouble with trying to write when you are financially insecure is that you are likely to insist to yourself that an idea is good simply because you most desperately need a good idea. Then you work on it, use your time; it isn't good—never was but you wouldn't let yourself realize it—and in the end you're more insecure than before. This is no spur to me any more—perhaps it once was. I am too scared of it for it to do me any good, any least good."

Miss Brush now works in a study overlooking St. Bartholomew's Church. "All the magazines in here I've read—they'd be too much temptation otherwise. But the weddings get me. I spend a lot of time when I should be writing leaning on my elbows watching the wedding parties go in and come out. The score is about three to two so far as the Army and Navy are concerned—three Army bridegrooms for every two Navy bridegrooms."

She has large filing cabinets filled with notes. In these cabinets are thick envelopes that contain both factual and imaginative material. One envelope was labeled "American Couple." Another, "College Girl." Another drawer holds masses of material for nonfiction articles, and another, thick journal volumes—closely typed thin pages that hold the record of what Miss Brush has seen and heard and done during the past fifteen years.

"Don't you waste a lot of time going through these notes?"

"I'm not sure. Perhaps it is a waste. But there are so many little details that I need to know—what the songs were in such and such a month of 1928, what night clubs were popular then, the slang, how women were wearing their hair, what the hats were like. Well, I have all that here. And right now—such facts as that the ferry pilots are in love with a dancer in a Cairo night club who is known as Mme. Putt-Putt, and the little things that you notice when you go to a shore resort and all the lights are dimmed—where am I going to get the little details that make the atmosphere of this time if I don't save them myself? Get them handily.

"And the long journals that I keep are good for warm-up. There's no mental block to sitting down and writing out exactly what happened yesterday and with that you have hit a pace and perhaps you can carry some of that pace over into your work.

"I suppose I shouldn't work as hard as I do. I start at eight each morning and work through lunch until two-thirty or so. Then I knock off for the afternoon and often work again in the evening. If I'm not going to work in the evening, I keep at it longer in the afternoon. That goes on for seven days a week, and the last vacation I had was in 1939.

"Undoubtedly there is the danger in that of going stale again. But I'm always promising myself a vacation and, anyway, I've come around again so that I enjoy working, look forward to eight o'clock in the morning, so probably it is all right."

AN INTERVIEW WITH LLOYD C. DOUGLAS

The author of "The Magnificent Obsession" talks of his life and work

July 19, 1942

"MR. DOUGLAS, why do you almost always have a rich young man as the hero of your stories and reform him and have him go around doing good?"

"Well, I think it is a good device," said Lloyd C. Douglas, the author of the enormously popular "The Magnificent Obsession" and "Green Light." "Sometimes I use a rich young heroine in the same way. Readers are interested in wealthy young people whose impulses are good and who discover that they have wasted their lives, have taken too much and given nothing and go about readjusting the balance. If they are rich, you see, they can do good without too much preparation and in a practical way."

"I suppose thousands of people dream that some day some one will come along and just hand them a lot of money."

"I'm certain that they do," said Mr. Douglas, "and so would you be if you read my mail. The letters steadily come in—I am offered up to 15 percent interest for loans and sometimes I stand to make even more, as, for example, from the young men who ask me to grubstake them while they write a story, the split presumably to be fifty-fifty. There are others who want to send me their life stories—I'm to write them and split fifty-fifty. My secretary answers most of these offers on her own stationery, as we have found that the introduction of a third person is a pretty good convincer that there is no soap. When I answer them myself the correspondence seems to go on and on. I am sympathetic but I have my own obligations, and there are too many requests."

"Mr. Douglas, do you believe your stories of human goodness as you write them? Do you see them as realism?"

"Yes, I believe in the philosophy that the stories express. As for realism, I certainly cannot argue that the characters and the events are of every day. The characters and events are changed and worked over to fit a thought—a point, or whatever you like to call it—to fit whatever ideal of living that I am trying to pass on. I can't pretend that you'll find my heroes or heroines walking about the streets in crowds, and why should that be? I've read a number of books of so-called realism; I don't read them altogether from choice. I knew without Steinbeck to tell me that there are great masses of the unwashed. I wish them well. I hope that they may rise in the world to the point that they may buy soap at least. I enjoyed 'The Yearling,' but why must Mrs. Rawlings follow that tender and moving tale with the account of pigs and backhouses and drunken orgies that she calls 'Cross Creek'?

"Hasn't the reader enough trouble—haven't we all? Why should a man pay $2.50 to pile more depression and trouble on the depression and trouble that he already has? Particularly at a time like this, isn't it better to give people the opportunity to believe that there is some good to hold onto, that idealism does exist? I realize that this is not a time when that is easy to prove. Just now all hell is broken loose but why not give—and take—such relief as is possible?

"Oh, I know what the critics think of me. I have a daughter—a young cynic—who kids me about my 'goody-goody' stories, as she calls them. And if I were a younger writer I should resent far more than I do being held up as a public laughingstock by the New York reviewers. But I'm not mad, whatever they say. I can see what they mean.

"I have, you see, a vein of cynicism that I don't express in my stories. Quite often after I have built up a hero to be thoroughly heroic I am strongly tempted to let him express not the heroic thought that he is expected to express but the thought that rises in my own mind as what I would say in his situation. However, I submerge this strain. In my plodding work I have insured my hero as a hero and he's going to be heroic come hell or high water. Yes, sir. I once broke down to the extent of writing a thousand words that ripped away at a hypocritical phase of religion. But I didn't publish it—no, no. I read it to my family and tore it up.

"If I were twenty-five years old, with a long future as a novelist before me, I probably would be concerned by what you might call my 'literary' position. But I was born in 1877—according to actuarial tables I have only nine years, six months and thirteen days still to go. That is my expectancy as the life insurance companies place their bets. With so short a time left it is natural that I should place first things first, that I should try to be constructive in my own way and as best I can.

"My mail is not all made up of letters asking for help. An astonishing number of letters come to me telling me that I have helped, that the philosophy expressed by this or that character has had a great effect on the life of the writer of the letter."

"Mr. Douglas, what was the history of your first book, 'The Magnificent Obsession'?"

"That wasn't my first book. I'm a parson, you know, and, not only that, a lecturer. Yes, I've had a long history as a windbag, talking and writing whenever I was given half a chance. I had written books of essays that had been published by Harpers and Scribner's, and had done moderately well. About a dozen years ago I was happily at work on yet another book of essays—on religious subjects, how to get more out of living—that I had planned for Harpers. But I always had wanted to write a story.

"My father had been a great storyteller. He hadn't written, but he told stories well. He was a country parson, a quite old man when I first began to think and notice. He was fifty years old when I was born. The fire in him was running out when I came along; he had reached a steadiness, a pronounced philosophical point of view, and he had time for me. He would take me out of school, sometimes for several weeks running, and I'd drive with him over the country roads on sick calls, to funerals, to weddings, behind a plodding old horse. I was an old hand at funerals when I was eight years old.

"Father had kept up his Greek and he coached me in Greek as we rode behind that old horse—he wanted to keep his Greek alive and he gave me a thorough grounding in it. He also stressed the importance of English—he'd rather have heard me cuss than make a grammatical mistake. But I never have had any mathematics.

"Father loved to tell stories and I've seen many a farmer right on the edge of a bench hanging on to every word Father said as he told some story from the pulpit. They were the old Bible stories—the farmers knew how they came out—but Father thought of every one in the Bible as alive and he made them seem alive. Yes, he did. And if he needed to throw in a little drama to make the story even more interesting, why he threw it in.

"Well, I grew up and became a preacher and told stories, but I wanted to write one. In mulling over the book of essays I found a theme—that the great joy is to do good secretly, that we lose a lot when we tell of the good we do, when the word is spread about. And at the same time I thought of a rich young man who had, not entirely through his fault, caused an accident in which a great brain surgeon was killed. And I had him remaking his life so that he might take the place of the surgeon and carry on his work.

"I wrote the story. Harpers had an Eastern minister read it and he said that the religion was no good—that it was dickering with the angels, commercializing the Christian impulse, that it wouldn't do. The story, I was told, might do, but the religion wouldn't do. I sent it to Doubleday, Doran and they turned it down, saying that the religion was all right but that the story didn't suit at all.

"Well, I was moving to Montreal, to a parish there, and on the way I gave the manuscript to my friends in Willett, Clark, the Chicago religious book publishers. They took a chance on it and published 2,500 copies. When every copy was sold they published 1,500 more. Then the book caught on and after it had gone through forty-nine editions it began to appear that we had something. Houghton Mifflin took it over and republished it and it sold more.

"No, I don't write easily or rapidly. Each morning at eight-thirty I start work and continue through lunch until about two-thirty. First I rewrite from the point that the story began to go bad the afternoon before. This gives me a start. I write four or five thousand words but if I can save 1,000 I'm satisfied.

"My secretary comes in at two-thirty and reads back to me what I've written. I can tell by the way she reads what is worth keeping and what must be thrown away and what changed. If she's not clear in her mind just what point I'm trying to make, it is no good. If she stumbles over a line of dialogue we mark it—if the dialogue were right she wouldn't stumble. Her manner gives me a pretty good idea of what I have.

"I've just completed a new book that will be published in the Fall. It is called 'The Robe.' A woman clerk in a store in Canton, Ohio, wrote me a fan letter saying that it seemed to her that there was a story in the robe of Christ—the robe that the soldiers threw dice for. I agreed with her. I've worked on that story for two years.

"A rich young Roman—Marcellus—is sent to Palestine and there learns the whole legend of Christ. . . .

"No, I don't write with my former parishioners in mind. I write for a wider audience. My parishioners were people who went to church every Sunday. They knew what they'd hear there. In my stories I write with the thought that I'm talking to people who don't know one thing of what Christianity is about and I try to tell them what it is about, tell them in simple words, through dramatic incident, of the joys of Christian living.

"Call it sentimental quasi-philosophy, say I'm a crude craftsman—I won't be mad. . . ."

MISS MacINNES ON THE PLEASURES OF WRITING

A natural story-teller describes her free-and-easy methods of work

July 26, 1942

HELEN MACINNES, who turned out a best-seller on her first attempt as a writer—that was "Above Suspicion"—and hit again on her second attempt—that was "Assignment in Brittany"—talked of the pleasures of writing, the delights of starting a yarn with no more than a basic thriller situation and letting the pencil work out the plot, open the door to new characters bringing unexpected complications, design a village and people it.

"As I write along, the man says something, the woman answers him, perhaps something unexpected and that I think is funny. I laugh at this and Gilbert (Gilbert Highet, her husband) looks up to see what I'm laughing at. I read him the dialogue. As he doesn't know what went before or is to come after, I'm afraid it doesn't amuse him much. But it might. He's not really paying much attention. And I write on through an encounter in the dark and an escape . . . It's a lot of fun.

"I've never tried to write anything but the sort of stories that I enjoy reading—the Buchan, Household kind of thing—and I'm sure that I couldn't do any other sort of writing. But I've been reading every good story that I could find ever since I began to read—Scott and Dumas and on through. I like the kind of story that you spend an evening with, and at the end you haven't learned anything at all or dug deep into any one's subconscious but you've had a thoroughly good time.

"I have no system about writing, don't keep hours or anything like that. After dark I start some music I like, sit on the living room couch with a pad and pencil and write a chapter. No, I don't change it much. I hate repetitions and get rid of those as I type very slowly and with great labor from the manuscript. I'm as long making the typed draft as the original."

It had been suspected that Mr. Highet might have had a hand in the writing of "Assignment in Brittany," as "Above Suspicion" had had a rather feminine tone in some of its rough action sequences, a tone far less marked in the second book. This suspicion, said Miss MacInnes, has no foundation. "Gilbert didn't see the manuscript until it was finished because I think it is unfair to ask some one to read a story that isn't complete and the best you can do—it is asking them to give you too much of a break in imagining how you'll do the rest of it. And it is risky, too, as a comment that this section is all right but that one isn't may be just the weight needed to throw the story out of focus for yourself and set you distrusting your imagination and the correctness of whatever plan you may have.

"If the second book is less feminine—well, it is a man's story with no woman tagging along through everything that happens. I didn't want to repeat, anyway. Practically every one took it for granted that the husband and wife in the first book were Gilbert and myself. This was not true. They were imagined, and all that happened to them was; I wanted to be certain that the second book couldn't even be thought autobiographical."

The first story told of a journey through Nazi-dominated sections of Europe just before the start of the war. Miss MacInnes's second story is a tale of action in France during the war. Her third story will be set in Poland after the defeat of that country.

Dominant in the background of Miss MacInnes' thrillers is a realization of the Nazi power, a warning of what the exercise of that power means.

Miss MacInnes said that she first became scared of Hitler just before he came to power. "We were in Munich on our honeymoon the last time that an election went against him. He spoke to an enormous crowd, including us. Before his speech he seemed rather a comic figure to me. But I couldn't miss the effect that he had on his audience—he got them. There couldn't be any doubt about it—you could feel them respond. Then he won not much later and his early moves in power made the pattern of what was to come seem quite clear to us. We did not doubt that he meant war.

"Of course, we talked about it. We went home to England—we lived at Oxford—and I remember the effect of our talk. One's mother and aunts and uncles could not take one seriously. You see, they remembered the other war so clearly and so bitterly that it was really unbelievable to them that any man or any group of men could be so inhuman as to start something like that again. It could not happen.

"Then in 1937 my husband was invited to come here to a teaching job. I found that I couldn't resist telling every one I met of how dangerous Hitler was. There were so many Cassandra statements in the top of my mind, so many warnings to people who didn't want warnings. I felt that I was becoming a bore and I thought that perhaps if I wrote what I thought of Hitler, I might spare acquaintances and friends some bad half hours. So I bought a journal and started filling it with prophecies of what the Nazis were likely to do.

"I had considered writing. Years before I half planned a detective story and once I filled a notebook with notes for a novel about Mad King Theodore of Abyssinia, a really fascinating character who wanted to modernize his country and invited experts to help him and then always became suspicious of them and threw them into really horrible dungeons. But instead of writing the novel I had a baby.

"But as I put down my thoughts in the journal I was very pleased to find that I wrote quite easily, simply sped along and seemed to have a great deal to say that was of interest to myself. And writing of Europe I recalled the towns I knew and the people, the inns where we'd stayed.

"So I started writing about two young married people leaving England to travel through the regions that I knew, and, of course, they'd need a good reason for traveling, so I gave them that, and they should have adventures . . . and I wrote when I felt like it and had a good time. When it was finished Gilbert read it and said that he thought it was all right, so the next step, of course, was to have a try at getting it published. One of our friends is a literary agent and in a very few days she telephoned me with the good news—I was astonished—that 'Above Suspicion' had been accepted.

"No, I didn't do any research into Gestapo methods or Secret Service lore to get incidents. I simply invented such action, feeling perfectly safe because, of course, the truth of how men are hunted down and how messages are secretly passed and so on would be much stranger and more improbable than anything I possibly could invent.

"But I'm most particular about settings, never describing a town or a street that I don't know quite thoroughly. Of course, that adds to the fun of it, as it lets me revisit regions that I liked so much and then there's the discipline of being exact about something—it keeps your feet on the ground and invention from straying too far."

AN INTERVIEW WITH E. B. WHITE, ESSAYIST

The author of "One Man's Meat" talks about writing and country living

August 2, 1942

E. B. WHITE, the reasonable, truthful writer who set the style for the "Notes and Comments" page of *The New Yorker,* wrote a lot of captions and headlines and tag lines for news breaks, and for many years (with James Thurber) wrote "Talk of the Town," came down from Maine last week and submitted to an interview—if you can call it an interview when the interviewee says, "Who? Me?" to a good many of the questions.

He did say, "The main thing I try to do is write as clearly as I can. Because I have the greatest respect for the reader, and if he's going to the trouble of reading what I've written—I'm a slow reader myself and I guess most people are—why, the least I can do is make it as easy as possible for him to find out what I'm trying to say, trying to get at. I rewrite a good deal to make it clear.

"All this about inspiration. . . . Now look, I can't tell you anything about methods of work. . . . But I do think that all this about inspiration—I think writing is mainly work. Like a mechanic's job. A mechanic might as well say he was waiting for inspiration before he greased your car, because, if he didn't feel just right, he'd miss a lot of the grease points—that he had to feel right up to it.

"And of how people get their effects. Every once in a while some one who is putting together a reader—you know, a book of extra reading for an English class—writes for permission to use a piece of mine. I always say, 'Sure—thanks very much,' but the last time I said, 'Go ahead and use what you want, but how about sending me one of the books?' When I was in school, books of that kind were full of Walter Pater. I thought they must be changing their pace a lot, wanting my stuff.

"He sent me the book and I read my piece in it. At the end there were a lot of questions: 'Why did Mr. White use repetition here?' was one question. And 'Explain the author's purpose in inserting this phrase.'

"Gosh, those questions aren't easy. I tried to answer them and flunked cold. I admit there was repetition there, but I hadn't realized it. Anyway, I couldn't think of a good sound reason why I'd used it . . ."

In his recently published book, "One Man's Meat," Mr. White gives as one reason why he threw up his job and went to live in Maine the desire to simplify his life. He said that he had 117 chairs divided about evenly between a city house and a country house.

During the interview he said early that he had desired to go to Maine and live on a farm "because it was something we'd always wanted to do, and we could do it, so that seemed the time. A good many people down here in New York seem to think that going to live on a farm the year round, especially a farm so far away, is some sort of height of affectation. They seem to think that you must be either washed up or very rich to do it. But we just wanted to do it."

Later he said: "I felt that I had to get away when I did because there seemed less and less integrity . . . more people easing off on their principles for some little advantage. There was this or that they didn't believe in, but if it made things easier for a little while they'd give in. . . ." But he didn't go on with this.

He said that he finds it more difficult to write in the country.

"When I was on *The New Yorker* I had to turn out a certain

amount each week—which isn't the ideal way. Perhaps the ideal way would be to have to produce every hour. That would keep you up to it, always conscious that there was a job. Now I write for *Harper's* each month and when there are twenty-eight days between one piece and the next you're a long time getting at it.

"Then, of course, the ideas—they are not so easy to package in the country. There isn't the same kind of stir. We're in the middle of a lot up there—animals, chickens, chores. I can't claim to be a real farmer but we do farm and I like to work outside. When I come in after working all day I want a drink or to go to sleep. A drink and a drink and sleep."

The Whites live away down East. They have stayed on the farm all year around since leaving New York except for one Winter when their son had sinus trouble—they took him to Florida. They have sheep, chickens, a dog, a cat and a pig. Mr. White figured at one time that he didn't lose more than a dollar a bird per year on his chickens.

The region seems less remote than it did at first, as patrol planes pass over frequently, Coast Guardsmen walk the shore, and the little town regularly practices blackouts.

"We talk about our tires a lot—and worry about them. Of course, we're pretty neighborly up there, but even so the present shortages and those that are expected have increased the neighborliness to some extent. You never think of driving to town any more without somebody's garbage can or an implement that needs mending or a package to be mailed in the back of the car. We take the blackouts seriously enough, though we can hardly be expected not to feel that if an enemy aviator drops a bomb on us, in that little town which is mostly a fishing town, he is either off his course or crazy. We're fifty miles from a railroad junction, twenty-five miles from a movie, so you can see it isn't likely we'll be bombed. But the patrol planes remind us how well we're being protected and we were considerably cheered up a short time ago when some men came back from fishing with the pretty clear certainty that they had seen a German submarine disposed of."

AN INTERVIEW WITH FAITH BALDWIN

Who discusses some of the general ideas on which her stories are based

August 9, 1942

MANY PERSONS who write well feel that they never can hope to reach a vast popular audience because neither their emotional nor intellectual reactions are attuned to the mental and emotional reactions of the mass of readers. Faith Baldwin, whose name on the cover of a fiction magazine is a guarantee of increased circulation, said that she had no theories about herself, but that she did have some general ideas that she supposed were at the base of many of her stories.

"I'm convinced, for example, that women are practical and that men are, comparatively, romanticists and sentimentalists. It is a biological thing. Men can go along with stars in their eyes, but if women aren't practical on major matters they will, as a general thing, find that there is no place for them in the community.

"When a boy and a girl fall in love, he's thinking about love. So is she, of course, but beyond his shoulder she also is looking to a new apartment and a baby carriage and deciding in a general way where to start looking for the dining-room furniture, and how much rent they'll be able to afford out of his wages. Men are often surprised when they find that they are about to become fathers and that there are bills to meet. They haven't thought about bills. The girl's surprise is less deep.

"I'm not talking about the career women and the women who

keep shifting about in their search for romance. They are minority types and though, of course, I hope to interest them and write about them often, the big reader audience is made up of average women, and to the average woman security, home and family ties still mean more than anything else.

"The majority of girls who work do so because they have to—they are waiting. Of course, this war, as all wars, will cause a terrific shortage of men and there'll be a lot of girls who'll have to sublimate themselves in careers or something. But the adjustment to marriage and responsibility is in the blood. It isn't so natural for men. Of course, there's an inexhaustible situation for writers just there."

"How about immorality in your books, Miss Baldwin? Don't some of your heroines steal the husbands of other women?"

"Oh, I don't know. I suppose you mean 'Office Wife'—as a matter of fact that wasn't my own idea; an editor gave it to me. But in any of my books or stories the only husbands permanently stolen are those married to mean and selfish women. Sometimes a man is temporarily eased away from his wife and he seems about to be stolen, but if the wife is halfway all right she gets him back.

"As for immorality, readers are more likely to kick if a man sticks to an unworthy wife than if he leaves her for the heroine. They say: 'What a lovely girl you left without a man!' But usually I think that I keep marriages together."

"What do you consider your main job in writing?"

"Emotion—that's my job. If you can put the reader through the paces of the emotions—even if they say that they wouldn't have reacted in the same way that your characters did, or that they didn't act that way when they were in the same situation—you've got something. You don't consciously say, 'Now I'll get emotional'—you just do it.

"Make two stories out of the same plot and in one concentrate on the emotions of the characters and in the other concentrate on the whys, the reasons, the mental roads to the solution—well, there's no argument about which story will be more popular.

"That's lucky for me, as a lot of action and plot always have been hard for me to contrive. In serial writing action and plot are demanded and I simply had to learn to deliver, but they are not my strong points. My interest is in the people—what they are and what made them what they are. I like to put down stories of their grandparents, of their name backgrounds, of what they were like when they were children. This makes the people dimensional.

"At first I'd devote a couple of installments to backgrounds of this kind, but they always were fired back at me by the editors with instructions to cut them in half. When that has happened often enough you learn to present the background material as you carry the action along."

"You write so much of young love. Do you find it difficult to keep up with the changes of setting and slang and viewpoint?"

"Oh, no. There are always young people about the house. And as for setting and slang, I read the gossip columns, and know who went to El Morocco, who lunched at Twenty-one, what stories were told last night at such and such a place. I don't traipse around, but it isn't at all necessary. Because how much does human nature change? There are changing conventions—but even in the wild 1920's some girls parked in cars and drank and some were reactionary as all get-out. Conventions just ebb and flow; freedom and strictness react against each other. But basically—life, death, birth, hunger, fear, love. Emotionally we don't change."

Miss Baldwin said that her first ambition was to be a poet and that she had a volume of poetry published in 1926. "I wrote short stories, too, and then novels. They were published, but had no success. Then I started writing newspaper serials, beauty columns, short stories for the pulp magazines—anything that was paid for. It was necessary to be paid.

"Then one day my agent heard that somebody who was supposed to have written a serial for *Good Housekeeping* had fallen down on it and that there was a hole in the magazine. She persuaded the editor to talk to me and he decided to take a chance, to assign me to the serial. I slaved over the serial—it was my big opportunity. And I just finished it in time, for I'd hardly written the last page before I had to go to the hospital. My twins were born."

She works very hard and very rapidly. At the time of the interview she had recently left a hospital where she had spent nearly two months and undergone two operations, but though she had not yet gone to her home in Connecticut and taken up her regular working schedule, she already was turning out some 2,000 words a day.

"Ordinarily I manage from 4,000 to 6,000 words a day but the operations seem to have taken the hurry out of me," said Miss Baldwin.

AN INTERVIEW WITH JAMES STREET

The author of "Tap Roots" and "The Biscuit Eater" talks of his work

August 30, 1942

To the question, "Just what are you trying to do, Mr. Street?" James Street, author of "Tap Roots," "O Promised Land" and "The Biscuit Eater," said, "Well, what I'd like to do is write a really good book. I think it is pretty doubtful that I ever will, but that is what I want to do and what I mean to try to do. I keep thinking that I am not ready because, though I am thirty-eight years old, I don't feel any too mature; in fact, I don't feel mature at all. I am cocky as a talker, and brag a lot, but I am not really sure of myself and when I think of writing a good book it is always in the future and the rather far future at that."

"When you talk of a 'good book', what novel do you have in mind?"

"I won't say 'War and Peace,'" said Mr. Street, moodily, after a short pause, "because I can't even pronounce a lot of words in it. Here am I, an American, trying to think of a good book, and I go wanting to bring in a novel about places and people I really don't know the first thing about. Mississippi today is my country, and it is there my material is.

"But, as I say, I don't know that I ever will have the stuff. Everything I am after in a book or a show is a lump in the throat or something to laugh at. If I can choke up or laugh, then I've had a good time, I'm satisfied with the entertainment. But I don't seem to be able to set my mind on what they call serious. The share-croppers aren't the whole South; they are not even very important. Why should 400,000 share-croppers matter so much in a nation of 130,000,000 people?

"I can do emotion—sometimes. Often there is so much corn in what I do that the whole thing is hopeless, and to other people it is not emotion at all; it is just corn. When that happens there is nothing to be done. When some writers turn out a story that doesn't click, they can doctor it here and there. Not me. When my stories don't quite go over they don't go over at all. There is no hope for them; they are all corn. To write a really good book you must be further from corn than that; it can't be so close a call.

"Sometimes I look through a book of mine and I wonder, 'Now why did I say that?' I come across some mighty unreasonable statements because I pop off so easy—I pop off from my mind and think with my heart, so I guess I am bound to make mistakes that might ruin a book I wanted to be really good.

"Also I overwrite. I make three words do what one word should do. You can't have that in a real good book.

"But, as I say, the stuff is there in Mississippi and if I were man enough I'd get it and set it down. There are a lot of habits of acting that I'd have to avoid—like sometimes I bra-a-g about the South and then I may write something that offends every one I know in Mississippi. That is just cantankerous, just mean. I think little people are mean, anyway, to say things that make other people want to fight. Because how can we lose? A fellow my size, if he gets in a fight with a big fellow, he's the winner whatever happens. If he hits the big fellow, everybody says, 'Look at that little fellow go; he's got spunk, he sure has.' If the big fellow hits the little fellow the people say, 'Look there, that big coward hittin' that little man.' We can't lose, so maybe we don't contain ourselves enough; we never learn to.

"I think of Peggy Mitchell—I happened to be in on the first moment of 'Gone With the Wind.' Peggy's little, too, not mean in any way, not a bit, but quick with her tongue. There were a lot of us at the club in Atlanta and a couple went by with their arms around one another—a Sunday evening. A girl from New Hampshire was with us and she happened to say something about loose morals, anyway, easy morals, in the South—not anything definite, just wondering. Peggy spoke up, quick, you know, 'We never bundled in the South!' And of course, in New Hampshire . . . Well, you know, Peggy is married to a newspaperman, a big fellow, and he never is excited. He said, 'Peggy, if you want to defend the South so bad, why don't you just write it in a book?' She sure did. What a storyteller she is! And how the South lapped up those big plantations and wonderful houses and the slaves running around. As I said, there are only 400,000 share-croppers, and they're not America. I don't know how many families there were that owned big plantations and lots of slaves, but they weren't the South. The South just loves to think so.

"There are members of my own family who think they came from that kind of life. They know better but they like to think it. We never had any such thing. My grandfather leased a slave or two when he needed them and my grandmother had a couple of linen petticoats, but she wasn't so long out of linsey-woolsey. And the tradition of culture which is honored and respected but not much followed any more is another aspect of that wishin'. There were cultured people down South, sure there were, but there was a lot of space, a lot of land to work. For culture you need leisure, and when you're building a new country, all that space and it all so new, why, you've got to go out and make a crop.

"You see, it's complicated. I want to brag about the South and I want to tell the truth. Doesn't always mix. I think there's no doubt but that most of the blood shed in this war by Americans has been Southern blood. There are good reasons for that. The military tradition hasn't died down there—Texas A. and M. makes West Point look like a prep school—it turns out so many students. And this fifty a month counts down there. It looks better to a boy off a Southern farm than to a man out of a Northern factory.

"Mississippi today—I hope to write it. I hope I get good enough.

But now I mine a gold mine with those historical novels, not a big gold mine but a handy one. They are full of faults but the people seem to read them; then, too, I write short stories and movies, so it works out.

"And the way I figure, even if those novels are full of faults, when you consider how little most people know about American history, so long as they will read at least some American history in even a poor novel they are learning something that they should know, that they need to know right now. If it takes a boy-and-girl story to bring their minds to history—well, that's what it takes and no harm done. It is better than nothing, for beyond the story is the bigness of the fight that made the country. You can't miss that no matter how much sensationalism you stick along with it."

Mr. Street was a newspaperman in the South for some years. "I started as a five-dollar-a-week reporter." He joined the staff of the Associated Press in Arkansas in 1927, worked in a number of cities, including a long tour of duty in Atlanta, and was transferred to New York on the strength of some color stories that were widely published and widely praised. On arriving here he wrote some tales of a saloon near Madison Square Garden, thus attracting the attention of William Randolph Hearst, who ordered that he be hired away from the news service. While working for Hearst he wrote a book called "Look Away," a memoir of his boyhood and youth in Mississippi, and on the strength of this became a free-lance writer. This strength was quickly dissipated, however, and he returned to newspaper work, finding a job on the *World-Telegram*. A short story, "Nothing Sacred," was sold to the movies and was made into a vehicle for Carole Lombard; it was his first published story. This set him out free-lancing again.

AN INTERVIEW WITH ELLEN GLASGOW

A major American novelist discusses her life and work

October 18, 1942

ELLEN GLASGOW said that the most striking fact that she had to impart was the news that she had been dead. For ten minutes, she said, at her Summer place in Maine, her life drained out. "The doctor had his fingers on my pulse. He said, 'She's gone,' to my sister. And I was gone. I was dead."

"What was it like?"

"It was like being taken up and carried, like being enveloped in a great, surging, slow tide—and it was bliss. Except for a half minute I was fully conscious, my eyes open, all my life crowding into my mind, knowing my room and the people in it and knowing what death was like—and it is bliss. A slow, heavy tide. Now I may have—with this heart—ten minutes or several years—"

"Does life seem more valuable?"

"Oh, yes. I am more detached from every one and everything in life. I am quite free."

"Miss Glasgow, when you thought you were dying, what did go through your mind?"

"I thought of the three things that I always have wanted and I thought that now I was to die with only one accomplished. I always have wanted to go around the world quite alone, but I never have been able to do that because of partial deafness. I have always wanted to live on a farm. (She apparently meant that she had wanted to live the year around on a farm but did not expand this.) And, third, I always wanted to write. I have written.

"I thought of these three desires."

Miss Glasgow was in New York briefly, a traveler from Maine to Richmond, where she lives in a "house in the slums," as she put it, referring to a fine, century-old house in a section of Virginia's beautiful capital that has been largely taken over by business and industry.

She warned: "If you use a photograph with this interview it must be an old one. I don't want a new picture taken. I have lost so much weight. I weigh only 106 pounds." But though she has been ill most of the time for three years she is zestful, happy seeming, tense with life. Her manner is entirely charming, almost exuberant for brief moments, and her speech is enriched by delicate, subtle shadings that cannot always be caught for quotation.

When she talked of the war, and she returned to it often, it was always in terms of its "cruelty." "There is only the one sin—to my mind anything else that is called a sin may be an error of manners or a mistake in conduct, but these are not sins—there is only the one sin, and that is cruelty. Truly I believe that. And there must be so much cruelty now—it is dreadful, the way it is re-entering all our lives. And not only human lives; even the animals are used in war and so cruelly used.

"We have never been civilized; I don't know that we ever shall be, but at least we were making progress. All through history there was beauty, but with the beauty, cruelty—it would have killed me, I could not have endured the cruelty of the Renaissance despite all the beauty that was created then. We drew away a little from cruelty; we learned—or began to learn—to accept responsibility for the poor and the mistreated, to learn that we must help where help was needed. We were even learning to be good to animals . . . How is your dog?"

"My dog?"

"My secretary saw you in the Berkshires with your dog. She described him to me. He must have been very handsome."

"Yes, he was. He lived to be thirteen and died four years ago. He belonged to my wife."

"I've always remembered my secretary's description of him," said Miss Glasgow, who founded the Richmond branch of the Society for the Prevention of Cruelty to Animals.

"Are you writing now?"

"Yes, though slowly. The days when I worked until two and three o'clock in the morning are over. When I was first recovering I could work for only fifteen minutes at a time. Now I can manage an hour."

She said that she is working on a sequel to "In This Our Life," her most recently published novel. "My theme was in the question of what it is that a man has that lets him go on and be a man after he has failed, as it would seem, at everything. So many people missed the point that I want to make it again."

The effort of writing, she said, exhausts her, but it is the greatest pleasure that she has known.

"The literary life offers little enough except the opportunity to aim at perfection and the momentary belief that you sometimes have in the middle of the work that you have achieved it."

Miss Glasgow said that she never has written for any reader or group of readers, that she has written wholly to please herself. No other writer, she is quite certain, has influenced her in any direct way.

"When I started to write [Miss Glasgow wrote her first novel before she was twenty and destroyed it and a second novel, "The Descendant," when she was twenty: that is, in 1895], all the novelists were trying to write in the manner of Henry James. I read everything that Mr. James ever wrote, but he did not influence my style. And when I was searching for a technique I read all of De Maupassant, but when I finally achieved a technique it came wholly through my own hard work, I was not helped to it. I am very sure of that."

As for her reading now, "I am too old to read, I sometimes think. I have read too long and too much. I don't know that I should say this, but I buy the new books and read very few of them." For some weeks she has been reading one book, the "Journals of Dorothy Wordsworth," edited by Ernest De Selincourt, and she talked with a lively, vital eloquence in praise of the genius of the author of these journals, and of the conditions of the Wordsworths' lives, which she accounts in some ways most enviable, as they understood how to use the simplicity that was made mandatory for them by their poverty and permitted poverty to do no damage to their thought or their emotions.

"But the other books, Miss Glasgow . . . why do you find them unreadable?"

"They are so raw. I do not like raw literature. I believe in the democratization of everything except literature."

She quoted an old Arabian saying to the effect that Allah delights in many kinds of truth and truth in many degrees, but that he does not desire the whole truth.

"In my work I have tried always to tell the truth but not the raw truth. I can believe that the novelists popular today are attempting to tell the truth, but they are so hurried to blurt it out and so little concerned with how they prepare it. When information has passed through the warmth of a vital mind, literature may result. But the process is slow.

"And, as I said, I have read so much. I was too poor to buy books when I was young, so I read everything in my grandfather's library. The books were old and most of them very good, and I read them thoroughly and I think that it was fortunate that my first books were the old ones."

Continuing on the subject of young writers Miss Glasgow said: "I thought for many years that a person should not write a novel until he was forty years old. Before that age so few men or women have enough to say or any mastery of the means for saying it. Now I wonder if sixty is not the right age. I told that to Van Wyck Brooks and he said we both must be about ready to start."

"How old were you when you started writing, Miss Glasgow?"

She said, "Seven," and laughed. "I found my first story not long ago. They burned most of my manuscripts when I left home, but not long ago in an old desk that I had used as a small child and that had been unopened for many years I found a manuscript that had not been burned. It was my first story, written in large, round letters, in pale ink. The title was 'A Lonely Daisy in a Field of Roses,' and that is interesting. I seem to have been born with my theme. The theme of so many of my novels has been just that—the lonely daisy, the field of roses, translated into the outsider, the man struggling up from an unprivileged status into a circle of inherited privilege; the lonely newcomer, the person who does not belong, entering a settled society and fighting for a place in it. Yes, I started on that theme when I was seven years old and have kept it all my life."

Miss Glasgow always has been a stylist, a precisionist. She once thought of allowing ten years to elapse between the completion of a manuscript and its publication, her theory being that there could be little doubt after a ten-year aging as to whether a novel was or was not worth publishing. She became convinced, however, that her friends were right in saying, "You change so much in ten years—all would be different. You would be obliged to write it all over again."

She said that she formerly wrote her novels a chapter at a time, working over each chapter until it satisfied her.

"But in late years I have changed my method, as I cannot be certain of sustained vitality. I have written the first drafts of my more recent novels straightaway in order to make certain that through their entire length they would be as vital, as alive, as I could make them, so that if illness interfered, the novel would not be ruined. For the life goes into a story when it first is written. The long period of revising or rewriting can do no more than perfect what first was there."

THE STORY BEHIND "THEY WERE EXPENDABLE"

An interview with W. L. White, who describes each step in the making of a notable book

November 1, 1942

To THE COMMENT THAT "They Were Expendable" had been a fine choice of title for his book on Lieutenant Bulkeley and his crew, W. L. White said: "I had to shove it down the throat of every one who had anything to do with the book before publication. All that saved my title was that, after they'd read the book, they could not think of a better title. There was a good reason for that. The title was built in.

"An interesting thing about titles that Harold Guinzberg, the head of Viking Press, told me is this: 'A good title is the title on a successful book.' You know, that's a truth. Look it over. When you think of 'Dodsworth'—well, it was a good novel, so 'Dodsworth' seems a fine title. So would 'Smith' or 'Russell' be a good title. All you need to go with it is a good book.

"Now for this interview—I hate to be in the position of asking you to pull punches but if I get too indiscreet I wish you would pull them, because of the four other guys who are in on this book—and they are Navy officers. They can't be indiscreet and I don't want to be indiscreet for them by proxy."

"How did you get the chance to write 'They Were Expendable'?"

"It was kicking around. Yes, you can almost say that. The Navy publicity people had the story and it seemed swell to them, but some of the people they put it up to couldn't seem to see it. The story had been turned down at least once. When the suggestion came to me that I might look into it on the chance that there was a good magazine story in interviews with Bulkeley and the other guys back from Bataan—well, I was in a good spot because of circumstances.

"You see, from the moment the war began I'd had an itching to get to the Philippines. I couldn't swing it—there was no room for correspondents in the planes—but I was eaten by the desire to get there and see the action at first hand, so naturally I thought about it a great deal, it was on my mind a lot. I didn't know anything about the individual figures, but I was enormously curious as to the mechanics of the business—of just how the plans of defense had been worked out, what the country was like, how the natives felt about the Japanese. I wanted to know the broad generalities of the campaign and what was behind the generalities.

"So when the suggestion was made I went to see Bulkeley, who is a first-rate Navy man, the kind of fellow who, if he tells you that he fired a torpedo from 2,000 yards, you know that it wasn't 2,200 or he'd have said so. If I asked him what he thought of that girl over there," said Mr. White, looking intently at a sparkling brunette who was seated at a near-by table in the restaurant, "he would tell me that she was just about five feet four inches tall and weighed about one hundred and twenty-three pounds. And I'll bet he'd be right," Mr. White added, in a considering way. "So that was fine and he gave me a lot of tough, solid stuff because he has a good, tough Navy mind, an engineer's mind.

"The Navy was running him around selling War Bonds and so on. I followed him to Washington, where he was spending quite a bit of his time hanging around the White House because the President wanted to talk to him and he was having lunch with admirals. I went to a couple of the lunches and couldn't get anything there. So I said, 'Look, how about my coming out to where you are staying in the evening and we can really dig into this.' He seemed relieved and said that this suggestion suited him fine. So each evening about nine I'd go to the suburban home of friends where he was staying and we'd go out on the screened porch and slap mosquitoes and talk for about three hours. I'd make notes.

"I had made the deal with the Navy publicity people that I was to see as many of the men of Bulkeley's squadron as were available because—you know how it is—if you have four or five men to talk to there usually is one who has that flair—who has seen and noticed the details you need and remembered what his mood was and what the sky looked like and can tell you the story. Kelly was that guy as it turned out.

"I went to the Newport base and the men gave their time; they were entirely co-operative. The system was to get up in what is the middle of the night for me—that is, before seven o'clock—have breakfast in the officers' mess and then pick one guy to interview and go to work on him. I guess I talked to Kelly most often and for the longest periods.

"The note-taking went on all day. I hadn't brought a typewriter or paper so I bought some of these big Lion brand notebooks that school kids use and some pencils, and the interviewing went on from eight in the morning until five in the afternoon with an hour out for lunch. That started on Monday, and on Thursday afternoon I was holding my pencil in my fist because of the callus on my index finger.

"Well, as I said, Kelly had the flair, and the first afternoon I recognized this and said, 'The first thing we must think of is structure, because if we don't get structure into this story we can't work it right.' Kelly understood about structure, of course, with his engineering training, so he said okay. Then I said that there were three lines, three themes, that we had to stick to. 'The first is this—you started with six boats and in the end there was only one. Now there is a clear line—what happened to each of these other boats and what were you doing when you heard what had happened to them? That's the first line. The second line is that you started out thinking that you were winning and then you learned bit by bit that you were losing and finally realized that you had lost. And then the third line—I think that should be the story of the girl.' Well, he felt the same way about letting the girl be brought into it that you would, but, of course, all I wanted was just the simple story, the absolute truth without decorations, and it was a fine, clear story. It seemed to me it belonged. Kelly realized that it belonged, so he said all right. The tough job later was in running that story through the book because the girl drops out mighty early. But there were those things that reminded him of her and so it was possible to carry this line through.

"So, you see, the background was pretty much established in my mind before the talking started and the themes were there—the plan of the structure. It seems to me that is a main thing when you are after a story. Invention isn't much in a story, anyway. You take the human hand. If you tried to invent the human hand, you'd be up against three billion years as a rival and you'd hit all kinds of unexpected snags. Same way when you're writing a story. If you try to invent something that is like truth or will pass for truth you have a very tough time and what is the sense of it? Because you can't invent anything as good and sound as the facts.

"When I make notes I am lazy—I just put down a word here, a phrase there. Then I type the stuff out and don't necessarily refer to those notes again because they have gone through my mind, have gone through it once when I made them and once when I typed them. They are there.

"I came back to New York and rented a ten-buck-a-week room at the Brevoort as a working place and set up a worktable and spread out the notes in chapter form on the bed. I didn't use chapters in the story but I had the material divided up into chapters in my head.

"I knocked out ten pages and read them over and it was plain that the best style for this yarn was dialogue—there was a slow-down when I left dialogue, when I stepped in myself. Well, I knew that if I wrote it all in dialogue—you know how it is—I was taking a chance of being pushed out of the picture altogether because people would say, 'Wasn't he the lucky guy to be there with a stenographer or a dictaphone handy and just take this down?' No one would consider the fact that their talk ran to better than a hundred thousand words, naturally, talking as they had for many days, and that what they had said was boiled down and had some good lines by me thrown in now and then. But I figured I am old enough to take a pushing around if it is coming to me. I'll do this right.

"Then I thought, 'Look, I am not going to fool with this story.' 'I will let this run its natural length. If it is a magazine story, fine, and if it turns out to be book length, why fine, but I'm not going to fool with it; I'll let it run as it likes.'

"That is what I did. It ran to about 44,000 words and I wrote fast on it, finished it in ten days. The last five days or so I'd work until four or five in the morning, go home, sleep a few hours, and then back to the sawmill. I kept it tight, but I didn't throw away anything just to make it tighter. I wanted it tight but complete.

"Every now and then I'd finish twenty pages, and a messenger boy would appear and take them away to my agent. He'd get on the telephone and give me news of how I was doing—that the Book of the Month Club was holding a special meeting on it, that the *Reader's Digest* thought it was fine, but wondered if I could keep it going as well as I'd started it."

"That must have been hard to take. Don't you find you work better if people tell you your stuff is lousy when you are in the middle of it?" I asked.

"Yes, the cheers might have bothered me—I know what you mean. I'd have tried to perfect the last part, to make it live up to the first—but, you see, my advantage there was that the work had really been done. It was all clear in my head. I was just typing it."

"Did you worry about censorship?"

"I tried not to. I knew that it had to be censored, but there was nothing I could do about that. Later I was pleased by a comment that Hans Habe, the author of 'A Thousand Shall Fall,' sent my publisher. He said in effect that only a country that was sound all the way through would permit a book such as mine to be published in wartime.'

"Yes, it has had a good play," said Mr. White of his book. "I seem to have hit the mood of that moment, of the moment that it appeared. You can't repeat on things like that, I suppose, but it is swell to do it."

W. L. White is the son of William Allen White, newspaper owner, of Emporia, Kansas. "You can't imagine what it is like," he said, "to be the son of a man like that unless you have lived through it. What I mean is, newspaper publishers who weren't quite sure of themselves and were wishing that they had some one like William Allen White to make decisions for them would think to themselves, 'Why, he has a son,' and they'd hire me. They'd feel fine then, thinking they had William Allen White around the place. The trouble was that I am just the son. I am another guy. I'm not for people such as Landon when they want to be President. So after a little while these publishers would hear that I was saying things that weren't solid Republican and they'd feel betrayed. They'd feel that I had gotten them to hire me under false pretenses. So I'd have to move on."

Now in his early forties, Mr. White has been a newspaperman for a good many years. At present he is a regular contributor to the *Reader's Digest*.

NANCY HALE...AN ANALYZER OF THE FEMININE

Comments and theories by the lively author of "The Prodigal Women"

November 8, 1942

NANCY HALE, who possibly shares with Virginia Creed, author of "Voyage of the Heart," the title of Prettiest Novelist Now at Work, had come early for the appointment and taken off her shoes and drawn up an extra office chair as a resting place for her feet. She had, she said, had an uneasy time since our last meeting five years before. "There's quite a bit of autobiography in my book," she said, referring to her novel, "The Prodigal Women," "and as the real theme of the book is cruelty and fear—well, you can see . . ." She wore a suit that apparently had been designed to suggest a forest ranger, and looked rather like an animated and happy Garbo playing Robin Hood. The years, it seemed, had left no permanent scars.

I asked: "Do you still sleep thirteen hours before writing a short story and then write it straight through at one sitting?"

"Did I ever do that?" Miss Hale asked.

"You told me you did."

"It sounds like a good system," Miss Hale commented.

"I see that you're still specializing in analyzing women in your writing."

"Did I ever say I was specializing in that?"

"Yes."

"That's quite interesting," said Miss Hale, "because I suppose that I have specialized in women—though I don't remember talking about it."

"I specialize in women," Miss Hale continued, "because they are so mysterious to me. I feel that I know men quite thoroughly, that I know how, in a given situation, a man is apt to react. But women puzzle me. At school the other girls always seemed mysterious to me—I'd expect them to react in one way and they'd twist it around in their feminine minds and come along with an action that I couldn't understand, that was incomprehensible to me. Naturally, at that age, I was miserable a great deal of the time as I felt that I was surrounded by enigmas.

"I think that men usually accept themselves in quite an objective way. If they have a picture of themselves, it is likely that it is drawn something like this: 'I'm Joe Smith, a sort of dull guy. I'm all right if I keep my mouth shut when I should and don't overplay my luck.' That kind of picture.

"Of course, I'm talking about good, sound men—not the literary set. What is all this masculinity that so many men who write have become so self-conscious about? Why must they cherish their masculinity so much? What makes it so delicate? If a woman writes a good story or makes a radio talk, why should her husband claim that she is destroying his masculinity?

"In other words, they have no sense of security about their own personalities. They have visions of themselves but any little thing can change the visions, and even destroy them. A woman can dress herself all up and be sure she's a knockout, the prettiest thing at the party, but then if the headwaiter doesn't respond to the sight of her in just the right way she collapses—that is, the vision that she has of herself collapses.

"I think that the reason that women love to wear uniforms—and they do love them—is that when in uniform they have their part provided for them. They are free of insecurity. They are Wacs or Waves or Postal Telegraph girls and all they need do is live up to the part—no headwaiter can destroy the vision. The uniform proves that they belong.

"You know, women's fears are really terribly interesting. They are changing. They used to be so afraid of being run over or having a baby and now that they are out in the world, going about on their own so much, some of the old fears are dying out and new ones are taking their places. It is like war—all the new ways to kill and all the new ways to cure. Perhaps the dominant fear now is the fear of being afraid, which probably means that they are moving farther toward maturity."

Miss Hale said that she is now the wife of a naval officer "who doesn't write at all." "We live in a house that is only twelve feet by twenty-two feet and is in Washington, and I like it, the small house, but the trouble is that there is almost always some one asleep there, as my younger boy must go to bed early, of course, so he is asleep in the evenings and my husband works at night much of the time and has to sleep mornings. So to do my writing I go around the corner to a rooming house, where they let me have the morning use of the parlor, the room that the tenants sit around in in the evening. That's the way it is in Washington—there simply are no spare rooms to work in. So that's my study—it has linoleum on the floor and lace curtains. I go to it each morning at about eight o'clock and work until lunchtime or sometimes later.

"I write fairly rapidly, and I seem to be going well—I enjoy it. I'm going to do six short stories now and then another novel. I feel as though I had dozens of novels still to write and all kinds of stories. The only difficulty is that I most want to write, it seems, about things that happened before I was twenty-five. I suppose that there is a good reason for that. I'm now thirty-four and perhaps as writers we just stay about ten years behind ourselves. Anyway, I hope that is it.

"The other possibility and the one that I am afraid of is that I'm just drawing on the life—the life that I really and fully lived—before I wrote much. Well, you can't draw on that forever. One reason there are so many one-book authors is that they used up the living years in the one book. And you do feel, if you write, that you are not so wholly involved in situations that come along as you once were. That is, all of you isn't in the situation as it once was—there is a part that sits aside and looks at the angles and sees the picture whole and studies what is happening on the other side of the fence, because this part of you realizes that it is being supplied with material.

"Well, of course, that is bound to decrease the vitality that is naturally in the situation, and as you are trying so hard to take it all in, through trying you miss a lot. The experience doesn't cut into you as deeply as it would have once.

"But I guess that is nothing to worry about because, as I said, I have an endless supply of stories—anyway, it seems endless—to look ahead to. And if the first possibility holds, and I am just ten years behind myself as a writer, I have a very great deal to catch up to," Miss Hale concluded happily.

"Oh, and by the way, if you do happen to say anything about my specializing in the analysis of women, remember that I'm not just talking about women alone—you know, as workers, or wasters or anything like that. My interest is in their relations with men. I think that should be clear."

AN INTERVIEW WITH CHRISTOPHER MORLEY

Author of "Thorofare" describes the process of Anglo-American osmosis

November 15, 1942

CHRISTOPHER MORLEY waited at the top of the four long flights of steep stairs that led to his workroom in midtown New York. He called encouragement. He never yet, he said, had had a visitor who wasn't panting when he reached the top. "I've been making this climb for years and still pant." The Three-Hours-for-Lunch Club that he founded is now disbanded and Mr. Morley has lost weight. His beard and this loss of weight have greatly changed his appearance, and his teeth, never particularly noticeable before, seem to flash a great deal. They look strong and sharp. His manner also seemed changed. There was less extra cheer in it and more energy. While still on the stair landing he said:

"I've changed my writing method." He showed the way into a sizable room where some dozens of the newest books were piled on the floor, having overflowed the several bookcases. Prominent on the big dining table that serves as a worktable is an hour glass that runs slow—sixty-two and a half minutes to the hour. "I dictate," said Mr. Morley, "while the sand runs through one time. That is my way of measuring the work session, of making myself keep going through an allotted time whether I have a cold or feel terrible, however much I want to stop. As the sand runs out—well, it has an effect. It hurries me along. Please don't call this a piece of whimsey because it very definitely is not."

"I'm sure you wouldn't call it whimsey," said Miss Winspeare,

Mr. Morley's attractive amanuensis, "if you realized how deeply it hurts the old guy to be considered whimsical."

Always before, Mr. Morley continued, he had labored alone on his work. "I'd write the first draft in long hand and make corrections as I typed the second draft. I enjoyed the actual writing when I got to it; but, you know, when you work alone there is a very powerful tendency—particularly if you are as procrastinating and lazy as I naturally am—to do whatever job is easiest. Oh, I turned out a lot of work, yes, I suppose I did, too much—particularly too much secondary stuff. I always planned to tackle the really big effort at some later time. Now I find with an amanuensis—well, as an example, I'll come in some days and look over the mail and say, 'There are a lot of letters here that should be answered, and that speech I've been asked to make—I should draw up an outline at least.' And Miss Winspeare looks at me stonily and says: 'Yes, but hadn't you better do the work first?' And of course that is true and I know that it is true and I put the letters off until later and do the work.

"And my schedule helps. I live in the country, twenty-five miles out, and how people ever retire to the country and write is beyond me. I'd go nuts. So I have bound myself to turn up here in this hideout every Monday, Wednesday and Friday morning prepared to dictate while the sand runs through—rain or shine, hot or cold, sick or well. I find that there is some stimulation in the very fact of being in New York, and the train ride helps put my thoughts in order. I average a little better than a thousand words while the sand flows and Miss Winspeare types her notes and I take the typescript to the country with me and rewrite when necessary. Sometimes I mess the script up so much that I type it again, but as a general thing the work stands up fairly well and I can spend all of my off day making notes on the episodes I'm to cover in the next session.

"I believe there is little doubt that this method has improved my writing. There is much less embroidery, much less loving fondling of words and phrasing, and so the line of the story is left clear and the story moves faster.

"My new novel, 'Thorofare,' was dictated on this schedule through thirteen months."

Mr. Morley crossed the room to a large wall map of the Atlantic Ocean. "The Atlantic is the hero of my novel—the ocean that is the thoroughfare between England and ourselves, that bridges us together and that keeps us apart. Do you see here?" He pointed to the marking of the Chaucer Banks. "On this map I found even the name for my book's leading character, young Geoffrey Barton. The Geoffrey—suggested by Chaucer, of course —and I started to call him Geoffrey Banks, but decided to use the Quaker name Barton, instead."

He detailed the origin and growth of his theme for this book and its plan. The beginning was a casual luncheon conversation with Jan Struther soon after Miss Struther had brought her children to this country from England in the Spring of 1940. "In what Jan said I seemed to feel the impact of this country on the children—the little strangenesses that add up. I was born in America, but my parents were English and I've spent considerable time in England, particularly when I was young, and I knew about those strangenesses."

Mr. Morley produced a memorandum that he had made chiefly for himself when his novel was in its early stages, a memorandum intended as a guide, a statement of what his meaning and purpose was to be. It read in part:

"If Fascism were to win the war, perhaps this would be one of the books most likely to be put out of print. For it suggests that in spite of magical and humorous westward changes the Anglo-American idea of freedom remains the same. In spite of plenty of mutual abrasive, the two races remain capable of smiling at themselves and laughing at each other. The author had felt for some time that a record of some kindlier phases of Anglo-American intercourse might be set down in the accidented relief of fiction. He tries to tell here the inward story of a mind in westward motion. The arrival of the British children in large numbers in this country in the early days of the war gave impulse to this thought. Just what might be happening in those children reflecting a life of double feeling? It is queer, the author reflected, that we have heard much for many years of the soul-process of all sorts of immigrants except the English Americans."

"In other words," said Mr. Morley, "I describe the process of Anglo-American osmosis—osmosis. You know that word, don't you?"

"Well, I know it when I see it. Isn't it the forming or grouping of cells—some sort of unfortunate grouping?"

"Let me see," said Mr. Morley, going for a dictionary. "My dentist was telling me that if I didn't quit using so much salt toothpaste I'd bring on osmosis. I think it is fluids interacting; it must be. Yes." He made a note of it. "That's a good and accurate word, exactly the right phrase—Anglo-American osmosis."

It is this, the furthering of good relations between the United States and England, Mr. Morley said, "that I have decided is to be my main job for the duration. I'll try not to be too obvious about it—that is, destructive—but it is my main job and I'll stick to it."

Or as he said in his notes for "Thorofare": "Even in his worst moments the author had some relieving hopes. He remembered that the rubble from shattered Bristol had been shipped and used to underfound the new East Side Highway in New York City. He remembered that even the smallest of thorofares is open at both ends and the Anglo-American genius for politics and poetry is still open for traffic. He remembered that if he didn't tell this story he could think of no one else who would be likely to. And that even if what was said was too little and too late, it was a tribute to a great adventure in human living."

Later, in a restaurant that, on first entrance, had nothing at all to distinguish it from a hundred other restaurants about the mid-town section but that, as might be expected of a Morley eating place, possessed a chef of rare worth, Mr. Morley explained his beard.

"You knew Felix Reisenberg—you must remember his beard. Felix grew his beard as a memorial to Herman Melville and I felt when Felix died that some similar memorial was due to him—so

I grew my beard. It is disconcerting to have so much gray in it."

"You seem to tend it well."

"I have it clipped about once in two weeks. That was a problem at first, as most of the barbers now have no interest in beards; in fact, they dislike them.

"I was very coldly treated by barbers until I happened to go into a little shop not far from here where the barber was a real beard fancier. He borrowed just the right shears from a friend—I doubt that they make beard shears any more—and he told me, 'I'll treat your beard perfect.' And, so far as that could be done, he has.

"I find that I enjoy a beaver. I believe that most men would; certainly I had the desire for a beard long before, with my fiftieth birthday coinciding with Felix's death, I decided to let one grow. I feel that I was not a coward about it. Some men hide away in the bush for those first two weeks when you look as though you had been on a very long drunk and that that is the only explanation for the fact that you haven't shaved. But I didn't hide. I went my accustomed way, and took the jeers as they came.

"And I feel that my beard is worth the jeers."

AN INTERVIEW WITH BEN AMES WILLIAMS

He tells why "formula" short-story writers wear out

February 14, 1943

"ONE OF THE tough problems of a writer," said Ben Ames Williams, an extremely likable man who has been established as a writer for twenty-seven years, "is rarely talked about. But it is a problem that always has bothered me. It is this: what to do with yourself in the afternoons. I've tried just about everything—golf, bridge, backgammon, mah jong, a couple of hookers of whisky and the movies. You see, there's this need for anything that will give your brain just a little to do, just enough action to get the work out of it, so that you can go to sleep at night. Otherwise, you're working endlessly.

"We spend about six months each year on our farm in Maine—go to bed before sunset and get up before sunrise—and there we have an elaborate croquet game that sometimes is good for five hours in the afternoon—the way we work that is, the ball never is out of bounds; you wander all over the countryside. That's good, but hardly a complete solution. Now Ken Roberts (author of "Northwest Passage") works in the mornings, then carves wood. He also manages his place, which is a fairly large one. However, at night he works for an hour just before dinner. Well, as you can see—no cocktails. And if it were me I'd be all steamed up again, would rush through dinner and keep right on working afterward. My system is to work for three or four hours very hard in the morning—only the first two hours are any good, but I never realize that I'm getting tired and make a lot of extra work for myself by continuing on beyond the time when I should quit."

Probably in the minds of most of his readers Mr. Williams is stamped as a Maine man. His imaginary Maine village of "Fraternity" was the background of many of his most popular stories. Actually he was born in Mississippi—a grandnephew of the Confederate General Longstreet—grew up in Ohio, and was schooled in Massachusetts, in Cardiff, Wales—where his father was United States Consul—and at Dartmouth College in New Hampshire.

"My wife comes from a Maine family—but she was born in China and lived there until she was thirteen. It was more or less of an accident that we went to Maine, but there I met A. L. McCorrison, the Bert McAusland of my stories, and we—well, we hit it off. Through Bert I got the feel of his country and so I used it often as a setting. Place means a lot to me—it is the conditions of life that make people—and I learned the conditions of life there. Then Bert died in 1931, willing us his farm. We spend a lot of time on the farm, but I haven't used Maine setting much in these last twelve years—a lot of the sting went out of the countryside with Bert.

"Of course, what it all comes down to—the meaning must be there for you, that's the first need when you sit down to write anything. When I was younger I suppose I was hardier when it came to accepting meanings—my first story that managed to get between book covers was written in ten days in 1919, and it came out of a glance through Polti's 'Thirty-six Dramatic Situations.' The situation was that of enmity between brothers. With only that to start, and some knowledge of whaling, I wrote 'All the Brothers Were Valiant'—which apparently still is read because I still get letters about it. In other words, I found the meaning after the start had been made. But usually the meaning, feeling whatever it is, comes first.

"One foggy night years ago I rowed a boat out to a bell buoy and sat alone, the bell clanging beside me—nothing but the sound, the water, the night, the fog—and smoked a pipe. Well, to me that situation meant a lot, it stirred my imagination, and at least a dozen—probably more—of my stories have come out of those few minutes by the bell buoy, though the bell buoy never has been in one of them. There's no explaining it. It's just that the moment had meaning for me."

Mr. Williams said that he had had proof early that he had no inborn ability as a writer. "Starting in 1910, I worked as a newspaperman for four years, and every night through those four years I spent two to three hours trying to write short stories, and the four years were up before one of my stories sold. Well, a man who works that hard and doesn't get anywhere for that long is no born writer. I finally taught myself enough to get along and since then have sold going on 400 short stories and serials. Yes, I used Polti—in fact I'm his translator. I learned what a short story must be. But I don't write them any more."

"Why did you stop?"

"Partly because I lost my respect for money back in the depression when I became overanxious and couldn't sell the stories that I wrote. And partly because they weren't fun any more.

"Four times in my life I've turned my back on easy money because I knew that for me easy money wasn't any good. When my stories were selling in the top markets, when the movies were snapping them up—I'd reverse my field and feel better when I'd turned out stuff that was different and that I thought was good, even if the editors didn't think so. You see, if you go along playing up to the standard you've set just because that standard happens to be popular, you get into a formula—and for you the formula inevitably wears out. It's too much like digging ditches when you're hired out to dig them. Some one else is telling you to dig here and dig there, and then go back and dig a little deeper where you dug before. There's no more fun in it. I repeat myself enough on my own when I go my own way.

"The last time I turned away from short-story writing it wasn't because I wanted to—I had lost the touch. Stories are becoming shorter and shorter as the big weeklies more and more imitate the picture magazines. They'll all be down to one word on a page one of these days.

"I can't turn around in those short lengths, and, anyway, I enjoy writing novels. For in them I can take the space I need, can say the things I want to say, can enjoy the work of writing, can be—completely—my own man, not hired out to any one."

Mr. Williams said that he does an enormous amount of preliminary blocking out of characters before he really settles into the work of a novel.

"For example, before writing 'The Strange Woman'—which is having a rebirth that astonishes me but makes me fairly happy, too, as it is selling well enough so that it is not necessary for me to rush on the books that I have in the works now—I wrote about 100,000 words of biographies of the main characters before I started the story.

"In most of my novels you'll find good-sized chunks of characterization as a new person is introduced. These usually represent a good many thousand words that I wrote when I was thinking out the person.

"I always write at length, getting it all down. I write rapidly and not too critically and revise slowly and with pains. I rewrote one chapter in 'Time of Peace'—my latest book—thirteen times.

"I'm happy writing books—it is unfortunate that I didn't start as a novelist instead of a short-story writer. But I had no choice. There was so much respect in my family for books that—well, the idea that I could write anything so impressive as a book did not occur to me until I was well along in my thirties. It was only after publishers had been putting hard covers on my stories for a number of years that I decided to make a try as a novelist."

AN INTERVIEW WITH MARCIA DAVENPORT

The author of "The Valley of Decision" describes childhood in the home of a great artist

February 28, 1943

"I'M A GUTTERSNIPE," said Marcia Davenport, the author of "The Valley of Decision." She talks rapidly and eagerly. "I'm a wharf rat. I was born in New York and I live overlooking the East River. I expect to go on living there because I must live in the city or I can't work, and near a large body of water or I can't function. I suppose the Freudians would know why I must live near a large body of water, but I hope none of them explains it to me—I don't want to hear about it."

The scene of the interview was an East Fifty-second Street restaurant where they give you only one pat of butter, but where you discover that your bread has been buttered in the kitchen and the slices stuck together. Mrs. Davenport didn't think much of this trick.

"It's all that damned insistence on 'business as usual,' on getting fat as usual, on pampering yourself as usual. This thing of specializing in keeping yourself happy seems to me the emptiest of aims. I have never seen a productive and functioning person much concerned with happiness. I doubt very much if there is any happiness, anyway, in escaping from grim reality into anything else."

"But how about all this time you spend listening to music?"

"That's no escape. Music to me is work. It's so identified for me with the labor that goes into it. When I listen to music it's with severe concentration. I don't loll back in a chair," she said, lolling back in her chair, "and say, 'Ah, isn't that lovely!' I follow the score. I know just what each instrument is doing. I listen for the special developments that I know are to come. Take a fugue. For me a fugue is a hyper-stimulant. It's a severe mental exercise. I am rigid when I listen to a fugue."

She said she learned that music was work very early. "I've made a habit of never talking about my mother [Mrs. Davenport is the daughter of Alma Gluck] for publication because my mother was simply fanatical in her adherence to the principle that nobody should rise to fame—that is, should try to rise to fame, or to celebrity, or even to notice—on the strength of somebody else's fame, of the work some one else has done. I feel the same way. I am fanatical on it. That's why, when I was starting out, I bent over backward to keep people from finding out my background because, you know, you're handicapping yourself dreadfully if you become associated in the minds of people as the child of some one who is famous. Oh, you rouse a momentary curiosity, but that cools off. I have never used her name as a springboard and wouldn't want any child of mine to use mine that way either.

"But, as I said, I did learn of the work that goes into music very early. I was in the middle of it from the time I was two years old."

"I should think you would have been in it from birth."

"No, my mother didn't become a singer until I was two years old. She was brought here from Rumania when she was six years old. The family was very poor. They landed at Ellis Island—no, it was Castle Garden—and went to live on the lower East Side. My mother went to public school and to high school. She was a very good student and graduated with honors. When she was still very young—seventeen or just eighteen—she was married. I was born a year later—in 1903.

"Her life was entirely domestic, keeping house and taking care of me. She'd sing now and then as she did housework. One night, just by accident, a business acquaintance of my father heard her sing. Well, this man was nuts about opera—an habitué of the upper regions of the Metropolitan Opera House. He was electrified. Of course, I don't know just what he said but you can imagine it—something like: 'Have you any idea what kind of voice you have?' And mother said no, she never had given her voice much thought. Well, this man, this businessman who loved opera, was the link between my mother and the teacher—Maestro Arturo Buzzi-Peccia. Buzzi-Peccia heard my mother sing and he said that she must work at music. She said that she had no time, that she had me to take care of, and that she had no money. He said that she must come to him every day, that he would see her whenever his regular pupils were not there, early in the morning, at the lunch-hour break, or late at night and when she had nothing else to do with me she must bring me too. And never mind about the money.

"I don't remember the trolley-car rides to the studio—I suppose we went on the trolley—but I do have a very dim recollection of the studio where I must have spent quite a lot of time between the ages of two and four. When I was four years old, Buzzi-Peccia went back to Europe. In order to continue her lessons my mother went also, taking me with her. I marvel at the self-discipline, the strong character of a young and beautiful woman who was working terribly hard at music and yet would let herself be encumbered by a small child and all the annoyances that go with it. In Switzerland, Gatti-Casazza heard my mother sing. It was just a practice session and he had come to the house of Buzzi-Peccia for lunch. He hired her on the spot for the Metropolitan.

"Of course, that story is a cliché. You find something quite like it in the life of dozens of singers. I used some elements of it in my book 'Of Leya Geyer'—all fiction must be a composite of reality, and if reality is made up of clichés—well, that's what you must use. Fiction is interwoven experience."

"What was it like to grow up in the home of a great artist?"

"It was hardly a home in the usual sense. My life was not what most people consider a normal life for a child. That is, my mother had no room in her world for a child. If I wanted companionship I had to come up to adult standards. I'll never forget one scene when I was learning this. My mother had taken a little house in the Adirondacks one Summer when I was eight years old. She had me practicing music not because I had the least talent for music —we both knew that I hadn't any—but because she believed, as I do, that work is most necessary for any human being; and because she also believed, as I do, that to permit a child to grow up an illiterate in music is as bad as to permit general illiteracy. I think that it is just as necessary for any one to know the way around in musical sources as to have read the classics of literature that every one is supposed to have read, and that it is no less desirable to be able to look at a sheet of music and to know what's on it and what the writer intended than it is to be able to look at a newspaper and understand what the print says.

"It was also partly for the discipline of work in music—my mother was a martinet—that I was made to practice piano and work hard. One day, there in the Adirondacks, I had been sloppy about the work, and I remember my mother's eyes as she stood at the bottom of the stairs in the cottage and looked up at me—I was on the top step. Her eyes seemed to be very large, and I was very frightened as she said to me: 'How can you ever expect to amount to anything if you won't work? You will be worthless—that's what you'll be!' And I said, in a very small voice, for after all I was very small and my mother did frighten me when she was angry, that I would amount to something. 'What?' my mother demanded. And I said, 'I'll write, I'll write.' "

"What did your mother say?"

" 'Humph!' I guess. But I did want to write books and I knew it even then. I had a very lonely childhood except for books. I read fairy stories, and the people in them were my first companions. I was so deeply in them that I was extremely fussy about the kind of fairy tales I read. For example, I didn't like Hans Christian Andersen at all. His stories were too folksy; they were about humble people, woodcutters and goose girls. The stories I liked had to have magic in them and be about extraordinary people—kings and princes, fairies and jinni—and the things that happened in them had to happen by magic.

"Although my mother was very strict with me in the European fashion—which means that every detail of my conduct was known to her and sharply criticized—she gave me absolute freedom in the range of my reading. When I was first given an allowance, I went directly to a bookstore and paid $65 for a seventeen-volume set of Burton's 'Arabian Nights' in the unexpurgated version. That was all right. I could read anything I could get my hands on.

"I don't know if that kind of bringing up is the right thing for a child. It's the kind of thing—the only kind of thing, that I can give my own children. I can't try to come down to the child's world. I can't function there. I was fitted into my mother's existence along with the other exigencies. For, after all, what can you do for a human being except equip him for accomplishment and hard work? I don't give a damn if a man writes a symphony or lays bricks so long as he does the job the way the job should be done. All this business of trying to give children a happy childhood with the thought you are fitting them for a happy life—well, I'm doubtful about it. Happiness must be incidental. If it comes along every once in a while, that's fine. But how are you going to learn to punch the world in the nose just by being happy?"

Talking about work, Mrs. Davenport said she didn't want to appear a monster—"though I may be a monster at that"—in slandering country living, but that, personally, she found it very hard to live in the country because she couldn't work in the country—"I can't function there."

"My husband [Russell Davenport, formerly managing editor of *Fortune* and the manager of Mr. Willkie's Presidential campaign] once bribed me to live in the country by giving me a little lion. It was the only time that Russell ever totally surprised me. I am mad about all cat animals, and on one of my birthdays, when we had a rented country place, Russell came home late, bringing two friends with him. Instead of stopping in front of the house, they went on down the drive to the barn. And then one of his friends came hurrying back, as I realized later, to forestall my going to the barn to see what they were up to. I am very near-sighted, and when I saw Russell coming toward me, leading what looked to be a Great Dane puppy, I thought, 'Damn the man. I don't want a dog. He knows I love cats.' Then, what was my delight to find that it was a baby lion."

She told enthusiastically of the household crises that result from having a lion about the place, of the jealousy of her cat that sat in an upstairs window and cried all the time because of the attention the lion was getting, and of the Negro butler who, at first sight of the lion, expressed the conviction, "He don't like me," but found that the lion did like him very much and afterward spent his afternoons dreamily picking flowers for the house with the chained lion at his side.

"How long did you keep your lion, Mrs. Davenport?"

"That's the worst of it. A lion is wonderful company until it gets to be eight or nine months old. They are very smart and play like kittens. While I had 'Kitty'—the lion—I agreed with Russell that we should have a farm. And we bought one. But then we had to give Kitty to a zoo and, naturally, my husband said that if I expected him to go on buying me lions to bribe me to live in the country, I was crazy. So we came back to town.

"Because it's only in town that I can work. When I'm really writing, I lock myself in a room overlooking the East River and keep at it for about ten hours a day."

AN INTERVIEW WITH BERNARD DE VOTO

Without assistance of "John August" he couldn't do "serious" books

April 25, 1943

AMONG THE ACKNOWLEDGMENTS in Bernard De Voto's "The Year of Decision: 1846," is the line: "Finally, I acknowledge that I could not possibly have written this book if I had not had periodic assistance from Mr. John August." John August is Mr. De Voto's pen name, under which he writes serial stories for the slick magazines, and which he took, he said, as a refuge because of the titles, such as "Life Begins on the Campus," with which magazine editors headed his work.

"You see, as John August I spend five or six months on a serial that brings me in $20,000. Well, we can live for two years on that—two years during which I can concentrate on my own work."

In this way Mr. De Voto has made the dream come true, the dream that must activate serried thousands of would-be writers. By learning the technique, first of the magazine short story and then of the serial, he has found it possible to devote large amounts of time to study of the American West and to his work with the Mark Twain papers. "Financially, the only thing I'm sure of getting for my work on Twain is the salary for my secretary." He told how he started on this happy course.

"It was when I was an instructor at Northwestern University, getting $1,700 a year, and filling that out by going downtown at night to teach an extension course. That was a tough life. In that extension course it was bad enough to be on my feet for three hours talking, without all that added work of getting up something to talk about. Then, too," said Mr. De Voto, with a kind of morose nostalgia, "I didn't fit in very well at Northwestern. It was at that period when they were changing over from being a good, small school into a metropolitan university, and standards were falling, well, wherever they happened to fall. They were advertising this and that, just trying to grow. But it offended me."

"You were probably pretty critically minded then, anyway, weren't you?"

"Sure. That was the Mencken period. It was then *The Mercury* was way up on top. That was my first outlet. I did a lot of stuff for Mencken. But he had a sliding pay rate of $90-125 an article, and Harper's paid $200 flat for the same stuff. So I switched to *Harper's*. Then in the Summer of 1927 I sold two or three pieces all at once; and I had been married four or five years then, and I was very tired of extension and so forth, so I said to my wife, who had never been East—she is a Michigan girl, 'Let's spend the Summer on Cape Cod.'

"We went to Chatham, Mass., and took one room in a boarding house. It was while we were there that the break came in a sort of odd way.

"One of my *Harper* pieces had been a short story, and it brought me a letter from an agent suggesting that I write more short stories, and let her sell them for me. It was just one of those form letters that agents send out all the time, but I didn't know that and wrote her a letter saying I'd like to hear more from her. Now it just so happened that one client of this agent was Conigsby Dawson, and that Dawson lived there in Chatham. Dawson's stepdaughter, Margaret Wright Clark, had been sort of filling in her time as an assistant to this agent, and was on vacation in Chatham at that time.

"So Margaret Wright Clark came around to see me and in the casual way of the prosperous girl with a social background, who finds everything pretty easy that other people do, asked me why I didn't write a story for *The Saturday Evening Post*. Well, to her that was very simple. And listening to her, it seemed very simple to me. So I tried it. I knocked off a story in about three weeks, sent it to the *Post,* and they paid me $600 for it.

"I know now that it must have been luck, but at the time I was astonished and delighted. I thought, 'How long has this been going on?' I wired Northwestern resigning my job and set up as a story writer. The next three or four that I wrote sold very readily, then they began to bounce around a little; and as rejections came in, I gave a great deal of attention to technique. For about two years I worked hard, trying to find out how I had done what I had done in the first place. And after about two years, I had the technique down fairly well. For a long time now I've known enough of what I was doing so that the stories usually land."

"Mr. De Voto, don't you write most of your stories through sheer force of mind?"

"Yes, I'm not a natural. And I say too proudly, 'I'm a hack.' That is probably the result of vestigial guilt left over from my youth, from the time when I wanted to be a great writer. Even after learning how to sell the stories, I still had a virginity left. I said that one thing I would not do was to write a hack novel. But then one day I was in Philadelphia and about four of the editors of *The Saturday Evening Post* took me to lunch. Ken Littauer of *Collier's* had been suggesting to me that I might write a serial. As he said, there is a lot more money in serial writing than in short stories—that is to say, per pound-inch of pressure on the writer the pay is better. So at this lunch I said I might do a serial. But this was in the old days and every one went very *Saturday Evening Post* on me, because you know in those days there was a very strong tendency down there to make you feel that though you might be a writer, you remained, in the eyes of the editor, only an ambitious worm—and a very fortunate worm, at that, if the editor was paying some attention to you. They told me that I didn't understand about serials and that I couldn't possibly write one, and so when I came back to New York that afternoon, still in a very bad temper, I telephoned Ken Littauer and told him that I had an idea for a serial. In a week the story was all lined up and in two months it was finished. I can't write 'em as fast as that now. I spend a lot more time trying to figure out the story line, which must be very direct and clear."

"What's your main problem in writing serials?"

"Well, it's that story line. I don't have a good story mind and the only way I can work it is through the writing. I write a comedy of manners that the magazines call a romantic mystery. Once the story itself is set, I go ahead at the rate of about 1,200-1,500 words a day, writing only in the mornings. I spend the afternoons in the Widener Library in Cambridge, doing research in history, going over the Mark Twain papers and so on. The only writing quirk I have is that I must write my first draft on a certain kind of cheap, orange paper. I hate to waste good paper. We bought a house in Cambridge not long ago and in the drawers of the desk in the study are several reams of the best Italian handmade paper. I can't bring myself to use it."

"How many drafts do you write?"

"Always at least three drafts. When I'm working out a story, I sit around using up pads of paper for penciled notes. I never look at these notes again. But they are useful for fixing the direction and the scenes in my head. As for characters, the main trouble I have is the villain. Oh, I've known a lot of saps and a lot of people who have been embittered by failure at one thing or another, and even some people who are malicious and maybe mean, but I never have known a real villain and I doubt if they exist outside the serials. As a result, I work on my villains overtime, trying to put in little touches that will bring them out, make them seem more lifelike."

"Do you do any research," I asked him, "for your comedies of manners? That is, do you hang around the Stork Club and places such as that for local color?"

"No, I never go into those places, unless an editor takes me for lunch. Hell, I can think of as good a Stork Club as Sherman Billingsley can. Lee Hartman of *Harper's* used to take me around to speakeasies now and then. And one time he introduced me at Twenty-One as a connoisseur of old brandies. They brought bottles by the dozen for me to taste. With my eyes wide open, looking at the label, I can tell the difference between whisky and brandy. But that's how expert I am. No, I don't bother with research for this stuff."

Mr. De Voto is of medium height, a durable-looking man. His manner was affable and he seemed far less ready to respond to minor provocation than might have been expected by one whose earlier meetings with him had been at literary cocktail parties, where he had seemed thoroughly unhappy, yet strangely eager—a puzzling combination.

But as he talked, with months of hard and steady work behind him, with one book newly published—"The 'Year of Decision' is the best job I've done"—and a John August serial newly completed, one had the feeling that here was a very capable man, pleasantly relaxed after a long time without ease, and not quite accustomed to ease but enjoying it as only good workmen ever do.

THREE YOUNG WRITERS IN UNIFORM REPORT FROM THE FRONTS

Sgts. McGurn, Meyers and Bernstein tell of war's effect on writing

January 28, 1945

A WRITER MUST know his own generation. Who can know the present male generation unless he has been in uniform—has experienced the intimacy and loneliness of troops in the field? I asked three young writing sergeants on the staff of *Yank*, the Army weekly, what they felt they had learned about men in war, what insight they had had that had impressed them most. These three sergeants are contributors to "The Best From Yank," an anthology that will be published by Dutton later this season. All of them have been around. One covered the Pacific for fourteen months; another served in Alaska and the Aleutians from 1942 until a few months ago; another was the first English-speaking correspondent to interview Tito: "I landed on the Adriatic coast of Yugoslavia and walked for a week—half the time through German-occupied territory . . ."

Sgt. Barret McGurn—former editor of *The Fordham Ram*, former sermon reporter and college correspondent for *The New York Times* and *The New York Herald Tribune*—had the Pacific as his beat from October, 1943, until last month. After training as a medical corpsman he was assigned to *Yank* and shipped out to Bougainville. He took part in the invasion of Green Island—"that was quiet"—of Peleliu—"I got there with a late wave, so it wasn't tough"—of Leyte in the Philippines.

"I think what most impressed me," said Sergeant McGurn, "is

the way people out there treat one another, and the way people here treat one another. My first day back in civilization I was walking on Market Street in San Francisco. And to get out of the way of some one coming toward me, I stepped into the path of a woman just behind me. Of course, I apologized. She didn't look at me. She stared straight ahead, and I could tell the way she felt about me was that she wouldn't take an apology from me, even for being jostled. She didn't want the contact of so much as an apology.

"Shock is too strong a word. I wasn't shocked, but I was surprised. Where I'd been every one was considerate of others, of everyone who was on our side. There was a man shot through the head on Leyte and all those who saw it hopped up out of their foxholes wanting to help. There was nothing much they could do but yell for the medics, but they wanted to do anything they could. The medics came and gave the guy plasma. It couldn't do him any good, but every one wanted to make use of every last chance of helping the fellow.

"And most of all I remember a trip aboard an LST going in for an invasion landing—there never was a group of men more one. We were all expecting tough combat, hand-to-hand stuff or grenade fighting. And it was as though, in looking forward to what we hoped to do to the Japs, we all especially prized one another. I actually heard one man congratulate the mess sergeant on the excellence of his coffee. Not kidding; quite solemnly. I guess the mess sergeant was amazed, but he was solemn, too. We were all thinking that day of whose turn it was. Maybe our turn or the turn of the guy just behind us, and we were trying very hard to give every one else all the little breaks. All that was petty or grasping for advantage—well, it was just wiped away. There was no pettiness left.

"I don't want to overemphasize this, but I wonder why civilians don't feel it more than they do—the oneness, the importance of every American to every American, of everyone who is on our side. It is tough going out there. The servicemen need to feel that there are a lot of people with them . . ."

Tech. Sgt. George N. Meyers was formerly city editor of the "Farthest North American Daily," the *Fairbanks News-Miner,* and news editor of KFAR at Fairbanks. Enlisting in the Army in May, 1942, he joined the staff of *Yank* a month later. He has flown over Paramushiro, has spent considerable periods in camps so remote that "when new movies arrive they run all the films through at once—twelve-hour shows. They can't get enough of movies. Of course, that's hard country, out on the Aleutian chain. There's no civilization at all—nowhere to go. I knew men who asked for and got three-day passes. Then they walked across the island they were on—to a camp on the other side which was just like the camp they had left. But it was a kind of change."

Sergeant Meyers covered the occupation of Adak in August, 1942, the occupation of Amchitka in January, 1943, the conquest of Attu that next May and the occupation of Kiska the following August. "Some of the boys grumbled because they didn't get a fight on Kiska. I didn't agree with them. I'd been in the valleys on Attu.

"I believe that the main thing I learned," said Sergeant Meyers, "is that most of us can take a lot more than we think we can, and that all of us are a lot more alike than we think we are. All this talk about differences in background making changes impossible —I don't believe such talk.

"The human mind and the human body are the most adaptable, most malleable entities that God ever made. I lived pretty well in Fairbanks and if any one had told me that I could move to a canvas cot over a floor ankle-deep in mud sharing a sixteen-foot pyramid tent with five other men—and go out and scoop up snow in a gallon can and melt it on a Sibley stove so that I'd have water with which to shave and wash—I'd have been staggered at the idea. But actually, that is luxury.

"Because when you make original landings in combat—well, on Attu we slept in holes we dug in the ground. And on Attu the hole begins to fill with water an hour after you've dug it. We had no sleeping bags, but we'd been under fire all day, climbing around in the mountains, dodging bullets and shooting at Japs, and at night we slept because we were exhausted. Every few hours we'd wake up and kick rocks to drive the numbness from our feet—then go back to sleep.

"After four nights we got sleeping bags. That was comfort. But what impressed me—I was doing all right under the original conditions, and so were the other men. We could have gone on four more nights and four after that. I didn't like it—I hope I'm never dope enough to say I like it. But I felt very much alive and very healthy.

"Out in the field we've discovered a great thing about ourselves —we've discovered that we won't cave in. And that discovery means that we have an added respect for ourselves and for one another. I used to think that a boy with seven years of college behind him might do a better job in the field than a boy who had only seven years of grammar school. Well, there may be those differences, but I didn't notice them on Attu. If they exist they are so slight that they can't be noticed."

Sgt. Walter Bernstein was graduated from Dartmouth in 1940 and went to work for *The New Yorker* as a writer. He has served as *Yank* correspondent in Africa and on Sicily, with headquarters at Cairo. In April, 1944, he landed on the Yugoslav coast and accompanied fifty young people who were on their way to Tito's headquarters to attend a youth congress. He remained at the headquarters for about ten days.

"What got me most was the way these people were standing up to crisis, the way they were fighting when they had nothing to fight with, the way the country was so cleanly split into those who were against Fascism, against the Germans, and those who were for the Germans. No fence sitting. In this country of fifteen million people it was known that a million had been killed. Probably even more had been killed, but they knew about the million.

"And they were operating on the principle that this was a fight that anybody could get into—men, women and children. And they weren't all just thrown into the fighting without organization. They had set up a law against illiteracy, for example. Every one who joined and was illiterate was given teachers and three weeks in which to learn to read and write. There were constant classes going on to tell the people what the war was all about. Every guerrilla unit had its newspaper, and once a month every one in the company had to contribute to that newspaper. I saw some poems written by a sixty-year-old woman.

"All the writing was straight black-and-white stuff, of course. But every one had to write to prove that he knew what the war was about. I talked to one lieutenant general who had been a surrealist in Paris and who had turned out to be one of Tito's best soldiers. He was keeping on writing, but I guess it was all direct black-and-white stuff, too.

"What really impressed me was the fusion of art with life. For me, it killed the notion of so-called pure art. The artist must know where he stands, where his roots are, where his strength is coming from. These people knew that their strength was coming from one another.

"Of course, the crisis carried some advantages so far as reaching that realization was concerned. Tito had to be on the move all the time and one of his great problems was the care of the wounded, so a technique was developed. They would enlarge caves in the mountains and put their wounded in these caves with supplies, a doctor and a couple of nurses. Then they'd seal up the caves. The Germans could be heard moving about outside, but the Germans didn't know about the caves. In a month or six weeks the guerrillas would come back if they possibly could and unseal the cave. If they couldn't come back, the wounded would break out and do the best they were able. You can imagine how all the little surface differences between people must disappear under conditions like that. The big landowner, the publisher of Belgrade's largest newspaper, and farmers and carpenters and writers, all in one cave—you get to know whom you're with under conditions like that. You get to know that you're with everybody who is in that cave with you, who is fighting the war with you.

"The crisis hasn't the same intensity over here, but it's here just the same. We're all against Germany and Japan, and we're all against depression, and hunger, and sickness. I think that writers will come more and more to realize that, and that out of identification with others they will draw new health, new affirmations . . ."

These sergeants are three among thousands of writers in uniform who range the world, supplying the material for thousands of publications that civilians never see, that are published by the Army, Navy and Marine Corps. Selected at random for interviewing, they did not confer with one another. They were seen separately. Yet, as can be noted, there was a striking similarity in their responses when they were asked to say what had impressed them most.

AN INTERVIEW WITH EDNA FERBER

Who thinks her generation of writers should "make room for the kids"

February 4, 1945

Edna Ferber waited for the publication of her new novel, "Great Son." Her hands and her talk were restless. The talk ranged over the hard drinking of some American writers and their wives: "She was like a little girl, a child, but after the cocktails and wine at dinner, she filled a whole tumbler full of Scotch and drank it down as I'd drink water; before long she looked like an old hag." The talk reached to Russia and Communism: "It's a good system for them; sure, it is. I visited there as a tourist and I know what they want. They want oranges and shoes and wrist watches and fountain pens and little cars to drive in. We have those things. What we want is here," said Miss Ferber, pointing to her heart, "and here," pointing to her head. Speaking of hearts, said Miss Ferber, she had recently come from Washington, where she had taken the "two-step," a physical test designed for young Navy fliers. The person being tested runs up and down two steps "about forty times, and the chart that they make afterward should be," said Miss Ferber wistfully, "all regular little cones." But hadn't the test been designed for the pick of the nation, the youngest, strongest, physically most perfect? "Yes, I suppose so," Miss Ferber said. "But the chart should be all regular little cones."

Miss Ferber spoke of "all the vitality that I have," but corrected herself to say, "that I had." She gives, however, an impression of great vitality. As she talks she acts, mimics, and though her eyes, which are striking, are alert for every response, they are not wary but have the look that expects and presumes response. One has the impression, watching her, of a person who after a fairly long and very full lifetime has reached an edge looking down into uncertainty, but who has never before quite known uncertainty, who has always filled up that pit with competence and work and pride in work and success.

She said: "I want to write five plays before I die." Had she been working on one recently? "No, the last thing that George (George S. Kaufman) and I did was 'Bright Land,' and that—as you probably remember—was a semi-flop. George and I haven't talked plays lately. I think I may try one alone."

She wants to write plays, she said, because there is some fun in doing them. "So much of the work on a novel is just lonely labor—the pile of manuscript that grows so very slowly as you slave through long stretches of description and narrative. But a play is all dialogue—that is, it is purely people that you are dealing with all the time. And I like to write dialogue.

"You know, it occurs to me as I speak, won't the new novels be largely dialogue? All swift pace and people? I've read that wonderful book, 'A Walk in the Sun,' by Harry Brown, and it is great, it's magnificent. What a beautiful job!" She quoted lines of the dialogue spoken by a soldier who is longing for an apple, a soldier who is writing a letter in his head. "Can't you just see the boy as he says that? So young, so concentrating . . ."

The mention of youth brought more animation to her voice and manner. "The best thing we can do—that is, my crowd, my generation—is to clear out of the way, make room for the kids, the young people who are twentyish, the soldiers and their girls and sisters. My goodness," exclaimed Miss Ferber, "what books they will write! Because they are honest and their world is debunked and they see it straight and clear. They even think straight, think honestly, and they are not afraid. Out of all of the mess of the

1920's and the miseries of the 1930's these amazing young people —the greatest generation, to my mind, since the people in the covered wagons.

"My generation was afraid and so was yours. Afraid of sex and inhibitions—well, of course, I can take inhibition or leave it alone; I don't really mind an inhibition—that is, it can be useful. But, anyway, the new generation isn't for them or afraid of them. My crowd was afraid of so many things—of words and emotion, of love. We had to be shocked with love. But these people can talk about love simply, naturally, and admit they love a home, or a Mom, or a Dad. We couldn't possibly have done that without quotation marks. But their voices are quiet, and they are controlled; they say what they feel as they feel it. They are sound people.

"They are a great hope in a world that for years has been gripped by an all-pervading fear, a fear that is everywhere as though it were a great sound from the sky. It is fear that is behind the hate, intolerance, bigotry, the verbal and actual slitting of throats. You see it on the streets—a woman and child walk along and the child isn't quick enough crossing the street, so the woman shouts at it, 'Why don't you come on!' " Miss Ferber shouted (and an echoing sound in the next room indicated that her startled, white-coated houseman had dropped a plate or an ash tray) "The woman slaps the child. Now that's fear, nothing more. We all feel it, except the young people. Perhaps they can save us from terrible times."

To the question of why, as she was so conscious of this fear and of the need to exorcise it, she did not use it as a theme for a novel, Miss Ferber closed her eyes and slowly responded: "One doesn't quite know the method."

She did use that theme, she said, in her autobiography, "A Peculiar Treasure." "Now you know—or rather, anyone who knows me knows—that if I lived to be 105 I wouldn't think it worth while to write my autobiography. I wouldn't do it. But with this theme, and feeling that I couldn't be entirely effective with the theme in a novel—because it is so vast, so overwhelming, so much our whole time—I decided to concentrate it in the story of the Jewish family that I knew best, and of course that was my own family. People like to know what is behind the scenes, they like a keyhole view, so I thought I'd give them that and this theme with it. I've had many, many readers.

"But as for themes in fiction—every one of my books has had a theme deep in it that was very important to me. I should say every book except 'Show Boat,' which hadn't any theme, which was just fun. But the rest have—though I suppose not many people know it.

"They didn't know it because—I think—if you write with humor, with lightness, entertainingly, you're not counted serious. If your writing is easy and pleasant for a great many readers, a phrase comes to be used on you—a phrase that I've begun to hate with a deep, strong, almost nauseating hatred. I don't even like to say it, the silly hybrid!"

It developed that the objectionable phrase is "best-seller."

"I was going over the advance publicity for my new book and I found in there—'best-seller.' I said, 'Please! Why? Why, even by my publisher, am I dismissed as a best-seller? 'Show Boat,' I said, 'was written in 1925. And this is the year 1945. 'So Big' was written in 1923, and this is 1945. 'Cimarron' came along in 1928—and they all are reprinted in those wonderful little books that are sent to the soldiers—yes, the Armed Services Editions. Well, goodness,' I said. 'Do you call books best-sellers—which means out today and gone tomorrow—and is a hateful, slurring derogatory phrase—when those books are being read and reread down through more than twenty years—and are being printed in the tens of thousands right today?'

"I shouldn't tell you this, I suppose," said Miss Ferber. "I've never told anyone, not one soul, of what a man said of my work in a letter not addressed to me but that I saw. The man was an Englishman. He wrote of me—I'm embarrassed saying this; repeating this rather, because certainly I'm not saying this. I'm only quoting—that it was probable that I would not be appreciated in my country and in my time. The man who said that was Rudyard

Kipling, and his letter is in the Doubleday, Doran offices. Another man, writing from England too, said the same thing. He was James M. Barrie."

Miss Ferber said that "Great Son" will be her last book in the field of historical fiction. "I want to live in today." She has been, she said, enchanted by certain phases in the development of this country, "by the figures—they were never people, but they were figures recognizable as people"—who had built the country, made it great. But now she was through with history. "I have that same feeling that I had when I finished with 'Emma McChesney.' "

"And that was?"

"Well, I wrote a good many stories about Emma McChesney. She was a good character and I was afraid to try a novel, and you know—when you write with some success you contract obligations. And Emma McChesney was so popular that she took care of my obligations. Of course, I was writing other stories along with those about her, but many of the others weren't really short stories—they were novels cut down. 'Old Man Minick' was a novel with a whole life crammed into a few thousand words. I had it in my mind that I was a short-story writer and no more. Yet my ideas were those that should go into a novel. It was as though I were taking enough clothes to fill a trunk and instead of putting them into a trunk put them into a suitcase. Then there I was sitting on the suitcase trying to close it. Ends of skirts and arms of blouses wouldn't go in, so I'd take the scissors and snip them off. That's what happens when you try to pack a novel into 5,000 words.

"Then a contract came from *Cosmopolitan* for more McChesney stories, and the line for payment was left blank. That meant that I could fill it in for any amount I wanted. Well, I knew that if I signed that contract I was a gone duck. I'd be writing Emma McChesney stories from then on. I sent back the contract unsigned and wrote 'The Girls'—and became a novelist.

"What's in my novels that will last? Well, I don't know. I'm not so old yet that I reread what I've done in the past, mourning among my souvenirs. But I do know that what you are emerges;

whether you are a writer or not, what you are becomes clear, and if you are a writer, then what you are is there in your writings for every one to read. As for me, if I don't last, if what I've done isn't good enough, I can't ever say I did it for the wife and kids. I've written what I wanted to write, and always the best I could do at the time."

AN INTERVIEW WITH CARLOS P. ROMULO

Hero of Bataan describes his newspaper days in Manila

February 11, 1945

THE SCENE WAS the Waldorf-Astoria's Peacock Alley and the time was midnight. Brig. Gen. Carlos P. Romulo, Resident Commissioner of the Philippines, aide to General MacArthur, and author of the forthcoming book "My Brother Americans," had had a full day. That noon he had addressed Congress and had received a rising ovation. He had then traveled from Washington to New York, attended a dinner given him by his publishers. In another hour he would start back for Washington, where he had a number of early morning appointments.

The day for him had not been unusual. Romulo has rarely relaxed since Manila fell to the Japanese. He went through the fighting on Bataan and then was sent here by General MacArthur to tell the story of Bataan. To tell that story he has traveled 99,000 miles through this country, has talked in 466 cities, has written three books and many articles, has granted innumerable interviews.

"When do you sleep?"

"I am very fortunate, for I can sleep anywhere. When I go to a station and have a five-minute wait for a train I sit down on a bench and sleep for five minutes. All I need is something to lean against."

General Romulo had returned to the Philippines to take part in the conquest of Leyte. What had he seen there that suggested themes for writers?

"The theme for a great book is there," he said, "a book not for America alone but for the whole world. Imagine what a Tolstoy could do with the story of American imperialism and its results. The Americans came as conquerors so short a time ago that my own father was a leader in the fight against them, and yet in those few years, a generation only, the Filipinos learned so much loyalty for America that—but let me tell you. . . .

"When we landed on Leyte the people waited for us waving American flags. The Japanese had made the possession of an American flag an offense punishable by death. But the people had kept their flags.

"Five days after the landing we reopened the schools. I had been named Commissioner of Education and I had feared that we could not open the schools for a long time because I knew that the Japanese had given orders that all American textbooks be burned, that they had burned all that they had found. But on Leyte I was told: 'Don't worry about textbooks. We have them.' And they had them, for they had buried them in the ground. Not as a group but as individuals. Now they dug up their textbooks, and though the covers were moldy the print was clear enough.

"Little incidents, little facts, but those flags would not have been hidden or those books buried except by a people who knew that the Americans would return and who wanted them to return.

"And beyond the loyalty is the acceptance, the recognition of that loyalty. I drove in a jeep with General MacArthur and we called the attention of each other to the passing scenes all about us. The soldiers had turned their packs inside out when they landed on Leyte. The people were hungry, and they gave them food, and they had no clothing, so the Americans gave them clothing. We saw girls wearing GI towels as sarongs—I remember one girl mincing along, and as she passed MacArthur nudged me; her sarong was stamped in big letters, 'Camp Hood.' We passed dozens of Filipinos wearing GI fatigue uniforms, and we came upon one soldier who was patiently showing a very old Filipino man how to shave with a Gillette razor.

"And in all these scenes—this is the important point that I am getting at—there was no consciousness of race. I thought of this as we drove in the jeep. I remembered one foxhole on Bataan where I had seen the bodies of two men who in life had occupied that foxhole together. They had been killed and their postures were grotesque, as so often in sudden violent death. Their bodies were grotesquely intertwined. These men who had shared the foxhole together and had died together were of different races. One was a tall blond American boy; the other was of Malay stock, short as I am, hair black as mine, his skin was brown. And as I had looked at them I had wondered if more honor ever would be paid to one than to the other, and I had thought that 'earth cannot be sifted to separate the one race from the other.'

"And as I looked about me on Leyte I thought, 'There is no difference here, either.' And as though General MacArthur had read my thought he said to me: 'Congress can give you political equality, Carlos, but no law could have given you social equality. That had to come another way.' And I said: 'I have just been thinking of that and that we seem to have it.' 'Yes, you do have it, Carlos,' the general said. 'You won it on Bataan.' "

Romulo said that his crammed hours and days represented his effort to go on living through all of the war years with Japan as he and the other men had existed on Bataan. When he mentioned sleepless nights and missed meals it is always in relating some tale of appreciation for America. His high-speed tours that sometimes call for two and three speeches a day in cities fairly distant from one another have been quite uniformly successful and have brought him considerable amounts of publicity. Many of his anecdotes of these tours have to do with his difficulty in giving tips.

"I had been talking at Butte, Montana, and my next speech was to be made at Great Falls, Montana. I remember it all very clearly because not only was the temperature 45 degrees below zero, but I had missed both lunch and dinner, and I think this made me feel the cold more. When I got to Great Falls, to the hotel, I said that I wanted the best dinner that could be had and that I wanted it in my room, as I was very tired. Soon a girl waitress appeared with one of those wonderful Montana beefsteaks. The bill for the whole dinner was $1.25, and I gave her two $1 bills and said that I did not want any change. But on her way out of the room she placed a 50-cent piece and a 25-cent piece on the table by the door. I called to her. I said, 'What is the matter with that tip? Isn't it enough?' She said that she would not take the tip because she had read in the paper that the Japanese had taken all I owned in the Philippines and that she would not like to take money from me."

Although it is said by lecture managers that General Romulo is the most popular visiting lecturer to have appeared in this country since Winston Churchill burned up the lecture circuit about a dozen years ago, he will not, he said, continue in this field. "I want to go back to the Philippines and return to publishing. Also I hope to write."

He told something of his beginnings when he left high school at the age of eighteen to become a reporter on the *Manila News* at a salary of four streetcar tickets a day. Wilmot Lewis (now Sir Wilmot Lewis) was the city editor. Before long he shifted to another newspaper where the pay was slightly higher and where, as the city editor was a man of irregular habits, there seemed more possibility of advancement.

"One night the city editor became so drunk that there was no one to manage things. I sat in and got out the paper, and from then on I had the rank of assistant city editor, which was the highest post on a newspaper printed in English that a Filipino had ever held. Not long after that the unfortunate city editor opened a drawer of his desk, and a large rat jumped out. This rat carried a flea. The flea bit the city editor, and he died of bubonic plague. I then became city editor."

Not long after this promotion Romulo came to New York as a ward of President Taft and entered Columbia. After graduation he returned to the Philippines, where his father had acquired control of a newspaper. At the time of Pearl Harbor, Romulo owned three newspapers, one published in English, one in Spanish and one in Tagalog. He was also the publisher of a photo magazine that he described as "our attempt to imitate *Life,*" and owned a radio station.

Behind his ambition to write is his conviction that the course of the United States in the Philippines has set a pattern for the proper relationship between races. "I want to tell about this," he said. "It is not all a flattering, rosy picture. Our relations have been no long honeymoon. There was bumbling and grumbling and bungling—but, finally, what of that?

"The obstacles that looked big at first became small when the Filipinos awoke to realize that there was no American business on the islands that a Filipino could not become the manager of if he was good enough at the job, if he was able, a good worker. The Americans got rich, sure they did, but also they paid better wages than Filipinos ever had had before, and the success of their businesses made business for us such as we never before had known.

"Even in my own family the course of the pattern is clear. My grandfather could not leave his own squalid village because he was bound there by debts—not debts that he had contracted but debts that his father, and before that his grandfather, had contracted, and that had been swollen by interest through the generations. He had no chance to improve his condition, for he was bound to the place where he was born by the debts he was born to.

"Then the Americans came, and my father fought them. My family hated the Americans, but as it became possible to see something of what they were doing the hate changed to wonder, the wonder to a desire to learn. With the satisfaction of that desire came understanding; out of understanding came respect, out of respect, loyalty.

"Six steps, you see. And why shouldn't it be possible for others to take those steps?

"No one believes in feudalism any more. That is a worn-out

idea, it has served its usefulness, it is past. The attitudes of feudalism have become repugnant to us; they are no part of our world. And so with the old-fashioned imperialism that exploited and gave nothing.

"The Filipinos with their guerrilla bands have proved the power of the American idea that brought to our islands education and opportunity. That we will not let go. We saved the flags and buried the schoolbooks and we were ready when the troops returned.

"I believe that the great theme that a writer will find in our islands is this: America brought us the realization of the incarnate dignity of the human soul, and won our everlasting loyalty in return.

"This is a realization that can be—and should be—brought home to all the peoples of the earth. Perhaps as a writer when the war is over I can help to bring it to them."

SAMUEL HOPKINS ADAMS DISCUSSES A LONG WRITING CAREER

The biographer of Woollcott gives rules for free-lance writing

June 17, 1945

SAMUEL HOPKINS ADAMS said that he wished that he had made more of Alexander Woollcott's courage in his book, "A. Woollcott: His Life and His World."

"I'm now convinced that it was courage that saved Woollcott from associations that would have finished him," said Mr. Adams. "Harold Ross admits that Woollcott had absolute courage but makes little of it. He says that such courage doesn't mean anything because Woollcott never knew fear. Well, that's too fine for me. Anyway, I'm not talking only of physical courage. Woollcott had moral courage, too, and great strength of will. There were times when he might have followed impulses that would have destroyed him. He didn't—too much will. I wish I'd made more of that."

"After all this association with them—what do you think of Woollcott's group?"

"Oh," said Mr. Adams, "people say they were a bunch of cheap self-advertisers. Of course they were self-advertisers. But I'm for them. Behind their exhibitionism there was a tremendous amount of real stuff, of faithful workmanship. They had conscientious scruples about their jobs and, on the whole, they've used their public influence well."

He is convinced that the extraordinary response his book has evoked is due to the hold that Woollcott and his friends had on readers.

"But the book's a swell job."

"Yes, I know it," said Mr. Adams, quickly. "It is a competent job," he then corrected. "But if it weren't, even if it were poorly done, it still would be a natural because of Woollcott."

"Do you feel that Woollcott introduced a new technique, a kind of advertising technique, into American letters?"

"Certainly," said Mr. Adams. "Woollcott was a slick publicity man. But he did his job so well, don't you see, that he becomes more than that. He becomes a fascinating, spectacular figure who stirs most of us emotionally. People aren't neutral about him."

In his two and one-half years of work on the book, Mr. Adams said, he wrote about 1,000 letters and talked Woollcott "to, I should guess, 500 people." "I asked practically every one I met what they knew about Woollcott—just on the chance, you know—and an amazing number of people had stories to tell."

"Did you find out much that you couldn't print?"

"Oh, yes. Some of Alec's writings—I think particularly of one satiric blurb he wrote for a recent best-seller—were unprintable. What I couldn't use I've sent up to Hamilton College to be kept under cover on the chance that it may be amusing in some more free-spoken age."

Except for suppressions that might reasonably have been required by the courts Mr. Adams has done little sparing in his account of A. Woollcott and his world. It is natural that this should be so, for one of his own sentences about Woollcott seems strikingly characteristic after meeting him. This sentence is:

"Early in his career I was able to do him a favor, which, I am sure, he never held against me."

As that sentence indicates, Mr. Adams hopes for common courtesy and not much more. And he is more concerned with what he himself is doing than with the emotions with which others respond to him, a way of looking upon the world that is rather rare among current authors.

Samuel Hopkins Adams is 74 years old. At a party given for

him by his publishers—appropriately in the Rose Room of the Algonquin—on the evening preceding the interview he had been all over the place, rarely faltering on a name though he hadn't seen some of the guests for twenty or more years. The next morning he put off his own breakfast until eight-thirty to suit the convenience of the interviewer and he came into the breakfast room wondering why New Yorkers insist on spending their evenings in night clubs. "We went around to one after the party last night," he said, "and were kept waiting in a drafty hall for nearly half an hour. I have a case of sniffles out of it. The cocktails were indifferent, so was the food, and although some one else took the check I'm sure it was expensive as the devil. I hate to pay for more than I get."

Graduated from Hamilton College in up-State New York in 1891, Mr. Adams came to New York City and became a reporter on the *Sun*. He says that he found good fortune there. Not only did his salary rise rapidly from a starting point of $15 a week to a booming guarantee of $75 a week, but he recalls doing fairly well in the practically permanent poker game that was played around the clock for, it is said, twenty-four years in the old *Sun* offices. "For the one and only time in my life I held a straight flush in diamonds at three o'clock one morning. No, it wasn't a very big pot; there was only a flush out against me."

He left the *Sun* in 1900 after nine years' service, which, he says, was four years too long. "Newspaper reporting is a good job for five years," he said, "but after that a man should move along."

In 1900 he went to the McClure Syndicate as managing editor, but he was "very bad" at that job and quit after a short time to become advertising manager for McClure, Phillips & Co., publishers, for a year. As he counts it, he has been a free lance since 1902, with any jobs he has held since being classified as assignments.

A first necessity for the free-lance writer is self-discipline. Mr. Adams set as his goal 1,000 publishable words per day. To fill out this budget he made it his habit for many years to get up each morning at five o'clock, and except for the interruption of breakfast, worked steadily and hard until noon. Since reaching seventy, he has slacked off somewhat in this, and allows himself the luxury of remaining in bed until six o'clock in the morning. He has spent his afternoons collecting early American glass and prints and furniture and, until fairly recently, playing golf. He and Mrs. Adams live at Wide Waters, a 300-acre place on the shores of Owasco Lake, eleven miles outside of Auburn, N. Y. "We have three houses on the place, all furnished from my collections, and while I could afford it we kept the farm stocked with blooded cattle. Wish we had them now. We could make money from the milk.

"A good life," said Mr. Adams, summing up. His books began appearing forty years ago, when he wrote "The Mystery," with Stewart Edward White. The next year, 1906, his "The Great American Fraud" was published—he had spent four years working on an exposé that earned him full place among the so-called muck-rakers of the time.

Mr. Adams has turned his hand at most sides of writing. He believes that his best fiction was a series of short stories that he wrote early in this century about the life that centered upon Stuyvesant Square here in New York City. "Those stories are out of print now, but people still write remembering them and wanting to buy them." He also spent a good deal of time writing mysteries a generation or so ago, and a radio agency is now at work adapting some of his yarns about a detective named Average Jones.

He says that there are only two really basic plots: that for the adventure story of which the mystery is an offshoot, and that for the love story. It was one of his love stories that was made into, with practically no rewriting, that remarkably pleasant movie "It Happened One Night."

He has done a good bit of digging into the sensational, and he called a turn with his "Flaming Youth," which he published under the name of Warner Fabian. Another great best-seller of its day was "Revelry," a fictional recapitulation of the Harding era. Less successful as to sales but still remembered is his novel, "Success," which had Arthur Brisbane as the main character.

Fifteen years ago Mr. Adams wrote a biography of Daniel Webster, "The God-Like Daniel," and since then he has spent much of his time working in American history. Tracking words and phrases through the new University of Chicago Press "Dictionary of the American Language on Historical Principles," he turned up oddities of speech and conduct from the American past.

"I make hundreds of notes each year for possible use in historical novels. Did you realize that mosquitoes were suspected of carrying malaria more than one hundred years ago? Did you know that fingerprinting was talked about as a means of identification early in the last century? Did you know that the word 'buncombe' was first used in a laudatory sense?"

The book of Woollcott has had a first printing of 60,000 copies. Mr. Adams said that he thoroughly enjoyed working on it, but that it is a relief now to return to his notes from history.

"Biography is easier to write. It is all mapped out for you topographically and chronologically. You find out where your subject went to and what he did. The outline is unchanged.

"Fiction is harder to do because no outline really serves and there are so many possible ways of making your effects. You may go completely off the track for several chapters, following your own interests and forgetting the reader, and then you must scrap a lot of the work that you like and get back on the track. But with all the difficulties there is a pleasure in creative writing that is in no other work I've ever found, and I don't know—I'm tempted by an assignment to do a biography and sometimes I think I'd like to write editorials. However, looking it all over, I think that now I might best stick to what I really enjoy. For some time, at least, I'm going to write historical fiction."

AN INTERVIEW WITH ERICH MARIA REMARQUE

Who outlines his rules for handling luck, loneliness and refugee living

January 27, 1946

"My father told me," said Erich Maria Remarque, the author of "All Quiet on the Western Front," "The Road Back," "Three Comrades," "Flotsam," and the newly published "Arch of Triumph," "my father, a good man, told me, 'Erich, never lose your ignorance; you cannot replace it but you always can become refined.' I have longed," Remarque continued, giving himself another treatment of liqueur (to ease the pains of "this arthritis that hits me here in the neck and goes to the top of my head"), "for a normal, simple life. My friends say, 'Erich, you are so at ease; you know how to accept what comes,' which is, of course, not true, though I try to make it seem true, as who does not? Naturally, I make the best of my life, following certain rules."

"What kind of rules?" I asked.

"Sound, solid rules," said Remarque. "As an example, after I wrote 'All Quiet'—well, you know how fantastic that was. A success—clippings this high in my publishers' office—and for me a completely unexpected success. There are two ways of accepting such fantastic success, such luck. One way is to hoard the windfall, to use it to build on, to use it as a means to bring in yet more money, to base security on it. The other way is to waste it. Of course, that is what I did.

"That is what a windfall is for. When it comes one should meet it happily and happily toss it about. What kind of person wants to put out luck at interest?" asked Remarque, smiling and gently shaking his head. "If you met a beautiful woman, a charming girl, the girl you had dreamed about as you sat in bars and walked in the streets and hoped all your life that some day you might meet —what would you do with such a girl? Would you say, 'Come, come home with me and cook my meals?' Oh, no, oh, no, not if you could get some one else to cook, not if you could take her to a fine restaurant, with good service, good wines, good coffee. Neither do you ask luck to cook for you, to supply your daily bread. You waste your luck, you toss it about. There is an old story that life is like a woman, loving a waster and despising a provider. Perhaps it is so."

He treated his arthritis with a sip. Remarque is a rather hardy, durable looking man in his late forties, his face alive and bright when he is talking with enjoyment. He does not want to go back to Germany. Knows no one who does. Soon he will become an American citizen. He lives and works in a corner suite at the Hotel Ambassador, Van Gogh's "Steel Bridge," above the fireplace, other of Remarque's excellent collection of paintings about the walls. Phonograph records are piled high on one large table, books are piled almost everywhere else. Only the big desk at which he writes is kept fairly clear. He has been a refugee since Hitler came to power in 1933, and among his rules are some for refugee living: have a phonograph and books if possible; take a room as near the center of a great city as you can get; be on friendly terms with a large number of people who are not refugees and who do not speak your native language; avoid the temptation to write an autobiography.

At his work Remarque is stubborn; when a novel is actually progressing he takes little time out. Formerly he did a great deal of rewriting, but Franz Werfel once told him that it is useless to write anything more than twice and he considers this advice sound.

"No, no, I never re-read what I have written until I have finished a draft; that is fatal. Nothing seems any good until it has been finished for some time; if you read it when it is unfinished you want to burn it and start all over, and then if you read the new version while it still is warm you want to burn that and start again. In that way one soon becomes a novelist without a novel—a pitiful state, and one that makes it difficult to pay one's bills. To write a bad novel is not good, but it is better to write a bad novel than to try to write a perfect one—and not write it. If for some reason I stay away from a piece of work for a long time and cannot remember the names of some of the characters, even so I don't re-read to find out. I know better than that. I give the characters new names. Such matters can be corrected at the second writing, but at least I have what I have done—I have not burned it up."

When he is stuck at some scene or situation he goes for long walks through the city. "I look at the faces. That is very important, to look at the faces, to try to guess what man or woman is behind the face. At parties I do that too, sometimes. I'm not interested, of course, in whether my guesses hit the truth. Precision of observation is of value to a policeman but not to me, for all that I require is the guess and if that seems to me true, and interesting, then it has served its purpose. There is no city like New York for faces, for you have faces from every continent, every country, many tribes, in endless variety, and at any hour of the day or night. And, of course, there are more beautiful and handsome faces here than anywhere else in the world. Oh, I am sure of it. And that is very pleasant, very, to see beautiful faces all about."

Remarque lived in Hollywood for several years before coming here. He said that he'd go out for walks and break them off and hurry back to his hotel and go to the bar and have a drink. "There always was some one in the bar, but the streets out there are deserted. No one walks. You know, that's ugly. In the country I take it for granted that I won't meet any one but there are animals, the life of the country. But to walk in a city where there are rows upon rows of buildings and sidewalks extending for miles and people nowhere to be seen, only buildings and automobiles—ah, ghastly. Hollywood is ghastly anyway. I had nothing to do with pictures, never went near a studio, but the ghastliness of it crept into me and I had to come away."

Remarque considers that he was late in finding himself as a writer: "I was so hungry for life, I was starved for it, and sitting alone, writing, was almost a waste of life, as it seemed to me." He went into the German Army as a boy fresh from school, fought through the first World War, then lived by odd jobs, taking up sports reporting simply because he found it easy and comparatively agreeable work. He kept trying to write and got nowhere with it until finally he took a few weeks off and worked very hard on a novel. "It was really simply a collection of the best stories that I told and my friends told as we sat over drinks and relived the war."

He took this novel, "All Quiet on the Western Front," to a publisher, who wanted him to change the ending in which the hero dies. The publisher wanted the hero to live so that he could go on and be the hero of a sequel. Remarque refused. "Naturally the reader identifies himself with the main character, and if that character lived then the story would be simply an adventure yarn. It is a truth about life that those periods that are the most difficult to live through become the basis of our thoughts, our interests, if we survive, and had the hero lived each chapter would have been just a good yarn of the death of others, of hard, difficult experiences, ending in the triumph of survival. His death gave the whole thing meaning, made it an anti-war novel. So, of course, I refused."

The book was a best seller through much of the world: "I used the money to grab at life." The Nazis recognized "All Quiet" as a force working against them. Remarque's agent found him one morning at about four o'clock and urged him to go to Switzerland and start work on a new book that he had contracted to write. "There was fantastic luck again," said Remarque. "I considered, should I order another drink and then go home to bed, or should I order another drink, get into my car and drive to Switzerland. I decided that it would be better if I woke in Switzerland the next day and started work at once than if I slept in Germany and drove to Switzerland the next day. That is why I was in Switzerland when the Nazis came to hunt for me."

The Nazis would have better served themselves, Remarque

says, had they followed him into Switzerland and killed him. It is his hope that he can write a novel that can live for some time and in living cause readers to long remember the attainments, progress and aims of the Nazis. He is convinced that nazism is far from wiped out in Germany and that many of its ideas still sweep through the world.

"The difficulty is, you see," he said, "that our imaginations cannot count. When I say five million died—the figure is a blank. Five million deaths does not equal one death. Five thousand dead in a concentration camp—there is that same difficulty. The figure is blank. But if I say five died, then perhaps. And if I say one died —a man I have made you know and understand—he lived so, this is what he thought, this is what he hoped, this was his faith, these were his difficulties, these his triumphs and then he—in this manner, on this day, at an hour when it rained and the room was stuffy—was killed, after torture, then perhaps I have told you something that you should know about the Nazis.

"The novel that I am working on is dated, it is dated now. The scene is a concentration camp—can you imagine anything more dated? But if it is a good book it will be widely read and through it some people who did not understand before may be made to understand what the Nazis were like and what they did and what their kind will try to do again. It is so dated, do you suppose any one will read it?"